Natural Resources and the Environment Series
Volume 12

Development without Destruction:
Evolving Environmental Perceptions

NATURAL RESOURCES AND THE ENVIRONMENT Series

SERIES DIRECTORS
Margaret R. Biswas and Asit K. Biswas.

EDITORIAL BOARD
Essam El-Hinnawi, Nairobi; Huang Ping-Wei, Beijing; Mohammed Kassas, Cairo; Victor A. Kovda, Moscow; Walther Manshard, Freiburg; W. H. Matthews, Hawaii; M. S. Swaminathan, New Delhi.

Volume 1: THE ENVIRONMENTAL IMPACTS OF PRODUCTION AND USE OF ENERGY
Essam El-Hinnawi, United Nations Environment Programme.

Volume 2: RENEWABLE NATURAL RESOURCES AND THE ENVIRONMENT: PRESSING PROBLEMS IN THE DEVELOPING WORLD
Kenneth Ruddle and Walther Manshard. United Nations University.

Volume 3; ASSESSING TROPICAL FOREST LANDS: THEIR SUITABILITY FOR SUSTAINABLE USES
Richard A. Carpenter, Editor, East West Center.

Volume 4: FUELWOOD AND RURAL ENERGY PRODUCTION AND SUPPLY IN THE HUMID TROPICS
W. B. Morgan and R. P. Moss, United Nations University.

Volume 5: ECONOMIC APPROACHES TO NATURAL RESOURCE AND ENVIRONMENTAL QUALITY ANALYSIS
Maynard M. Hufschmidt and Eric L. Hyman, Editors, East-West Center.

Volume 6: RENEWABLE SOURCES OF ENERGY AND THE ENVIRONMENT
Essam El-Hinnawi and Asit K. Biswas, Editors.

Volume 7: GLOBAL ENVIRONMENTAL ISSUES
Essam El-Hinnawi, Editor, United Nations Environment Programme.

Volume 8: THE WORLD ENVIRONMENT 1972-1982
Martin Holdgate, Mohammed Kassas, Gilbert White, Editors; *Essam El-Hinnawi,* Study Director, United Nations Environment Programme.

Volume 9: ENERGY ALTERNATIVES IN LATIN AMERICA
Francisco Szekely, Editor, United Nations Environment Programme.

Volume 10: INTEGRATED PHYSICAL SOCIO-ECONOMIC AND ENVIRONMENTAL PLANNING
Yusuf J. Ahmad, Editor, United Nations Environment Programme.

Volume 11: THIRD WORLD AND THE ENVIRONMENT
Essam El-Hinnawi and Asit K. Biswas, Editors.

Volume 12: DEVELOPMENT WITHOUT DESTRUCTION: EVOLVING ENVIRONMENTAL PERCEPTIONS
Mostafa K. Tolba.

Volume 13: LONG DISTANCE WATER TRANSFER IN CHINA
Asit K. Biswas, Zuo Da-kang, J. Nickum and Liu Chang-Ming, United Nations University.

Development without Destruction:
Evolving Environmental Perceptions

MOSTAFA KAMAL TOLBA

Published by
TYCOOLY INTERNATIONAL PUBLISHING LTD.
DUBLIN

All rights reserved. No part of this publication may be reproduced, stored in a retrievable system or transmitted in any form or by any means; electronic, electrostatic, magnetic tape, mechanical, photocopying, recording or otherwise, without permission in writing from the publishers.

Tycooly International Publishing Ltd.,
6, Crofton Terrace,
Dun Laoghaire,
Co. Dublin, Ireland
Tel: (+353-1) 807221

First edition 1982.

© Copyright 1982 Mostafa Kamal Tolba

Typeset by Printset and Design Ltd., Dublin and printed by Cahill Printers Ltd., Dublin, Ireland.

ISBN 0 907567 22 3 Hardback
ISBN 0 907567 23 1 Softcover

CONTENTS

		Page
Preface		vii
Acknowledgements		ix
1.	Food and the Environment	1
2.	Natural and Man-Made Environment	6
3.	Development without Destruction	10
4.	Environment: Global Concerns	19
5.	Are Development and Environmental Protection Compatible?	28
6.	Social Justice, Peace and Environmentally Sound Development	35
7.	Environmental Management	45
8.	Water and the Environment	59
9.	Human Needs Satisfaction	63
10.	Desertification can be Arrested	71
11.	Environmental Education	82
12.	Disarmament and the Environment	88
13.	Environment in the Technical Cooperation among Developing Countries	93

14.	Climate, Environment and Society	97
15.	Rural Development and Environment	101
16.	Science, Technology, Environment and Development	106
17.	The State of the Earth	111
18.	Environmental Protection and Economic Development	118
19.	Alternative Patterns of Development and Lifestyles	127
20.	World Conservation Strategy	136
21.	UNEP: Retrospect and Prospects	139
22.	Air Quality Management	147
23.	Water Systems and the Environment	153
24.	Urbanization and the Environment	163
25.	Interrelationships between People, Resources, Environment and Development	165
26.	Renewable Energy and the Environment	168
27.	The Holistic Concept of the Environment	171
28.	The Environment in 1982	181
Abbreviations		188
Index		191

Preface

ONE of the most fundamental problems confronting mankind at present is how to meet the basic needs and requirements of all people on earth without simultaneously destroying the resource base, that is the environment, from which ultimately these needs have to be met. Hence an understanding of the interrelationship between environment and development is absolutely essential for successful implementation of any strategy for the protection and management of the environment. Similarly for development strategies to be sustainable over a long-term, they must explicitly recognise the opportunities and constraints provided by the environment. This is a process I have often termed *development without destruction,* and it has been a major emphasis of the United Nations Environment Programme from its very beginning. This overall philosophy of *development without destruction* permeates all my writings and speeches and thus I believe it is an appropriate title for this book.

The present book contains a selection of my speeches and reports during the period 1974 to 1981. During this 8-year period, as to be normally expected, our knowledge of environment-development processes has increased. There have also been a series of world conferences at the policy-making level held under the auspices of the United Nations, to discuss the critical problems of this era — Population at Bucharest, Food at Rome, Human Settlements at Vancouver, Water at Mar del Plata, Desertification at Nairobi, Science and Technology for Development at Vienna, and Renewable Energy at Nairobi. In addition there have been several other conferences convened by various UN agencies on important subject areas such as employment, technical cooperation among developing countries, world climate, agrarian reform and rural development and primary health care. All of these subjects have an important environmental dimension. Each of these factors have contributed to the evolution of our thinking and changes in our perception of environmental issues during this period. As to be expected, this evolution can be discerned in my speeches spanning this period. For this reason speeches have been chronologically arranged, rather than under specific subject areas.

Since the speeches were given in my capacity as the Executive Director of the United Nations Environment Programme, they cover primarily broad areas of interest of UNEP's programmes and policies. This means there is some duplication in terms of issues dealt with. To a major extent, this problem has been dealt with by careful editing, but in some cases it was not possible to do so without seriously interrupting the flow. However, such duplications have been kept to an absolute minimum and cross-referencing has been provided in appropriate places. Furthermore, some duplication is necessary since the issues are closely interrelated.

Nairobi, December 1981   Mostafa Kamal Tolba

Acknowledgements

This volume would not have been possible without the assistance given to me by my colleagues, both past and present, and many policy-makers and scientists from all over the world, which has not only significantly increased our knowledge of the environment and development processes but also has enabled us to formulate appropriate policies and actions. I am truly grateful for their generous assistance and cooperation.

I would especially like to express my deep gratitude and thanks to my colleague and friend, Dr. Asit K. Biswas, President of the International Society of Ecological Modelling, Oxford, England, who has been one of my Senior Scientific Advisors since the early days of UNEP, for helping me select and edit the speeches.

1
FOOD AND THE ENVIRONMENT

Statement to the World Food Conference

Rome, Italy, November 1974

DEVELOPMENT without destruction — the maximization of the production of food without destroying the ecological basis to sustain production — is in essence the theme we in the United Nations Environment Programme wish to bring to this Conference.

We consider that any strategy to increase food production on a sustained basis should explicitly take account of the complementarity of environment and development. Indeed, there is no area where the objectives of environment and development are more interrelated and mutually-supportive than in the production of food on a sustained basis, a view which was reflected at the seventeenth session of the FAO Conference.[1]

The urgency and magnitude of the task of more than doubling world food production by the end of the century, while assuring the supplies of basic requirements to all, cannot be underestimated. It is vitally important to ensure that the measures taken to increase food production on a short term basis can be sustained and effectively integrated with long term policies.

From amongst the various elements of the three major issues identified by the Secretary-General of this Conference for its consideration, namely, food production, food consumption, aid and distribution and world food security, let me indicate some of the elements which rank especially high from the environmental point of view.

[1] "The major environmental problems facing agriculture, forestry and fisheries were not only the avoidance of environmental pollution but the ensuring, in the development process, of the maintenance of the productive capacity of the basic natural resource for food and agriculture through rational management and conservation measures."

Expansion of Land Under Agriculture

Pressure to expand the area under agriculture has often resulted in serious environmental disruptions. To cite but a few examples, the expansion of agriculture to steep hillsides led to serious erosion in Indonesia, increasing pressure of slash-and-burn agriculture, and is adversely affecting tropical forests in the Philippines; deforestation in the Himalayas is contributing to the increase in frequency and severity of flooding in Pakistan, India and Bangladesh; and overgrazing and deforestation is contributing to the southward march of the Sahara in the Sahelian Zone of Africa. There are numerous other similar examples where short-term agricultural benefits have been negated by the ensuing long-term environmental costs, leading eventually to an actual decline in food production.

Rational management of arable agricultural land is thus becoming an increasingly critical factor for the survival of mankind.

Technology

Technology transfers have often not taken root because in their planning proper account was not taken of local, social, cultural, educational, economic and ecological conditions. Equally dismal has been man's frequent inability to use locally available technology. For instance, simple inexpensive countermeasures known over the centuries, like the use of terracing, are often not applied widely enough to prevent soil erosion.

Existing technical and scientific knowledge must be better mobilized and more effectively applied. What is necessary is to provide better services to move available technology to the field level, and to ensure that the steps taken provide sustained rather than short-term benefits.

Energy

There is an intimate relation between inputs of energy and the output of food. Scientifically planned inputs of energy to the land yield extraordinarily favourable results. But a saturation point can be reached where any extra inputs are wasted and cause serious environmental degradation. As an example of favourable results, energy inputs to corn production in the USA increased by about 33 per cent from 5.6 kilojoules/kg in 1945 to 7.5 kilojoules/kg in 1970, yet the increase in actual production was over 138 per cent. Enormous amounts of the energy spent on producing packaging materials like paper and plastics, and on transport, storage, marketing, etc. can be conserved, and the marginal utility of the application of energy on the land may be greater.

Fertilizers

Fertilizers are indispensable for increasing food production but their excessive use has occasioned much concern as a possible environmental threat. In this regard there is no basic difference between the objectives of increasing food production and of environmental protection, and the common aim is to maximize food production on a sustainable basis, in a way consistent with minimum harmful effects on man and his environment. The achievement of this objective requires that fertilizers be used with maximum efficiency on the farm. For example, new types of nitrogen fertilizers must be developed which release their nitrogen as nitrate into the soil solution during the growing season at a rate comparable to the crop's demand for nitrates. Although technically feasible, no satisfactory slow-release fertilizer is currently available for general agricultural use.

Special attention should be paid, and sufficient resources channelled, to the promotion of the most efficient and effective use of available fertilizers and to the development of biological sources of fertilizer, especially microbiological nitrogen fixation and compost.

Pest Control

Pests cause significant losses to crops worldwide. There has been a tendency to control them through continued and even increased use of pesticides. This has resulted, through the processes of natural selection and evolution, in the appearance and proliferation of new strains of pests which generally turn out to be more vicious and more immune to chemicals. Increasing dosages or using different pesticides provide no final solution.[1]

Another major problem is that existing modes of application of chemical pesticides have extremely low efficiency rates. Several studies indicate that a very high percentage of pesticides applied by aircraft never reach the target, creating totally unnecessary ecological hazards.

A third element of concern is that the distribution of pesticides through ecosystems takes place most commonly by selective concentration as they pass through successive levels of food chains and food webs. This means that high pesticide levels are most readily noticeable in the higher animals and in man.

It is, therefore, essential to develop effective new methods of integrated pest management, an ecological approach to pest control. The programme of UNEP places a special emphasis on this. Where the use of pesticides cannot as yet be circumvented, there should be conentration on increasing the efficiency of their application. The motto should be "efficient use of pesticides: more on target, less outside".

---

[1]See also p. 114.

Food Losses

Current losses during food storage, processing and handling could well have fed hundreds of millions of people. These losses occur in all countries, developed or developing, in temperate or in tropical regions. According to some estimates, rodents eat or destroy a quantity which could have fed on an average nearly two hundred million people. The US Federal Authorities estimate the cost to the US economy of losses due to rats at well over one thousand million dollars per year. In Africa, almost 30 per cent of all crops (which would suffice to feed an additional fifty-five million Africans per year) are lost in storage. Thus, the application of new and better techniques in the conservation of food by preventing losses and wastes during storage, processing or handling is of great importance in improving the world food situation.

Weather and Climate

Weather and climate have always been of great importance to crop production, often outweighing the factors subject to human management. Today there are increasing signs of possible changes in climate and weather patterns, but also a great development in man's capacity to anticipate and possibly influence these. The capacity to forecast must be developed, to the extent that it does not already exist, to permit the planning of crops. There is also an urgent need to develop mathematical models which interface physical climatic models with those of agricultural products.

Irrigation

Irrigation schemes are undoubtedly needed to accelerate development in the developing countries. In some cases, however, certain environmental hazards result which may include the spread of waterborne diseases. The application of ecological and environmental principles right from the planning stage of irrigation schemes would enable even greater benefits to accrue, leading to a positive improvement in the health, well-being and productive capacity of the population of the region.

In each of these, and in other relevant areas, like the development of an internationally coordinated food contamination monitoring programme, I offer full support and cooperation by the United Nations Environment Programme in the light of the recommendations of and within the framework of the follow-up action to be decided upon by this historic Conference.

Food Surpluses

Let me now refer briefly to a few of the broader issues before this Conference. We know that the world can produce surpluses of food. We know that more, much more, should be produced where the direct need exists. We realise, however, that there are certain regions of the world where, because of such reasons as climate, soil, topography and water availability, the application of additional resources and inputs would lead to the production of more food than in others. The generation of surpluses in the favoured regions must be linked with changes in the economic and social patterns which affect distribution. The international community must develop mechanisms of distribution which can act equitably, also to prevent and remedy an unjustifiable form of international coexistence — that of overconsumption with starvation.

Interdependance

Strategies to solve the world food problem must be developed in full knowledge of the web of interdependence that exists between this and the other major problems facing mankind — those of population, the availability of energy and other raw materials and the lack of development. It is not in any one of them, but in the interaction amongst them, that the future of mankind will be decided and shaped.

May I conclude by quoting from the Cocoyoc Declaration which emanated from a Symposium convened jointed by UNCTAD and UNEP last month at Mexico on Patterns of Resource Use — Environment and Development Strategies:

> "The world is today not only faced with the anomaly of underdevelopment. We may also talk about overconsumptive types of development that violate the inner limits of man and the outer limits of nature. Seen in this perspective, we are all in need of a redefinition of our goals, of new development strategies, of new life styles, including more modest patterns of consumption among the rich. Even though the first priority goes to securing the minima we shall be looking for those development strategies that also may help the affluent countries, in their enlightened self-interest, in finding more human patterns of life, less exploitative of nature, of others, of oneself."[1]

---

[1] For the full text of the Cocoyoc Declaration, see "In Defence of the Earth," Executive Series 1, UNEP, Nairobi, 1981.

2
NATURAL AND MAN-MADE ENVIRONMENT

Statement to HABITAT: UN Conference on Human Settlements

Vancouver, Canada, May 1976

WE IN UNEP are looking to HABITAT to achieve a shift in vision which will bring the urgency of human settlements issues sharply into focus and so promote a coherent strategy and related actions to deal with the problems facing the world's cities, town and villages. Experience teaches us not to be starry-eyed about the results of international conferences, but I am encouraged to believe that this Conference will have a most profound impact on thinking and practice in the world over during the next twenty or twenty-five years. It could — and must — be the occasion for a fundamental reorientation of our approach to an issue which is central to the future welfare of mankind.

UNEP is wholeheartedly committed to the success of this Conference; indeed we have supported HABITAT since its inception and have a deep and close interest in its outcome. Our Governing Council was the initial forum for discussing the purposes of HABITAT and it has, each year, since 1973, considered a progress report from the Secretary-General of the Conference. Moreover, the Council authorized an expenditure of $3 million, in addition to the United Nations regular budgetary appropriation, to assist with the audio-visual part of the Conference, especially in meeting costs incurred by developing countries. Consequently, we are very involved partners with a major stake in the success of the HABITAT enterprise. For these reasons, I feel it proper to speak of our hopes and expectations for HABITAT.

In contributing to your deliberations on the complex of issues that you will be tackling in the next few days, UNEP has two particular dimensions which appear relevant to your consideration of human settlements issues.

1. The problems which arise in the context of human settlements are but a part — though certainly a major part — of those which concern the environment as a whole;
2. The struggle to improve human settlements must be seen within the wider context of the relationship between environment and development, and the building of the New International Economic Order.

These are no mere academic concerns; they are essential to the understanding of the nature of the human settlements crisis and to selecting the proper course of action to deal with that crisis.

Relationships between Settlements and the Human Environment

The first dimension, the integral relationship between human settlements and the human environment[1], is a relationship which was given recognition and prominence at Stockholm almost four years ago, in the Declaration adopted then, in the recommendations contained in the Action Plan and in the institutions proposed to deal with environmental problems.

With the guidance from Stockholm, UNEP has attempted to define a conceptual base and programme that satisfies the many and complex relationship between the human settlements and the other sub-systems of the environment. In doing this, we borrowed from the principles developed in the appropriate disciplines of the natural and social sciences. After debating this issue at length, Governments agreed that a promising new direction could be developed around the concept that human settlements are man-made ecosystems. In the context of this concept, a satisfactory human settlement is one which provides shelter, sustenance, communications and employment, and which meets social and cultural needs without seriously polluting or destroying the natural environment upon which the continued life of the settlement and its inhabitants depends.

It was with these views in mind that the Governing Council of UNEP, at its fourth session in 1976, took several decisions which reaffirmed the close link between human settlements and the environment of which they form a part.

In particular, the Council invited the delegations participating in the HABITAT conference to take the following two points into account when considering the institutional arrangements for human settlements within the United Nations system:

1. "The Stockholm Conference proclaimed that both aspects of man's environment, the natural and the man-made, were essential to his well-being and to the enjoyment of basic human rights, even the right to life itself. The first recommendation of the Conference emphasised

---
[1]See also p. 163.

that the planning, improvement and management of rural and urban settlements demanded an approach, at all levels, embracing every aspect of the human environment, both natural and man-made."

2. "The linkage between the man-made environment and the natural environment is of prime importance, and their interrelationships must be considered in all forums dealing with international co-operation in order to ensure the improvement of the quality of life of all peoples."

These considerations have from the outset guided UNEP's own human settlements programme whose objectives are:

1. to assist governments in formulating national strategies for human settlements which take the environmental dimension into account;
2. to train those responsible for planning and managing human settlements;
3. to demonstrate on a pilot project basis the feasibility of a comprehensive approach to problems of human settlements and to coordinate activities – especially international activities – in this field so as to avoid duplication and to encourage transfer of experience.

A central feature of the programme is the promotion of environmentally sound, low-cost technologies for use in human settlements.

Human Settlements: Environment and Development

The second dimension is the place of human settlements within the theme of environment and development. Human settlements take on a special significance in this context because it is in human settlements that both the need for development, and the dangers to the human environment, are most evident and concentrated. If we cannot resolve the apparent conflicts between environment and development objectives in human settlements, we cannot solve them anywhere.

I say 'apparent' advisedly, because I do not believe there need be such a conflict; on the contrary, the relationship between the two is inevitable, intimate and inseparable. Environment and development could be considered as the two sides of the same coin; conflicts only arise when one objective is pursued in ignorance of the other.[1]

For this reason, UNEP's commitment to environment implies an intense

---

[1] See also p. 28

concern with development. Putting this concern into a human settlements perspective, I believe that in your deliberations you may wish to bear in mind the following related sequence of principles:

1. in so doing, great care must be taken to minimise the impact on resources and environment at large and so ensure the environment's sustained productivity;
2. the purpose of our concern with human settlements should be the positive improvement of the human environment; this will not come about, though, if our approach is haphazard, uncoordinated or ignores ecological constraints;
3. at every level from the international, where UNEP has a key role to play through its environmental assessment programme of Earthwatch, to the individual city or town, we need to monitor changes in human settlements and be alert to the danger signals of environmental sickness;
4. all this will come about only if we can promote alternative patterns of development and life styles in rich and poor countries.

Thus, human settlements are seen to have a central place in the environment/development nexus. If the changes we hope to set in train through our participation in this conference are to be effective and sustained, then the planning of human settlements must now take account of the need for alternative patterns of development, for the widespread use of environmentally sound technologies, for the encouragement of self-reliance and for the discouragement of the wasteful and irrational use of natural resources. These are all prominent elements in the New International Economic Order; they are also key features in the environmentally healthy world which UNEP advocates; and they should be at the core of our approach to the human settlements issue.

The HABITAT Conference is unique. Human settlements problems, being what they are, primarily local and national problems, have now engaged the earnest attention of the international community. This Conference can very well go down in history as a landmark in man's effort to assert his dignity and not only to make this one Earth a better place to live in but to make life itself worth living. For all our efforts to succeed it is imperative that the noble decisions we take here are backed by the unwaivering political will of Governments. It is hoped that we will all rise to this opportunity and challenge which HABITAT will throw at us and we will fulfil the hopes of millions of people in this "Home of Mankind".

3
DEVELOPMENT WITHOUT DESTRUCTION

Address at Chelsea College
London, United Kingdom, June 1976

I BELIEVE that the fundamental question which confronts us is that of meeting the basic needs of man without simultaneously destroying the resource base — that is the environment — from which those needs must be met. I wish to share with you my views on this issue, not so much as to relate the progress which may or may not have been made by us in recent years, but so as to associate you with the quest for answers.

Why Development?

Many of the negative aspects of development have so impressed themselves on the minds of those concerned with the environment, that the question is often asked "why development?". Some indeed advocate environmental protection through arresting economic growth.

It is true that past industrial and agricultural develoment have created many environmental problems, ranging from the pollution of water, soil and air, and the consequent costs to human health and well-being, to the spread of the deserts, largely due to the mismanagement by man of natural ecosystems. These threats are not localized, and by themselves or through their interactions with other factors, become matters of regional or global concern. An example which has been much quoted recently is the possible impact on global climate of the continued combustion of fossil fuels to meet energy demands. Such cases constitute dangers to the "outer limits" which man must respect for his long-term well-being, even for his survival.

But environmental problems are caused also by a lack of adequate development. Today there are hundreds of millions of people without the basic human needs of adequate food, shelter, clothing and health; hundreds of millions more lack access to even a rudimentary education or regular employment. This is not only an intolerable situation in human terms, but it also has serious environmental consequences. The relentless pressures that arise where basic human needs are not met can erase the resource base from which man must inevitably gain his sustenance. The destruction of forests, the loss of arable soil, the loss of productivity through disease and malnutrition and the increasing pressure on fragile ecosystems which so often result from poverty are as significant as the pollution created by industry, technology and over-consumption by the affluent; both lead to the rapid depletion of basic natural resources. Many human settlements problems also arise from a lack of adequate development; consideration of these problems was, of course, the object of HABITAT, the UN Conference on Human Settlements, held at Vancouver.[1]

With these thoughts in mind, I conclude three things in answer to the question "why development?". First, that for the developing countries in the world, in which more than two-thirds of mankind live, there is no alternative to pursuing economic and social change so as to meet basic human needs and secure better prospects for their citizens. What is more, the lesson of the United Nations Conference on Population, held at Bucharest in 1974, is that only when this has been done, and the poor in the world experience a more satisfactory existence, will the population increase — itself a major contributory factor to environmental problems — decelerate markedly. Next, I conclude that the manner in which development takes place is too often destructive to the environment and thereby threatens the basis for continued development. Even so, my third conclusion is that, far from being in conflict, environmental and development objectives are complementary.

This last point needs a little elaboration. A few years ago, it was commonplace to characterise the environmental problem solely in terms of pollution and to measure economic and social development solely in terms of the growth in gross national product. Given these premises, the pursuit of environmental objectives through pollution control would be a check on development. But in fact there have been significant advances in recent years in our understanding of what is meant by environmental and development objectives and a growing acceptance that these converge. We may now look upon environment as the stock of physical or social resources available at a given time for the satisfaction of human needs, and upon development as a process pursued by all societies with the aim of increasing human well-being. Thus the ultimate purpose of both environmental and development policies is the enhancement of the quality of life, beginning with the satisfaction of the basic human needs. In recognition of this, we see the emergence of terms like

[1] For the statement to the UN Conference on Human Settlements, see p. 6.

'the new development' or 'alternative styles of development', which suggest a more rounded way of looking at the purposes of development, in which environmental considerations play a central role.

A new kind of development is needed because it is essential to relate development to the limitations and opportunities created by the natural resource base to all human activities. It is also required because it is now clear that past patterns of development in both developed and developing countries have been characterized by such serious environmental damage that they are simply not sustainable.

A New Kind of Development

What are the features of this new kind of development? I believe there are three aspects which are particularly relevant: it has implications for all countries, rich and poor; it presupposes new directions for growth and development, not their cessation; and it incorporates the environmental dimension.

There are, though, certain important differences between the form that new kind of development might take in industrialized countries and that which would be evident in developing ones. In the industrialized countries, it will be necessary to reorient societies' aims so that the entire population has more opportunity for self-expression in the fields of culture, education, the arts and humanities — those non-physical areas of development which represent the highest levels of human achievement. This new orientation must be less demanding of natural resources, energy and the environment. Present patterns of production and consumption, based on waste, extravagance and planned obsolescence, must be replaced by patterns based on conservation and reuse of resources. I am encouraged by signs from several industrialised countries that such a reorientation of life styles and societal aims can now be discussed seriously, though clearly the change implied by this approach is an immense one, which it will take many years to carry through.

In the developing world, which still lacks the infrastructure and readily-useable resources required to meet the growing needs and aspirations of its peoples, the new kind of development must continue to have a strong physical orientation. But each country should be helped to follow a path to development best suited to its own needs and accords with its own culture and value systems. Developing countries should have access to the technologies that they require to support this kind of development under conditions which will enable them to adapt these technologies to their own requirements, rather than have alien technologies dictate or unduly distort their development process. Most of all, the new forms of development in the developing world should be based on environmentally sound development of their natural resources of soil, water, plant and animal life to avoid the destruction of the resource base on which sustained development depends.

The pursuit of these new approaches to development also has important international implications. The 'debate' around the New International Economic Order, with its emphasis on meeting basic human needs, a fairer use of the world's natural resources and the need for development to be of a form appropriate to each country's requirements, shows that there is already a widespread, if still partial, recognition of these implications. I hope the international community, and especially the developing nations, in advocating and designing the much-needed new economic order, will not forget that there will be no sustained development or meaningful growth without a clear commitment at the same time to preserve the environment and promote the rational use of natural resources.

Irrational and Wasteful Use of Resources

It is clear that the new kind of development should avoid the irrational and wasteful use of resources. The use of natural resources can be called irrational if they are not used in the best possible known ways to further the aims which a given society has set itself, taking account of all effects known to follow from the choice. Wastefulness is the particular form of irrationality in which a given level of fulfilment of human purposes is achieved with the use of more resources than necessary. Three examples should explain what I mean: the pollution of the environment by effluents from industry, the resource of wildlife, and life styles based on conspicuous consumption.

Effluents from industry are commonly regarded in terms of their effects as threats to human health and well-being. It has been remarked that a pollutant is a resource in the wrong place, and certainly the well-known example of sulphur which could be retrieved from factory chimneys and used for industrial purposes is a case in point. I do not think it rational to lose ever-increasing quantities of resources as pollutants and then to use greater quanta of resources to deal with the effects of that pollution.

Our headquarters are in Nairobi, surrounded by countryside containing the greatest array of wildlife in the world. It has already been demonstrated that such resources like wildlife, if wisely used, the world over, can provide food in a manner which is less destructive to the soils and vegetation of the area than the 'traditional' pastorage of cattle; and that through tourism, wild animals can earn valuable foreign exchange. Yet, despite the efforts of Governments, this resource is being steadily destroyed for short-term profit — used irrationally and wastefully.

The most blatant instance of the irrational and wasteful use of resources results from the projection of wasteful life styles as desirable ways of achieving human happiness. To take just one example: much extra energy is used at the manufacturing stage to produce tins of drink with pull-tab stoppers, so as to save the miniscule effort of punching the hole; and resources are deliberately designed to be lost when throw-away tins are produced rather than reuseable glass bottles.

Development without Destruction: the Example of Food

This analysis and these examples should make clear what I mean by development without destruction. I mean sustainable development, which takes due regard of environmental constraints. Nowhere is that need more in evidence than in the satisfaction of the most basic human need of all: the provision of food.

On the assumption that the objective is to maximise food production, without destroying the ecological basis to sustainable production, there are ten considerations that need to be given special attention. These are: expansion of the land area under agriculture, technology in the field of agriculture, energy and food, fertilizers, pest control, food losses, weather and climate, irrigation, food surpluses and interdependence between food problems and those of population, the availability of energy and other raw materials, the lack of development and the environment.[1]

I have spoken about the food issue because it illustrates so well the importance of assessing the environmental impact of food production and therefore the need to build environmental considerations into every aspect of food policy. And as for food, so for development as a whole. If development is to be sustained, its environmental impact must be assessed and an environmental approach adopted to the management of the activities which make up the development process. The concepts of environmental assessment and environmental management were first formulated at the United Nations Conference on the Human Environment, which took place in 1972 in Stockholm. Assessment and management provide a conceptual basis for UNEP's own programme and both exercises are essential to the pursuit of development without destruction. I wish to devote the remaining part of my lecture to an explanation of what these terms mean, and what we in UNEP are doing to promote them. In so doing I hope to give you some insight into the ambitious programme of activities supported or encouraged by UNEP.

Environmental Assessment

The Stockholm Conference considered that environmental assessment — or Earthwatch as its global application has come to be called — contained four functions: evaluation and review, research, monitoring and information exchange. Evaluation and review provides the analysis to identify the gaps in knowledge and action. Research provides new information, or new interpretations of old information, which may lead to a better understanding of environmental problems and thus provide guidance for the decision-making process. Monitoring gathers in a continuous and systematic fashion certain

---

[1] For a detailed discussion of these ten points, see pp. 2–5.

data on specific environmental variables, and evaluates such data to determine and predict important short and long-term environmental trends. Information exchange provides data to the scientific and technological communities and so ensures that decision-makers at all levels have the benefit of the best information available at the appropriate time and in the most useable form.

Since its inception a few months after the Stockholm Conference, UNEP has begun to develop and apply this theoretical concept in practical terms, the most marked progress being made in the field of monitoring and information exchange. Thus a Global Environmental Monitoring System (GEMS), an International Referral System (INFOTERRA) and an International Register of Potentially Toxic Chemicals (IRPTC) have been established.

The purpose of GEMS, which is a global network of monitoring systems, coordinated through the efforts of UNEP but executed by a number of UN agencies and other bodies, is to establish the means to understand rapidly and correctly the changes brought about in the global environment by mankind's actions. Seven goals have been set for GEMS: to establish an expanded human health warning system; to assess global atmospheric pollution and its impact on climate; to assess the extent and distribution of contaminants in biological systems, particularly food chains; to assess the critical environmental problems relating to agriculture and land and water use; to asses the response of terrestrial ecosystems to the human pressures exerted on them; to assess the state of marine pollution and its impact on marine ecosystems; and finally to improve the monitoring of the factors necessary to understand and forecast natural disasters. As you see, it is an extensive system which it will take many years to establish in its entirety but already we have made substantial progress.

The International Referral System does not deal in the information itself but provides a switchboard to put the seeker of information in touch with the provider of it. Thus, when fully operational, and supported by a network of national focal points. INFOTERRA will be a most valuable tool in helping governments, decision-makers, professionals, research workers, educationalists and others to gain ready access to sources of environmental information. The International Register of Potentially Toxic Chemicals will provide the means to handle data and answer queries about environmentally significant chemical substances; we hope that the IRPTC, which like INFOTERRA, will depend upon the support of the national centres for the supply and updating of data, will be operational within eighteen months or so.

The ultimate purpose of the assessment programme must be to provide early warnings of any global threats to human welfare, or even survival, brought about through man's activities which transgress the outer limits. Thus as part of Earthwatch, UNEP has developed a programme on the outer limits. The time is not available to describe this programme at length, though you may be interested that it contains two subjects currently of much interest to the scientific community — and of concern to the lay one — threats to the ozone layer and climatic change. In each case, and several others, we are designing programmes of research and monitoring, coupled with an evaluation mechanism, and thus building up the ability to inform the world community of the situation.

Let me expand somewhat on that example of ozone because it illustrates well the way in which each component of Earthwatch — evaluation, monitoring, research, and information exchange — are being pursued by UNEP to construct a comprehensive assessment programme. Thus evaluation reveals that the ozone layer, and hence its effectiveness as a filter of harmful rays from the sun, may be reduced by the release of fluorocarbons, and, indirectly, from the manufacture and application of nitrogen fertilizers. An evaluation of the possible impact of supersonic aircraft on the ozone layer has been made by the World Meteorological Organisation which has recently issued a statement on the situation, the conclusions of which are not too alarming in respect of this particular possible hazard. A coherent programme of monitoring of total ozone and its vertical distribution is under design. UNEP intends to support research into the effect of fluorocarbons and fertilizers on the ozone layer, and also into the consequences for life on earth of a reduced ozone layer and increased ultraviolet radiation. Aware of the important issues at stake, Governments have requested me to convene a meeting to review all aspects of the risks to the ozone layer. This meeting, which will be held in 1977 and to which industrialists and others will be invited as well as governments, will provide a forum for the exchange of information and give added impetus to other aspects of ozone assessment.[1]

The ozone programme, and other similar studies which UNEP supports, are meant to provide data which indicate the priorities for environmental management and suggest the form that management should take.

Environmental Management [2]

The concept of environmental management, as advocated by UNEP, is a broad one. It is not the management of the environment, but management of all those human activities which have a significant impact on the environment, with due regard to environmental considerations. The most processing objective of environmental management is to meet basic human needs within the potentials and constraints of environmental systems, including natural resources. Environmental management brings two new dimensions to the development process: it *broadens* the concept to include environmental quality, and it *expands* it in time to include development over the long-term on a sustainable basis. At present environmental management is too often neglected because governments and others whose activities can affect the environment lack the necessary information, political will or resources, or find

---

[1] Biswas, Asit K., Editor, "The Ozone Layer," Pergamon Press, Oxford, 1979.
[2] See also Tom Mboya Lecture, p. 45.

it hard to respond to the long-term and trans-sectoral nature of environmental problems; or because existing administrative, professional, legal, financial and other institutions are poorly adapted to the need for environmental management.

In collaboration with a host of UN and other bodies, UNEP now has a great many activities underway which could help further the application of environmental management. To take a few examples: we are demonstrating new environmental approaches to the improvement of marginal settlements in Indonesia and the Philippines; we shall be advocating an ecological approach to the management of arid and semi-arid rangelands at the United Nations Conference on Desertification in 1977; we have helped prepare a world action plan for an environmentally sound approach to schistosomiasis control; we are establishing pilot schemes to illustrate the ecodevelopment approach, that is the application at the local level of environmental management principles within the development context; and we are establishing demonstration centres to show how renewable sources of energy can be utilized to provide the basic needs of small rural communities in developing countries. All these examples show that it is perfectly practical to introduce environmental management into every level of human activity.

The Mediterranean

In my closing remarks, I wish to come back to the theme of development without destruction, and demonstrate, with the specific example of the Mediterranean Sea, that assessment and management, along the lines indicated, can be employed to attain that end.

There has been a serious and sharp decline in recent years in the quality of the marine environment of the Mediterranean. If this is not soon halted and reversed, it will have a disastrous impact on the many communities dependent upon fishing and tourism, will greatly detract from the quality of life of the people living in the region and would demonstrate appalling contempt on the part of modern man towards a region which has played such a central role in his cultural evolution. To let the Mediterranean die would be an outstanding example of the pointlessness of development *with* destruction.

After several years of preparation, UNEP convened in January 1975 a meeting of Mediterranean Governments in Barcelona which agreed upon an action plan for the protection of the Mediterranean. This plan contains a major assessment programme involving monitoring of, and research into the health of the marine environment through the joint and co-ordinated efforts of many regional and national institutions. On the management side, the action plan contains two elements, integrated planning of the region up to the end of the century, and legal measures. At a second conference in Barcelona in

February 1976, the sixteen nations present adopted unanimously a final act embodying a convention and two protocols to protect the marine environment; fifteen of them signed the act and twelve of these also signed the convention and protocols, an unprecedented proportion of states to sign a convention immediately after its finalisation. The meeting also agreed to establish a centre in Malta to enable States to combat major oil spills in the Mediterranean.

Such conspicuous achievements in a region as politically sensitive as the Mediterranean is striking proof that, where the political will exists, the goal of development without destruction is attainable. But we should not delude ourselves: that act of political will does not come easily because it implies very large changes in public attitudes and expectations.

Conclusion

In the years ahead, we face the task of meeting the minimum human needs of mankind and of avoiding environmental catastrophes. I have spoken encouragingly about the prospects because I am convinced that disaster is not inevitable. But the urgency is extreme; we have very little time in which to set right our approach to the environment and to meet the legitimate demands of the world's poor. We shall need to act far more thoroughly and speedily than hitherto to redress environmental and human grievances, and we shall need to harness the energies of all sectors of society in this effort. No sector has a more important role than the scientific community. It is the duty of science to bring the problems and solutions to light and to display them with appropriate objectivity. Through the diligence and thoroughness which is the mark of all sound scientific endeavour, scientists can help mankind see the dangers which confront him and to understand that it is essential that he adopts wiser and safer approaches to managing his planet.

4

ENVIRONMENT: GLOBAL CONCERNS

Lecture delivered at the Ministry of Administration,
Local Economy and Environment Protection

Warsaw, Poland, July 1976

I AM particularly interested to have this opportunity to exchange ideas with you. I hope to present to you some of the principles and general considerations which guide our approach to environmental issues. I also hope that, through your eyes, I shall see how you think the actual problems that face you could be tackled and could relate to those global concerns.

Today, in seeing Warsaw again, I was struck by how large a contribution your own man-made environment makes to the spirit of your people. This beautiful city of Warsaw, 80 per cent of which was destroyed during the last war, has lovingly been rebuilt by you and restored to its former glory. This was done at a time of severe economic strain, at a time when the necessity to rebuild the industrial economy of your country was at its greatest. As you know, problems of human settlements constitute an area of high priority in the work of UNEP. We solidly believe that human settlements are an integral part of the human environment. We treat them as an ecosystem.

Over the last five years, Poland has enjoyed one of the highest economic growth rates in the world and I am sure that the importance of restoring your natural and man-made environment, of protecting and enhancing it, is for you all the greater. Some of the environmental consequences of past development were apparent to me when I visited Katowice, as were some of your efforts to deal with these consequences, for instance, in reclaiming land despoiled by mining and establishing a Park of Culture and Recreation, an act not only important, but symbolic.

Before explaining the way UNEP approaches its specific tasks and before describing some of our detailed activities, I shall first give you the general background to our thinking about environment and development, a matter central to our concerns.

The Development Process

At UNEP, we consider that, important as it is to cure the environmental problems created by the development process, it is more important to establish a development process which, instead of creating adverse consequences, in itself enhances the environment. I think this observation is true for all countries, be they at different stages of economic and social development. At the level of the individual, the process of development must contribute to the provision of his basic needs.

The perception of human needs naturally differs at different stages of development. But, at the poorest level, basic needs which have to be met include food, adequate shelter and potable water, clothing, medical care, education and productive employment. The achievement of such goals, the meeting of the basic human needs of the poor in each and every society, are a must if we are really serious about our concern over the environment at the global level. Environmental problems are not only caused by what may be called over-development, they are equally, and even more seriously, caused by a lack of adequate development. The relentless pressures that arise where basic human needs are not meet can erase the resource base from which man must inevitably gain his sustenance. The destruction of forests, the loss of arable soil, the loss of productivity through disease and malnutrition and the increasing pressure on fragile ecosystems which so often result from poverty are of the greatest significance and lead to the rapid depletion of basic natural resources. Of course, many human settlements problems also arise from a lack of adequate development.

It is sometimes not recognised that at higher levels of development, the satisfaction of human needs also constitutes a package and that an inbalance towards certain needs does not lead to correspondingly greater levels of welfare or satisfaction. The satisfaction of consumer needs at the expense of the destruction of the environment does not even lead to a greater total satisfaction, quite the converse. In most industrialized countries with basically consumer societies, we see how greater and greater increments of material goods fail to provide corresponding increases in satisfaction, while succeeding in damaging the environment. We believe that, at higher levels of welfare, the concept of a total look at human needs should be seriously considered. In such societies, new styles of life should be designed which are directed more towards the highest levels of development, the non-material levels: expression in arts and culture is just one example. Such life styles should be less demanding on the resources and the environment at large and in the meantime more capable of meeting the aspirations and needs of peoples who are already enjoying high standards of living in the material sense.

I believe we all agree that the overwhelming proportion of man's needs are met by the common service provided by natural processes and it should be understood that the relationship of man with these processes is symbiotic. It is sometimes difficult in our modern age for the symbiotic nature of this relationship to be conceded since we prefer to think that, standing unique, man orders and dominates the processes around him. Yet it is still beyond our knowledge to manufacture a plant and the economic, not to mention the environmental, cost of replacing the pollinating function of the bee would be truly formidable. Food does not grow exclusively, mostly or even largely, because of man's efforts. These efforts succeed mainly because of the natural properties of the soil and the microorganisms which live in it, the biological absorption and use of nitrogen, the energy of the sun. More pests are controlled by their natural predators than by chemical means. Such examples can be multiplied and they point to the great scope of the services provided by the natural environment. These are our natural partners, whose worth we supplement by our efforts, whose destruction constitutes an outer limit, and causes irreversible damage. The truly sustainable development process must reflect man's symbiotic dependence and provide for management of man's relationships with the environment. In the long term, the objectives of development and environment must be seen to be, if I may use the term in this context, symbiotic. Neither set of objectives has meaning without the other, both must be mutually supportive. It is entirely unrealistic to believe that the future is best assured by a development process which does not recognise our interdependence with the tropical forests, with the maintenance of the ozone layer, with the common services provided by the environment and the natural resources available to us. It is a singularly ineffective development which exploits the present without regard to future consequencs. The world of the future may indeed, as some forecast, present a gloomy prospect — but it may equally well be one which may join the satisfaction of the planned use of the wealth of the biosphere and the serendipity of new discoveries, to assure the fundamental well-being of future generations. In our linkages of the biosphere, in a better understanding of the complex biological, biochemical, ecological, socio-economic and technological factors affecting the processes of development, lie the clues to furthering our welfare through new kinds of development.

Seen in the context of these ideas, the need to develop technologies which are environmentally sound, patterns of production which are not wasteful of non renewable resources and which recycle and reuse such resources, sources of energy which are renewable and those which pollute less, assume their importance. Here is an important role for the natural scientist: the ethic of being miserly with our limited resources, of conserving and reusing, needs to be translated into concrete techniques, and knowledge of these techniques made available to the world community at large. For instance, effluents from industry are commonly regarded in terms of their effects as threats to human health and well-being. However, it has to be remarked that a pollutant is a resource in the wrong place, and certainly the well known example of sulphur which could be retrieved from factory chimneys and used for industrial purposes is a case in point. It is not rational to lose ever-increasing quantities of resources as pollutants and then to use greater quanta of resources to deal with the effects of that pollution and the scientist and technologist should turn his attention to evolving more truly efficient patterns of production.

Monitoring the Environment

The world community, in addition to fostering and encouraging the application of the approaches I have mentioned, also has tasks which largely fall into two main categories. The first is that of monitoring the environment and assessing the results of such monitoring. This is the essential basis for spotting emerging environmental problems, and ultimately for ensuring that the outer limits of the biosphere's capacity to sustain human life are not transgressed. It is essential for environmental management to ensure sustainable development and an enhanced environment. The exchange of information regarding the results of this monitoring and the evaluation thereof, thus identifying the impact of man's actions on the environment, and the carrying out of research to deal with such impacts, all enter into the international programme known as Earthwatch.

Protecting the Global Commons

In the second category falls the task of protecting the global commons and providing for its more rational use. The oceans of the world, for instance, are, to a very large extent, the property of no nation, yet each nation, by law and by tradition and by necessity, uses the oceans and their living resources without great thought to their protection. The issue of the pollution of the seas by oil has alerted the world community to the risks involved in treating our common heritage in so cavalier a fashion, and today we realise the joint responsibility that we, through our efforts at the regional and global level, must exercize in respect of actions which may affect our global commons. An aspect of this approach is to be seen in the efforts of the Economic Commission for Europe in dealing with the issue of transfrontier air pollution, and in the references to the environment in the Declaration of the Helsinki Conference on Peace and Security in Europe.

Let me now proceed to tell you how UNEP has acted with regard to the perceptions to which I have referred. Time does not permit me to dwell on what we are doing in regard to various priority areas defined by our Governing Council. I will give only a few illustrations.

Environmental Assessment

The Stockholm Conference considered that environmental assessment — or Earthwatch as its global application has come to be called — contained four functions: evaluation and review, research, monitoring and information exchange. Evaluation and review provide the analysis to identify the gaps in knowledge and action. Research provides new information, or new interpretations of old information, which may lead to a better understanding of environmental problems and thus provide guidance for the decision-making process. Monitoring gathers in a continuous and systematic fashion certain data on specific environmental variables, and evaluates such data to determine and predict important short- and long-term environmental trends. Information exchange provides data to the scientific and technological communities and so ensures that decision-makers at all levels have the benefit of the best information available at the appropriate time and in the most useable form.

Since its inception a few months after the Stockholm Conference, UNEP has begun to develop and apply this theoretical concept in practical terms, the most marked progress being made in the field of monitoring and information exchange. Thus a Global Environmental Monitoring System (GEMS), an International Referral System (INFOTERRA) and an International Register of Potentially Toxic Chemicsl (IRPTC) have been established.

The purpose of GEMS, which is a global network of monitoring systems, co-ordinated through the efforts of UNEP but executed by a number of UN Agencies and other bodies, is to establish the means to understand rapidly and correctly the changes brought about in the global environment by mankind's actions. Seven goals have been set for GEMS:

> to establish an expanded human health warning system;
> to assess global atmospheric pollution and its impact on climate;
> to assess the extent and distribution of contaminants in biological systems, particularly food chains;
> to assess the critical environmental problems relating to agriculture and land and water use;
> to assess the response of terrestrial ecosystems to the human pressures exerted on them;
> to assess the state of marine pollution and its impact on marine ecosystems;
> and finally to improve the monitoring of the factors necessary to understand and forecast natural disasters.

As you see, it is an extensive system which it will take many years to establish in its entirety, but already we have made substantial progress.

The International Referral System does not deal in the information itself, but provides a switchboard to put the seeker of information in touch with the provider of it. Thus, when fully operational, INFOTERRA will be a most valuable tool in helping governments, decision-makers, professionals, research workers, educationalists and others to gain ready access to sources of environmental information. INFOTERRA functions on the basis of support by a network of focal points at the national level. Its operational capacity and quality is thus dependent on the information governments provide.

The International Register of Potentially Toxic Chemicals will provide the means to handle data and answer queries about environmentally significant chemical substances; we hope that the IRPTC, which like INFOTERRA, will depend upon the support of the national centres for the supply and updating of data, will be operational within eighteen months or so.

The ultimate purpose of the assessment programme must be to provide early warnings of any global threats to human welfare, or even survival, brought about through man's activities which transgress the outer limits. Thus, as part of Earthwatch, UNEP has developed a programme on the outer limits. The time is not available to describe this programme at length, though you may be interestred that it contains two subjects currently of much interest to the scientific community — and of concern to the lay one — threats to the ozone layer and climatic change. In each area, and several others, we are designing programmes of research and monitoring, coupled with an evaluation mechanism, and thus building up the ability to inform the world community of the situation.

Let me expand somewhat on that example of ozone because it illustrates well the way in which each component of Earthwatch — evaluation, monitoring, research and information exchange — are being pursued by UNEP to construct a comprehensive assessment programme. Thus evaluation reveals that the ozone layer, and hence its effectiveness as a filter of harmful rays from the sun, may be reduced by the release of fluorocarbons, and, indirectly, from the manufacture and application of nitrogen fertilizers. An evaluation of the possible impact of supersonic aircraft on the ozone layer has been made by the World Meteorological Organisation which has recently issued a statement on the situation, the conclusions of which are not too alarming in respect of this particular possible hazard. A coherent programme of monitoring of total ozone and its vertical distribution is under design. UNEP intends to support research into the effect of fluorocarbons and fertilizers on the ozone layer, and also into the consequencs for life on earth of a reduced ozone layer and increased ultraviolet radiation.

The ozone programme, and other similar studies which UNEP supports, are meant to provide data which indicate the priorities for environmental management and suggest the form that management should take.

Environmental Management[1]

The concept of environmental management, as advocated by UNEP, is a broad one. It is not the management of the environment, but management of

---

[1]See also Tom Mboya lecture, p. 45.

all those human activities which have a significant impact on the environment, with due regard to environmental considerations. The most pressing objective of environmental management is to meet basic human needs within the potentials and constraints of environmental systems, including natural resources. Environmental management brings two new dimensions to the devleopment process: it *broadens* the concept to include environmental quality, and it *extends* it in time to include development over the long-term on a sustainable basis. At present environmental management is too often neglected because governments and others whose activities can affect the environment lack the necessary information, political will or resources, or find it hard to respond to the long-term and trans-sectoral nature of environmental problems; or because existing administrative, professional, legal, financial and other institutions are poorly adapted to the need for environmental management.

In collaboration with a host of UN and other bodies, UNEP has now a great many activities underway which could help further the appliction of environmental management. To take a few examples: we are demonstrating new environmental approaches to the improvement of marginal settlements in Indonesia and the Philippines; we shall be advocating an ecological approach to the management of arid and semi-arid rangelands at the United Nations Conference on Desertification in 1977; we have helped to prepare a world action plan for an environmentally sound approach to schistosomiasis control; we are establishing pilot schemes to illustrate the ecodevelopment approach, that is the application at the local level of environmental management principles within the development context; and we are establishing demonstration centres to show how renewable sources of energy can be utilized to provide the basic needs of small rural communities in developing countries. All these examples show that it is perfectly practical to introduce environmental management into every level of human acticity.

Human Settlements

The Stockholm Conference recognised the integral relationships between the man-made and natural human environment and reflected this recognition in the recommendations contained in the Action Plan. Through UNEP governments have agreed that, in the context of the concept that human settlements are man-made ecosystems, a satisfactory human settlement is one which provides shelter, sustenance, communications and employment, and which meets social and cultural needs without seriously polluting or destroying the natural environment upon which the continued life of the settlement and its inhabitants depends.

---

[1]See also the statement to the UN Conference on Human Settlements, p. 6, and the statement to the 4th Session of the Commission on Human Settlements, p. 63.

Soil Degradation

It has been estimated that the total area of destroyed and degraded soils once biologically productive amounts to about 20 million square kilometres, or more than all the arable land used for agriculture at present. Much of this degradation is due to effects of man's activities on soils, ranging from unsustainable patterns of cultivation and land use, including petrifaction, soil compaction and erosion, to strip mining and the adverse effect of industrial wastes and pollutants. The Governing Council has considered the prevention of degradation to be a priority for UNEP and activities include the preparation, in co-operation with other UN Agencies, of a world soil degradation map, the encouragement of studies on soil loss, support to the development of a methodology for processing soil data, and the establishment of a soil data bank by FAO, together with the encouragement of national research centres and institutions on soil study and reclamation.

Regional Seas

There has been a serious and sharp decline in recent years in the quality of the marine environment of several regional seas. It was quite apparent that if this is not soon halted and reversed, it will have a disastrous impact on the many communities living around them. This fact applies to all regional seas where we started, or are considering, actions, including the Mediterranean, the Caribbean, the Red Sea Malacca Straits and adjacent waters, the west coast of Africa and several gulfs. UNEP highly values the work done by Poland and other Baltic States on the protection of the Baltic Sea. The Gdansk and Helsinki Conferences are landmarks which were and will continue to be a source of inspiration in drawing up urgently needed legal instruments for protection of other regional seas. After several years of preparation, in January 1975 UNEP convened a meeting of Mediterranean Governments in Barcelona which agreed upon an action plan for the protection of the Mediterranean. This plan contains a major assessment programme involving monitoring of, and research into the health of the marine environment through the joint and co-ordinated efforts of many regional and national institutions. On the management side, the action plan contains two elements, integrated planning of the region up to the end of the century, and legal measures. At a second conference in Barcelona in February 1975, the sixteen nations present adopted unanimously a final act embodying a convention and two protocols to protect the marine environment; fifteen of them signed the act and twelve of these also signed the convention and protocols, an unprecedented proportion of states to sign a convention immediately after its finalization. The meeting also agreed to establish a centre in Malta to enable states to combat major oil spills in the Mediterranean.

Such conspicuous achievements in a region as politically sensitive as the Mediterranean are striking proof that, where the political will exists, the goal of development without destruction is attainable. But we should not delude ourselves: that act of political will does not come easily because it implies very large changes in public attitudes and expectations.

These are but a few examples of how we function. In a nutshell, what UNEP is all about is to help governments ensure a rational management of the environment, leading to a sustainable development and an enhanced environment. As I said earlier, proper management of the environment requires proper environment assessment: monitoring and evaluation of the impact of actions taken to develop the environment, an exchange of information regarding these impacts and carrying out research to deal with them. To succeed in this respect, we need supporting measures, including education and training and technical assistance. Proper environmental management also requires legislation, if enforcement of environmental measures is to be effective. The work in the priority subject areas defined by the Governing Council, e.g. human health, human settlements, oceans, arid lands, tropical forests, natural disasters, renewable sources of energy, etc. is meant to illustrate how better management of all these elements of the environment, based on the best available knowledge, may be ensured. UNEP will be better positioned when the earth component of its work has reached the stage where it can supply the necessary solid information base on which policy and decision-makers could take the most appropriate decisions with the whole series of involved interrelationships explicitly considered.

Conclusion

At UNEP we have come to realise that emerging environmental problems will be the product of the interrelationship between whole networks of factors. In such synergic systems, simple direct solutions do not produce the expected results and solutions must also involve whole networks of elements. The capacity to postulate such solutions will require efforts by scientists in transcending disciplinary frontiers, and in joining together the efforts of both natural and social scientists. We realise that the lead time required to avoid problems is now great and that a capacity has to be developed to forecast accurately results of alternative policies and to choose the best track. This is an intellectual challenge which strains present techniques of management and, in the resolution which established UNEP, the General Assembly has called on our Organisation to seek to use the capacities of the scientific and professional communities across the world. In presenting to you this overview of the nature of the problems that face the environment, and the way in which we visualise our actions in the resolution of these problems, I invite you to join with us in making your contribution.

5

ARE DEVELOPMENT AND ENVIRONMENTAL PROTECTION COMPATIBLE?

Statement to the Economic and Social Council of the United Nations at its sixty-first session

Abidjan, Ivory Coast, July 1976

THE interdependence between the problems of population and resources, environment and development[1] has come to dominate the world's agenda at such recent conferences as those on the Human Environment, Food[2], Population, Trade and Development, HABITAT,[3] and the World Employment Conference, and has also been recognised by the General Assembly of the United Nations.

In each of these forums, we have faced the inescapable truth that the remedies we propose in any particular regard must equally be remedies when seen in the wider context. I wish to address myself to one aspect of the composite environment-development-population-resources nexus, that of the relationship between environment and development.

Environment and Development

It is our belief in UNEP that this relationship is one of the central topics confronting the world community. If we are to face up to the complexities of this relationship, if we are to cope with its full implications, we have to adopt the right policies at every level.

However, we do realise that behind the external expression of the

---

[1] For a detailed discussion, see p. 28.
[2] For the statement to the World Food Conference, see p. 1.
[3] For the statement to the UN Conference on Human Settlements, see p. 6.

problems inherent in such a relationship lie more deeply rooted social and political forces, whose true dimensions are still exceedingly difficult to assess. To mention only the most striking of these uncertainties, the significance of man's impact on nature and society has been tremendously augmented by this century's breakthroughs in the nuclear, chemical and biological sciences. It is not nature that is at the root of many of the world's most urgent problems, but man's manipulation of nature. To muster the social consensus needed to redefine and refocus these manipulations has become a fundamental necessity of our times.

Many of the negative aspects of development have so impressed themselves on the minds of those concerned with the environment that the question is often asked "Why development"? Some in the developed countries go so far as to advocate protecting the environment by arresting economic growth.

It is true that past industrial and agricultural development has, largely through mismanagement by man of natural ecosystems, created many environmental problems, including pollution of water, soil and air and its consequent costs to human health and well-being. These threats are not localized; by themselves or through their interactions with other factors, they become matters of regional or global concern. An example which has been much quoted recently is the possible impact on global climate of the continued combustion of fossil fuels to meet energy demands. Such cases constitute dangers to the "outer limits" which man must respect for his long-term well-being, even for his survival.

But environmental problems are caused also by a lack of adequate development. Today there are hundreds of millions of people without the basic human needs of adequate food, shelter, clothing and health; hundreds of millions more lack access to even a rudimentary education or regular employment. This is not only an intolerable situation in human terms; it also has serious environmental consequences. The relentless pressures that arise where basic human needs are not met can erase the resource base from which man must inevitably gain his sustenance. The destruction of forests, the loss of arable soil, the loss of productivity through disease and malnutrition and the increasing pressure on fragile ecosystems which so often result from poverty are as significant as the pollution created by industry, technology and overconsumption by the affluent; both lead to the rapid depletion of basic natural resources.

With these thoughts in mind, I reach three conclusions in answer to the question "Why development"? First, that for the developing countries in the world, in which more than two thirds of mankind live, there is no alternative to pursuing economic and social development so as to secure better prospects for their citizens. What is more, the lesson of the United Nations Conference on Population, held at Bucharest in 1974, is that only when this has been done, and the poor in the world experience a more satisfactory existence, can there be any marked slowing of the population increase which is in itself a major contributory factor to environmental problems.

Next, I conclude that the nature and extent of destruction or otherwise of the natural environment depends to a large degree on the manner in which development takes place. My third conclusion is that far from being in conflict, environmental and development objectives are complementary.

Complementarity of Environmental and Development Objectives

A few years ago, it was commonplace to characterize the environmental problem solely in terms of pollution, and to measure economic and social development solely in terms of the increase in gross national product. Given these premises, the pursuit of environmental objectives through pollution control would be a check on development. But in fact there have been significant advances in recent years in our understanding of what is meant by environmental and development objectives and a growing acceptance that these converge.

We may now look upon environment as the stock, seen in dynamic terms, of physical or social resources available at a given time for the satisfaction of human needs, and upon development as a process pursued by all societies, with the aim of increasing human well-being. Thus the ultimate purpose of both environmental and development policies is to improve the quality of life. In recognition of this, terms emerge like "the new development" or "alternative styles of development", which suggest a more rounded way of looking at the purposes of development, in which environmental considerations play a central role.

It is conventional wisdom that today we stand at the high point of an age of technological advance, that we know what are the requirements of development and how it may be managed, how it may be achieved rapidly using modern technology. Yet do the industrialized countries of this world themselves believe that they have achieved a sustainable development, within our current concepts of resources and their availability, and of the fragility of the biosphere of this "only one earth"?

We believe that new kinds of development are needed. They are needed because it is essential to relate development to the limitations and opportunities created by the natural resource base to all human activities. They are required because it is now clear that past patterns of development in both developed and developing countries have been characterised by such serious environmental damage that they are simply not sustainable. They are required because of increasing inequalities, especially internationally. They are also required because past patterns have not met the expectations of peoples in the developing world.

There should, however, be certain important differences between the forms that the new kinds of development might take in rich and poor countries. In the industrialized countries society's aims must be reoriented so that the entire population has more opportunity for self-expression in the fields of culture, education, the arts and humanities — those non-physical areas of development which represent the highest levels of human achievement.

This new orientation must be less demanding of natural resources, energy and the environment. Present patterns of production and consumption, based on waste, extravagance and planned obsolescence, must be replaced by patterns based on conservation and reuse of resources. I am encouraged by signs from several industrialized countries that such a reorientation of life styles and societal aims can now be discussed seriously, though clearly the change implied by this approach is an immense one, which it will take many years to carry through.

In the developing world, which still lacks the infrastructure and readily useable resources required to meet the growing needs and aspirations of its peoples, the new kind of development must continue to have a strong physical orientation. But each country should be helped to follow a path to development best suited to its needs and accords with its own culture and value systems. Developing countries should have access to the technologies that they require to support this kind of development under conditions which will enable them to adapt these technologies to their own requirements, rather than have alien technologies dictate or unduly distort their development process. Most of all, the new forms of development in the developing world should be based on environmentally sound use of their natural resources of soil, water, plant and animal life to avoid the destruction of the resource base on which sustained development depends.

The rich industrialized countries have an enormous investment in or commitment to a technological *status quo*, one which in its profligate use of resources and support of overconsumption may not even be the most efficient model under present circumstances. A striking example of this phenomenon may be seen in some countries where railways and public transportation systems are inadequate because of economies geared to the production of private automobiles. Radical and rapid changes of direction for such economies are the more difficult, and I would say, at the risk of exaggeration, that it is not easy for the overdeveloped to take quick advantage of technological innovations which conserve resources, compromise production patterns in which heavy investments have been made, or require a greater input of human labour. Such advances are to the advantage of countries on the threshold of a more modern development, and may give them competitive advantages as yet unconsidered. A more efficient form of development may in many respects now be possible for the developing countries than for the developed countries.

Let us be assured that we have not come to the end of the age of discovery of our inner space, our biosphere, but may stand yet on the very threshold of it. Many advances to the benefit of all of us may yet await us as we seek to learn from natural processes. In harmony with them we may further our welfare.

The power of the tides and currents, and the secrets of the genetic diversity and biochemical complexity surrounding us, are among the many features of our world which are as yet unexplored. And yet these are the riches, full of promise, which we compromise through heedless action, actions mighty in their possible destructive impact but which are nevertheless dependent on natural processes if they are to yield us the fullest benefit. Food does not grow exclusively, mostly, or even largely, because of man's efforts. These efforts succeed because of the natural properties of the soil and the microorganisms which live in it, the biological absorption and use of nitrogen, the energy of the sun. More pests are controlled by their natural predators than by chemical means. Such examples can be multiplied and they point to the great scope of the services provided by the natural predators than by chemical means. Such examples can be multiplied and they point to the great scope of the services provided by the natural environment. These are our natural partners, whose worth we supplement by our efforts, whose destruction violates the outer limits and causes irreversible and irretrievable damage. Yet each year, we add to the biosphere thousands of new chemical compounds unknown in nature and, in terms of their long-term effects on our children and their children, equally unknown to us. Each year we engage in actions which may compromise by permitting increasing quantities of biologically significant ultraviolet radiation to pass through it at considerable risk to our health and well-being.

It is entirely unrealistic to believe that the future is best assured by a development process which does not recognize our interdependence with the tropical forests, with the maintenance of the ozone layer, with the common services provided by the environment and the natural resources available to us. It is a singularly ineffective development which does not take this interdependence into account, or which exploits the present without regard to future consequences. The world of the future may indeed, as some forecast, be a gloomy prospect — but it may equally well be a world which joins planned use of the wealth of the biosphere and the opportunities offered by new discoveries to assure the basic well-being of future generations.

In our linkages with the biosphere, in a better understanding of the complex biological, biochemical, ecological, socio-economic and technological factors affecting the process of development, lie the clues to furthering our welfare through new kinds of development.

I hope that I have shown the mutually supportive nature of environment and development objectives within the environment-development-population-resources nexus. The pursuit of harmonized environment and development goals may thus lead to a faster, more sustainable development than is the case for conventional development goals alone, and may lead also to more positive protection and improvement of the environment than purely environmental goals as such. Across the whole series of interactions between environment, development, population and resources, harmonized objectives need to be articulated. This must, we believe, be an immediate priority when states review the goals of the Development Decade and the implementation of the Programme of Action for the establishment of a New International Economic Order.

Principles of Development

We believe, in UNEP, that each nation must accept the responsibility for planning and managing its own development so as to achieve a sustainable balance between its resources, its population and its capacity to meet the needs and aspirations of its people. And all nations must join in creating a more equitable and viable world system based on a realistic and achievable set of common principles. I submit that such principles guide UNEP's activities. These are:

1. that the starting point for the world community must be to meet basic human needs;
2. that the immediate purpose of development should be to satisfy those needs;
3. that the process of development itself can and should improve the environment. Deleterious effects often result when development activities are haphazard and unmanaged and do not take account of ecological constraints. When this happens the natural resource base upon which continued development depends is placed in jeopardy;
4. that we must monitor the impact of development processes and identify when this threatens the life-supporting systems of the biosphere and thus endangers human well-being;
5. that in order to meet this objective of sustainable development without destruction of the natural resource base, we need to promote alternative patterns of development, and life styles, in both rich and poor countries.

Conclusion

The attitude to environment and development I have been attempting to describe in the preceding paragraphs is perhaps best exemplified in the Cocoyoc Declaration adopted by the joint UNEP/United Nations Conference on Trade and Development Symposium on Patterns of Resource Use, Environment and Development Strategies, held in Mexico in October 1974:

"We have faith in the future of mankind on this planet. We believe that ways of life and social systems can be evolved that are more just, less arrogant in their material demands, more respectful of the whole planetary environment. The road forward does not lie through the despair of doom-watching nor through the easy optimism of successive technological fixes. It lies through a careful and dispassionate assessment of the 'outer limits', through the co-operative search for ways to achieve the 'inner limits' of fundamental human rights, and through all the patient work of devising techniques and styles of development which enhance and preserve our planetary inheritance".[1]

---

[1] For the full text of Cocoyoc Declaration, see "In Defence of the Earth," Executive Series 1, UNEP, Nairobi, 1981.

6

SOCIAL JUSTICE, PEACE AND ENVIRONMENTALLY SOUND DEVELOPMENT

Statement to the World Conference on Development convened by the World Peace Council

Budapest, Hungary, October 1976

SOCIAL JUSTICE, peace and environmentally sound development are complex and vital subjects in today's world. Each one of these three issues is of critical importance in the enhancement of man's welfare including the quality of his life. Moreover, a dispassionate and deep appreciation of the interrelationships among these vital issues, especially at the level of national policy formulation, is crucial to the achievement of sustainable and internationally harmonious enhancement in the quality of human life. There is no doubt that without this the notion of development is bereft of much meaning in human terms.

Three principal aspects of the broad notion of "social justice" are pertinent here:
1. eradication of acute mass poverty;
2. an equitable distribution of income, consumption and wealth;
3. popular participation in work and decision-making.

Social justice must be sought within and between nations and for this and coming generations. And when I speak of peace, I do not mean merely an absence of political conflict but rather a state of harmonious and mutually satisfying relationships among peoples and countries.

Economic Development

It is now recognised that past trends and patterns of economic growth have not been generally satisfactory. Benefits of growth have been distributed very unequally between and within countries, while the production and consumption patterns accompanying that growth have led to a rapid depletion of natural resources and have often caused unacceptable levels of environmental degradation.

Extrapolations based on past growth have at times led to cautionary warnings against economic growth as such. However, it is important that concerns about economic growth are placed in a correct global perspective, because the experience of growth, and of the attendant improvements in standards of living, have been widely divergent both among countries and within countries. Growth is not bad *per se*, and if we ignored the variable pattern of growth and the benefits which have occurred, we would fail to make a scientifically rigorous examination of the issues involved in the contemporary problem of world development. Moreover, we would encounter difficulty in our search for development patterns which are consistent with international harmony, social jutice and peace.

It is depressing and deplorable that there are today hundreds of millions of people who live in grave conditions of poverty — conditions in which they are denied such basic needs of decent human living as adequate food, water, health, shelter, clothing, education and employment. The World Food Conference,[1] the important work by the World Bank on poverty and income distribution, the World Health Organization's initiatives in the area of basic health needs of people in developing countries, the Conference on Human Settlements (HABITAT),[2] the World Conference on Employment, Income Distribution and Social Progress and International Division of Labour, as well as the work done by UNEP since its establishment, have all helped clarify the nature and dimensions of the task of eradication of acute mass poverty. It is estimated, for example, that something like 70 per cent of the world's population does not have access to safe water, that more than 450 million people may actually be starving, that 200 million people may be without jobs and that the lowest 40 per cent of the population in developing countries are on average receiving only 12.5 per cent of the national incomes generated.

While the imperative for continued economic development is compelling enough in view of the urgency and the magnitude of the task of eradicating mass poverty, there are also other reasons for the argument that continued economic development is essential to the global enhancement of the quality of human life. There are at least three important aspects to this point.

The impact of population growth

As we all know, there is no unanimity regarding the cause-effect relationships involved or on the most appropriate policies necessary in this

---
[1] For the statement to the World Food Conference, see p. 1.
[2] For the statement to the UN Conference on the Human Settlements, see p. 6.

highly charged field. However, a consensus has emerged, especially since the World Population Conference at Bucharest in August 1974, to the effect that while high rates of population increase in relation to resource availability create environmental problems and hinder the task of development, minimum needs for decent human living must be satisfied if success is to crown any policy to control birth rates. Concurrent historical observation of improvements in levels of living of people on the one hand and falls in birth rates on the other hand, in most developed countries and in some developing countries, supports this view. Thus, to those environmentalists who are rightly concerned about the environmental consequences of expanding populations, I say that the vicious circle of poverty and population growth can only be broken by accelerated socio-economic development.

Impact of material deprivation

Widespread material deprivation engenders patterns of human behaviour which are environmentally damaging — a phenomemon which, with its cumulative impact over time, makes living conditions of the poor still more precarious and vulnerable to natural forces. A common and tragic example of such a poverty-environment relationship is the widespread dependence of the poor on firewood for domestic fuel. To a poor household, firewood is often the only source of energy for cooking and heating. But the resultant feeling of trees in poverty-striken areas, unless properly compensated for by public action, eventually leads to cumulative erosion of good agricultural soil and finally to desertification. Similarly, pressures of subsistence living may force farmers to cultivate marginal lands intensively, year after year. Such poverty-induced environmentally imprudent farming practices will in time turn once productive soils into barren lands. Neither of these examples should be taken as conjecture or theory; there is ample proof that ecological catastrophes are being brought about in precisely this fashion.

In the urban sectors, dwellers in shanty towns, deprived of access to basic facilities for drinking water and waste disposal are frequently forced to use open water for washing, cleaning and waste in unhygienic ways, to break open municipal water mains; to use public places such as parks and open grounds to relieve themselves, and to live in makeshift shelters surrounded by accumulating domestic waste. The humanly degrading conditions of life in urban slums already call out for urgent amelioration not only in the interest of social justice and peace but also of protection and enhancement of the human environment. It is well known, for example, that unhygienic living conditions in slums can spread diseases like typhoid, cholera, malaria and hepatitis among entire settlements. Furthermore, it is estimated that world's urban population will grow by about 1,300 million people in the next twenty-five years. If present trends continue, 75 per cent of these people would live in slums — thus creating a truly serious human environment problem. Therefore, in both the rural and the urban context, there are sound environmental reasons for promoting the enhancement of living conditions of the poor.

Economic benefit to developed countries

Economic development of the low income countries or groups of populations within developed countries is conducive to the economic well-being and environmental enhancement in developed countries or regions as well. The maintenance of profits, market demand, investments and employment at high levels in the developed areas has often appeared to require the artificial creation, for example through advertising, of all kinds of new wants in developed as well as developing countries. Production patterns and consumption styles which these drives have engendered have been costly in terms of depletion of the world's key natural resources and of environmental degradation. There is little doubt that the means employed in pursuing economic stability and employment levels in the developed countries have often been inefficient and wasteful both from a global environmental standpoint and from the standpoint of world development. If developed and developing countries see their own economic well-being and social progress in the global perspective of sustainable and harmonious world development, a mutually beneficial collaboration could ensue. This collaboration could take the form of appropriate trade, investment, development assistance and technology cooperation that would not only be conducive to improvement of living conditions of populations at large in developing countries but also to fostering economic well-being and social progress in developed countries while protecting the integrity and beauty of the human environment everywhere.

Therefore, the case can never be against economic development *per se*, but rather against the course it has taken in many developed countries, and several developing countries in the last few decades.

Development Strategies

One other point which is now generally agreed is that strategies of development focussing merely on acceleration of growth of national output in aggregative terms are simply not viable. There are two main criticisms of this: First, exclusive reliance on growth has failed to bring about a broadly based participation in the benefits of development; in particular, it has failed to achieve reductions in the extent of poverty or to generate employment on significant scales; and that, in some instances, it has even exacerbated already glaring income, consumption and wealth inequalities. Second, such strategies have been, as I said earlier, very costly in terms of resource depletion, environmental pollution and the lowering of the quality of human life.

The first argument is advanced particularly in respect of growth strategies adopted in developing countries while the second argument is mainly advanced in respect of growth policies of developed countries. However, both criticisms are applicable to developing as well as developed countries, though in differing degrees. Further, the emerging patterns of production and life styles in developed as well as developing countries have exacerbated already existing extreme inequalities in levels of living and wealth internationally. It has been estimated, for example, that 80 per cent of the increase in world's wealth during 1960 – 71 accrued to countries with per capita income of $1,000 and above, while only six per cent accrued to countries with per capita income of $200 and below. These growing extremes in income and wealth distributions are prejudicial to the protection of human environment and to world peace.

Economic Development and the Quality of Human Life

Given that economic development is a must, but that our experience of the results of growth in recent decades cannot be considered very satisfactory, it becomes necessary to explain why recent events have failed to meet expectations.

1. First, there has been an uncritical dependence on the market mechanism to determine choice in what is to be produced, in what proportions how it is to be produced and where the production activity is to be located. While markets may often given valuable guidance to public policy, even the most perfect of all markets cannot appropriately reflect human needs because they typically do not take fully into account social and environmental considerations (which are often regarded by economists as externalities). While market forces respond to prevailing distributions of purchasing power these distributions may themselves be far different from what would be desirable from the standpoint of social justice, or of guaranteeing conditions of decent human living for all.

2. Another fundamental cause has been that priorities for public investment have not necessarily been guided by a conscious concern for improving levels of living of the poor in particular, or for protecting and enhancing the human environment in general. In many developing countries, governments' direction of growth has been dominated by the urge to adopt quickly foreign production patterns, technologies and life styles. In the process, much that had been good in their own tradition, culture and ways of living has been lost in the effort to "develop". Moreover, such patterns of growth have eroded the foundation of self-reliance at national and local levels. They have also failed to foster mutually beneficial cooperation between developing countries themselves.

   In developed countries, on the other hand, the drive towards increasing sophistication and advancement of material consumption have led to wasteful use of mineral resources that are today critically important to the industrial and agricultural development of the world at large, developed and developing countries alike and thereby raised the price of the remaining reserves.

3. A third main cause of the failure of the growth experience to enhance globally the quality of human life has been the absence of enough knowledge about the changing condition of human life and too much readiness to accept blindly simple economic indicators of national success. We have chosen to measure our accomplishments in very narrow terms such as growth of industrial or aggregate production and growth of income per capita. We have not looked at our quality of life comprehensively enough; nor have we looked far enough into the future. It is only now that we are beginning to be confronted with such statistics as that the world spends about 300,000 million dollars a year on armaments and only about 15,000 million by way of aid; or that the average consumption of resources or energy in a rich country may be more than a thousand times their average consumption in a poor country. What that means for this generation is alarming enough; for further generations it implies a dim prospect, unless fundamental changes take place soon in the policies which national states pursue.

It is unrealistic to hope for peace, tranquillity and harmony within societies or among nations while development patterns remain environmentally destructive and socially unsatisfactory. There is no peace for the man who is denied basic material necessities of life. Nor is there peace in the heart of the man who is denied the psychological and social satisfaction of living and working as a human being in a community of people. The discontent and the frustration generated under such conditions is liable to find expression in the form of spreading crime, violence, the breaking up of deeply valued institutions like the family, and outright social and political unheavals with consequent human suffering. Moreover, under such circumstances, there are risks that governments might be tempted to indulge in adventurism, regional conflicts and international confrontations; they may be prodded by internal pressures of military-industrial growth, moved by the quest to obtain command over vital but rapidly depleting resources, or act in a calculated effort to induce artificially the lacking social unity and national purpose.

Thus conditions in our world are not very favourable and since we have to live together in it, it is essential that we adopt a cooperative and global approach to the problems of world poverty and of the contemporary human condition. Of course every country is free to choose the path of development it considers most appropriate to its own historical, social, economic, political and physical circumstances. Nevertheless, considerations of rationality, humanity and of interdependence require that national development policies now be guided by lessons learnt from past growth experience and by a vision of achieving a global enhancement in the quality of human life.

The complexity and the magnitude of the task of world development is such that one can only be extremely modest and cautious in putting forth suggestions by way of suitable strategies, policies and measures. Yet I believe there are available some signposts that we must not ignore if we are to achieve durable enhancement in the quality of human life. Let me merely point to the more outstanding of these signposts.

Signposts for Development

Basic Human Needs

Developing countries should make a serious effort to evolve and pursue decent minimum standards for housing, including water supply and sanitation, health services, nutrition, clothing, education and employment. Public policies bearing on investment, production, trade, income distribution and prices should be consciously guided with a view to achieving, in a phased manner, the satisfaction of basic human needs in accordance with these standards.

Policies are needed to expand productive employment so as, *inter alia,* to attain minimum incomes; to ensure equitable income distribution patterns; and careful spatial planning to ensure at least a minimum access of the poor to essential services and facilities. Policies are also required to guide growth and trade so that the excessive preemption of wealth by an affluent minority is avoided and the population at large has better access to the goods and services which are produced.

Various dimensions of this unified context of planning development along lines that would facilitate a broadly based satisfaction of basic human needs are reflected in the recent work of various international agencies in the field of development. For example, one sees a growing emphasis on primary and preventive health services in the work of WHO, on basic education in the work of UNESCO and on improving the productivities and incomes of small farmers and landless labourers in the development loan policies of the World Bank. Further, since 1974 the international community has been attaching a great deal of significance to expanding production and storage and improving distribution of primary cereals. The investigative and advisory work of ILO in the field of employment expansion and the work of the World Bank and UNEP in the field of improvement of marginal urban settlements are also part of the growing concern for satisfaction of basic human needs in development.

In developed countries, as well, it is essential to reorientate patterns of production and consumption in ways which accord to rational, just and humane social orders and to economic justice and environmental protection and enhancement. Policies should be adopted which pursue these aims within the richer countries and through their trading and other relationships with developing countries, in the Third World too. Actions towards this end should include curbs in production of armaments, growing involvement in the peaceful settlement of regional conflicts, curbs on the wasteful uses of energy and of natural resources now obvious in the consumption patterns, development of resource-saving and energy-saving technologies, schemes addressed specifically to improving blighted living conditions especially for urban popualtions, and a growing emphasis on cultural, artistic and other non-materialist sources of human happiness. Further, there should be increasing assistance from developed countries to developing countries to assist them to improve their human environment.

Environmentally Sound Development

Spatial location of productive activity, and therefore of settlements, must be guided within and among countries along such lines as would respect the carrying capacities of ecosystems, basic social institutions like the family and fundamental individual and social values. This principle has several important implictions at the level of practical policy. For example, through dissemination of relevant information, through legislation and by means of systems of incentives, private decision-making should be made to reflect the long-term evaluation of social costs and benefits involved in questions of size and location of production. The issues involved here are of course complex and their satisfactory resolution will vary with the kind of production activity involved and with other aspects of the situation concerned. But I think at least the direction in which decisions ought to be influenced is clear enough. There is today a considerable opportunity and a need to spread industrial development widely over rural areas of developing countries, to foster growth of small and medium-sized towns and to relieve the extraordinary pressures on the human environment inherent in the uncontrolled growth of cities.

Industries processing agricultural produce, those manufacturing agricultural inputs or light consumer goods as well as industries processing bulky natural resources can, with advantage, be located in the countryside where more people in developing countries live. There is growing evidence that widely held beliefs about the advantages of the economies of scale are not always justified. The statement that 'Small is beautiful' has some truth and relevance to those pursuing environmentally sound forms of development.

Further, the imperatives of social justice as well as environmental protection require that rural areas of developing countries be fully integrated in the mainstream of development. A proper spread of industrial activity is one aspect of this integration; another, is the planned provison of facilities and services for basic consumption such as water supply, sanitation, public health, education and public transport. Still another is the promotion of sustained increases in rural employment, productivities and incomes. Finally, there is the urgent need to take direct steps to arrest deforestation, soil erosion, spread of desertification and to improve water management practices in rural areas.

An important implication of spatial planning for environmental enhancement and social justice relates to the international distribution of new industrial capacity. The establishment of a New International Economic Order agreed upon by the General Assembly implies, in part, that developing countries strengthen their industrial base. The International Conference on Industrialization held in Lima in 1975, declared that by the year 2000 the share of developing countries in world industrial production should have increased to 25 per cent from its 1974 level of 7 per cent. The achievement of that target should, of course, be pursued on the basis of environmentally sound programmes.

Appropriate Technology

Innovation in technology and its adoption, whether in industry, agriculture or infrastructure should be guided by public policy designed to conserve resources, save energy, minimise waste and generate employment.

There is likely to be considerable coincidence between considerations of environmental protection and enhancement and those on technologies which are more appropriate. Small-scale well and pump irrigation for water supply, and the use of village refuse and wastes to make biogas energy and fertilizer are two cases in point. Moreoever, the responsibility for evolving appropriate technology is not to be confined to developing countries alone. An excellent instance of the emergence of an appropriate technique from a developed country has been the recent American concept of drilling seeds into untilled, mulched, contoured and terraced soils. This new farming technique bears the promise of extending the nutritive life of topsoils several times their normal spans, while saving energy and expanding employment.

Popular Participation

No matter how sound the public policies for environmentally responsible and socially just development, it is crucial that administrative and institutional mechanisms mobilise popular participation in their implementation and their continued evolution. Since the notion "quality of life" has an abiding subjective aspect, it is essential that the population at large participates actively in the formulation and implementation of development programmes and projects. Participation is a two way concept: the citizen at large comes to understand the aims of the society in which he lives and thus to respond positively to public policies; and second, the planning aurhorities derive benefit from the first hand experience of citizens in facing development and environment problems and working out their own, often traditional, solutions. Of course, the perception of developmental-environmental issues at the level of an individual or a group may not always coincide with the society's long term and broader perception.

Conclusion

I should say that when development and environmental goals are defined appropriately following considerations of social justice and global enhancement in the quality of human life, there are no conflicts between environmental improvement and development. In fact, they will be complementary and will actually tend to coincide. Further, pursuit of development along environmentally responsible and socially just lines by all countries will contribute greatly to healthy international cooperation and to the emergence of a just and lasting new international economic order and to international peace.

To realise this ideal and as implicit in what I have been saying, it is necessary to evolve alternative patterns of development and lifestyles in both rich and poor countries. Evolution of such alternatives underscores the urgent need for prudent environmental management. By environmental management we do not mean management of the environment but management of the actions of man that affect the environment. Prudent environmental management requires us to master the social consensus and economic means necessary to guide man's activities so that they enhance the environment; it is a fundamental necessity of our times to match up to this challenge, at the community, national and international levels.

In the years ahead, we face the task of meeting the minimum human needs of mankind and of avoiding environmental catastrophes. Contrary to doomsday prophecies we do not believe that disaster is inevitable. But the urgency is extreme: there is very little time in which to set right our approach to environmental management and to meet the legitimate demands of the world's poor. What is required is not incremental *ad hoc* steps taken for environmental protection, but prudent environmental management accompanied by the realisation that the ultimate self-interest of all nations is inevitably merged in an inescapable web of interdependence. We need to act far more thoroughly and speedily than hitherto to redress environmental and human grievances; to do so, we must harness the energies of all sectors of society in this effort. The job is difficult but not impossible: given enough political will, adequate resources and sound scientific advice, the obstacles will be overcome.

7

ENVIRONMENTAL MANAGEMENT

The Tom Mboya[1] Lecture delivered at The Kenya Institute of Management

Nairobi, Kenya, November 1976

I HAVE chosen the topic of environmental management as the title of my address for two reasons: First, it is a natural theme upon which to speak to the Institute of Management. But I have selected it, too, because the subject has become the chief concern of UNEP. I will present some of the basic issues concerning the evolution of our thinking and understanding about the environment and, in so doing, put the relatively new concept of environmental management into its proper context.

Evolution of Environmental Thinking

An international organization like UNEP has no sovereign power. Such authority as it has, flows from the quality of the arguments it musters and the effectiveness of its attempts to catalyze others into action. Inevitably this is a long, slow, process. Anybody who studies the history of international organizations will be familiar with the time given over to discussion and negotiation, through which concepts painfully evolve, and from which our thinking and perception of international problems gradually change. One of the inescapable facts bearing on this process is the universality of the membership of United Nations organizations; this requires the identification

---

[1]Tom Mboya (1930 – 1969) was a distinguished Kenyan who at the time of his death was the Minister for Economic Planning and Development of the Government of Kenya. He was the first National Chairman of the Kenya Institute of Management (KIM). The Lecture Series was instituted in his honour, and every year a distinguished personality is invited to give the Tom Mboya Lecture.

of shared ground between nations and accommodation of their legitimately different views and interests. The evolution of the concept of "environment" and our understanding of environmental problems, offers a good illustration of this process, and, at the same time, illuminates the evolution of our concept of environmental management.

Under the impact of problems facing the industrialized societies, and prior to the United Nations Conference on Human Environment which was held at Stockholm in 1972, environment used to be considered essentially a problem of pollution, the solution to which lay in pollution abatement. It was seen as a technical question, amenable to technological, legal and administrative answers. Though this narrow definition may still be prevalent in some places, and many people still tend to think of environmental problems solely in terms of polluted streams, air and seas, few who are well acquainted with the matter would be satisfied with this limited, restrictive interpretation.

You may recall that, in the pre-Stockholm days, many developing countries were very suspicious of "environment" as a public issue on a global scale. Of course they were not unaware of the threats which uncontrolled pollution posed to the global environment and of the possible impacts of these on them; they realized, too, that problems of pollution would be increasingly faced by their own societies; and some leaders, at least, felt that they should avoid the mistakes already committed by the industrialized countries. Moreover, the positive potential of environmental concern was also recognized; for example, developing countries might benefit from the dispersal of polluting but productive industries from industrialized countries, and there was a possibility of substituting natural products produced in developing countries at the expense of the environmentally suspect synthetic ones.

Yet many developing countries had misgivings. Some saw environment as a ploy of the rich countries to prevent the poor nations from industrializing, and to keep them as sources of essential supplies for the continued development and prosperity of the industrial countries. Some argued that if pollution meant industry, they would welcome pollution whole-heartedly. More realistically, perhaps, some feared that aid from developed countries would be diverted to the "new" problem of environment, to the detriment of their development ambitions. If anyone should be disadvantaged by a concern for environment, they argued, it was the rich countries who were largely responsible for pollution. Developing countries also feared that environmental concerns would impose extra burdens on them, for example, by paying more for imported technology and machinery which had to meet stringent environmental standards; and they suspected that their export trade with the industrialized societies would be harmed because of the environmental measures and standards that the importing nations were likely to adopt. All in all, therefore, environment and development were seen as being in conflict, and it was feared that a commitment by the international community to environment was likely to detract from its commitment to development.

To clarify the issues and to point out the linkages and interdependencies between development and environment, a panel of experts from both developed and developing countries met in 1971 in Founex, Switzerland. The Founex report[1] represents a landmark in the evolution of the concept of environment. The panel identified the interests of the developing countries in the environment and the many and serious environmental problems which were largely concentrated in the Third World. Environmental problems of developing countries are very often the result of extreme poverty and the lack of economic and social development. For example, it is in the developing countries that the quality of water is lowest, the standards of housing least satisfactory, sanitation and nutrition worst, disease most prevalent and natural disasters most destructive; it is in the poorer countries, too, that the destruction of vital natural resources, such as soils, vegetation cover and wildlife is most alarmingly evident, and the impact of a fast-growing population most apparent. The panel also made it clear that many of the environmental problems already distressingly familiar in the richer countries would emerge in the developing countries — perhaps sooner than many realised — through industrial and agricultural growth, and the growth of transport and communications sytems. Though the Founex panel indicated differences between the environmental problems of rich and poor countries, they established that many were shared concerns and, demonstrated beyond doubt, that developing countries themselves faced vast environmental difficulties.

The conclusions of the Founex panel were elaborated at the regional seminars held in the developing world which helped to provide the basis on which the Stockholm Conference[2] could deal with the relationship between environment and development. In particular five broad understandings emerged from Founex and Stockholm:

> First, the understanding of environment was broadened from an approach which heavily emphasized the natural sciences, was essentially technocratic and dealt primarily with consequences, to a more holistic approach, encompassing socio-economic factors which are the ultimate causes of many environmental problems.

> Second, the link between development and environment concerns was clarified.

> Third, there was a wider understanding of the proper aims of development so that quality of life rather than a limitless pursuit of material possessions became the principal criterion of success.

---

[1] For the Founex Report, see "In Defence of the Earth," Executive Series 1, UNEP, Nairobi, 1981.
[2] For the full text of Stockholm Declaration and the Action Plan, see "In Defence of the Earth," Executive Series 1, UNEP, Nairobi, 1981.

Fourth, developing countries came to appreciate the need to incorporate environmental considerations into their development efforts.

And finally, it became understood that the environment agenda should be expanded, and that an already complex issue had become even more complex.

Following the Stockholm Conference, the United Nations General Assembly had to decide on the location of the new organisation which would be entrusted with the implementation of the Stockholm Action Plan[1]. One of the key reasons for locating UNEP in a Third World country was to ensure that it would be sensitive to the environmental needs of developing countries and to their perception of the problems. Further, it was expected that the interest of the developing countries in the field of environment would be greater if the organisation were located in the Third World. On both counts, I think, this reasoning has proved correct.

Thinking advanced considerably beyond Founex and Stockholm at the Cocoyoc Symposium on Patterns of Resource Use, Environment and Development Strategies[1], which was jointly organised by UNEP and UNCTAD, and held in Mexico in 1974. The symposium reached agreement on these points:

1. Economic and social factors, for example, patterns of wealth and income distribution, and economic behaviour within and between countries, which lead to development problems and inequities, are often the root cause of environmental degradation.

2. Satisfaction of the basic human needs of the world's population was a chief goal for the international community and of nation states. It was especially important to meet the requirements of the poorest strata of mankind, but needs must be met without impinging upon the outer limits of the carrying capacity of the biosphere.

3. Different nations, and different groups within them, placed widely different demands on the biosphere; access to many cheap natural resources was preempted by the rich. However, irrational and wasteful uses of natural resources were by no means solely a characteristic of conspicuous life styles; the poor, too, were often left with no option but to destroy vital natural resources.

4. Developing countries should not follow in the footsteps of the industrialised countries, but should develop their own self-reliant approach to development.

---

[1] For the full text of the Cocoyoc Declaration, and the Stockholm Action Plan, see "In Defence of the Earth," Executive Series 1, UNEP, Nairobi, 1981.

5. The search for alternative patterns of development and new life styles, in both developed and developing countries, was the principal means of achieving environmental and development goals.

6. Finally, this generation should have the vision to take account of the needs of future generations and not so preempt the plant's limited resources, and so pollute its life supporting systems, that the future well-being of man, even his existence, was jeopardised.

I believe that three messages emerged from Cocoyoc which offer a key — I would say the *only* key — to a better, fairer future for mankind. These are:
— the satisfaction of basic human needs for all;
— the need to do this without transgressing the planet's outer limits of biological tolerance;
— the means to harmonise these two aims is the process we call 'environmental management'.

Since the Cocoyoc symposium of 1974, these ideas have gained currency in international discussions and are increasingly talked about in the context of revising the present international development strategy, and implementing the New International Economic Order.

Environmental Management

This brief history of the evolution of a concept reveals why we in UNEP believe that environmental and development objectives are complementary, and that if we look upon environment as the stock, seen in dynamic terms, of physical and social resources available at a given time for the satisfaction of human needs, and upon development as a process, pursued by all societies, aimed at increasing human well-being and maintaining it in the long term, we will have no choice but to direct and manage development along lines that are environmentally appropriate.

Recognition and reflection of environmental considerations at every stage of the development process is the practical essence of environmental management. Its purpose is to ensure that development is sustainable and produces net benefits to the community.

Environmental management cannot be effectively undertaken without information on the condition of, and trends of change in, the environment. Information of this sort, obtained by the process of environmental assessment, not only provides the basis for environmental management decisions that must be made from time to time, but also enables an evaluation of the effectiveness of environmental management decisions already made. National and international policies must be based on adequate information about the understanding of the environment.

Environmental assessment, the global application of which we call Earthwatch, is itself a complex process. It consists of monitoring, research, information exchange, review and evaluation. Monitoring systems generate a continuous flow of information about the condition of the environment. Research enhances our understanding of environmental processes and enables interpretation of environmental data. Information exchange is an obvious requirement if the benefits of monitoring and research are to be enjoyed by all. Review is an analytic process. it enables the definition of problems and identification of gaps in knowledge and understanding which further research and/or monitoring should fill. Evolution is a synthetic process. It involves collating, correlating and interpreting the results of monitoring and research, and is, in fact, the culmination of the assessment process providing one of the main inputs to the policy formulation and planning functions of environmental management.

UNEP has made a start in its Earthwatch programme to focus on those problems that seem to the international community to be of priority concern — threats to human health and the health of the biosphere, and the effects of man's impact on various ecosystems. The Global Environmental Monitoring System (GEMS) is evolving in response to these priorities. You will be interested to know that UNEP is supporting a feasibility study for the establishment of an atmospheric monitoring station at Mount Kenya, which will be a vital link in a global atmospheric monitoring system, one of the most important components of GEMS.

The processes of environmental assessment and environmental management about which I have been speaking are directed towards air, water, soil, minerals and living resources not only as elements of the human environment but also as stocks of substances that are used by man as material resources.

In the last twenty years, developments in technology have led to spectacular increases of affluence, particularly in the industrialised countries. But, this affluence is a result of exploitation of natural resources on a scale unparalleled in human history. No wonder that, over the past decade, concern has been expressed about irrational and wasteful use of natural resources. More effective management of natural resources on a worldwide scale has become an urgent matter, requiring that we recognise the symptoms of poor management, understand the causes and take effective remedial action.

The main symptons of the current crisis in resource management are irrationality and wastefulness. The use of natural resources is rational when resources known to be available are used in the best possible known ways to further the aims which a society has set for itself, taking account of social, economic and environmental effects known, or suspected, to follow from the choice. Irrational use of resources arises from a failure to choose wisely from alternative means and objectives of resource use. Wastefulness is a particular form of irrationality that occurs when an aim of society is achieved with the use of more resources than necessary.

Irrationality and wastefulness have two effects — exhaustion and encroachment. They are most pronounced in the case of non-renewable resources, but also include the extermination of species of plants and animals. The seriousness of resource exhaustion cannot be over-emphasised.

Encroachment effects occur when one resource-using acticivty interferes with others through the changes it makes to the social and physical setting in which those other activities take place. For example, air pollution from factories may require enhanced expenditures for health reasons, or pollution of water by the wastes of a resource-using plant may increase the costs of downstream water treatment.[1]

Whether resource use is rational or irrational depends on a number of factors, most of which have a global dimension. UNEP is devoting considerable effort to the definition of these factors, as a contribution to improved environmental management. I do not propose to define and describe the operation of all these factors here, but one in particular may be of interest.

The methods of production and delivery of goods and services can have a significant effect on the rationality of resource use. This is largely a matter of technology, each technology encouraging certain patterns of resource use and resulting in certain external effects. Many technologies now in common use, and currently attracting the interest of developing countries, were developed before the magnitude of their exhaustion and encroachment effects were realised; for example, they take no account of the importance of recycling waste product.

UNEP is supporting work on the development and adoption of environmentally sound technologies. It is well known that many African countries have a considerable capacity for sugar production. The inevitable increase in the capacity for sugar production should be achieved in a manner which will maintain or enhance environmental quality. Thus the main objectives of a UNEP supported project are consideration of the environmental impact of different sugar technologies under African conditions; appraisal of selected alternative sugar technologies in terms of their environmental consequences; and the technology. The results of this and other projects are planned to be fed into a network of African institutions concerned with development so that information is provided with the widest possible field for practical application.

One of the indispensable techniques of environmental management is the development of legal principles that can be translated into simple enforceable rules applied at the international and national levels. To this effect, UNEP has decided to help the Governments of Africa to develop their own environmental law institutions and national environmental laws.

Thus far, I have spoken mainly in theoretical terms about generalized concepts, although I have mentioned some UNEP activities to illustrate the main thoughts in our promotion of the concept of environmental management. I have done this because I want to remove any lingering

---

[1] See also pp. 67-68.

misconceptions about the breadth of UNEP's view of the environment, and to dispel any remaining doubts about the relevance to the developing world of what we are trying to do at Gigiri.

But now I want to move to a more specific discussion of the environmental problems facing the world today and how we in UNEP hope to counter them through encouraging the practice of environmental management.

Practice of Environmental Management

Let me start by looking at a few aspects of the situation in Kenya itself. If I focus on problems rather than success — and there have been substantial successes — it is because the problems need solutions now.

Although Kenya has not been as generously endowed with natural resources as some other developing countries, she has well-watered uplands, significant stretches of fertile soils, a splendid variety of scenery, a vast array of wildlife, a magnificent coast and fine forests. Kenya has a very talented people who have been innovative and pragmatic in developing the institutions and procedures to enable effective solutions to their problems. Kenya is indeed a land of promise; its future should be bright. But fulfilment of the promise must not be taken for granted. Because of various forces and pressures, including a high rate of increase of population, precious resources upon which hopes for Kenya's future rest, are being eroded and some are in danger of being lost forever.

Nearly nine out of ten Kenyans live in the countryside and three out of four live directly off the land, and thus agriculture must remain the foundation of development. Kenya is thus inescapably dependent upon the life-supporting natural ecosystems which sustain agriculture. But in many parts of Kenya the soil is being eroded, its fertility diminished, its vegetative cover cut or burned. The natural fertility of some areas has already been badly damaged and many other areas are similarly threatened. Land has a finite carrying capacity; for example, when the carrying capacity of the nearby plains is over-stressed, the herdsmen bring their cattle into Nairobi. Exceed carrying capacity through overgrazing or inappropriate cropping and the results can only be tragic to the people involved and damaging to the country's economy. Since less than 30 per cent of the land area of Kenya is truly productive, the loss of soils and vegetation resulting from the pressure of a growing number of people and inappropriate agricultural and pastoral practices should be a matter of careful consideration.

Only three per cent of the land in Kenya is now covered by forests. This is far less than was the case half a century ago. Forests play a vital ecological role for the environment as a whole and their destruction for charcoal burning, for timber production, or to make room for agriculture may not be the most rational way of utilizing them. Despite the re-afforestation efforts of the Kenya Government and the existence of laws which regulate deforestation, there is little doubt that every year sees an increase in the amount of forest land lost. This problem calls for not only positive and regulatory measures but also the development of new sources of energy and building materials. In a very true sense this problem indicates clearly the energy problem of most developing countries.

The threat to Kenya's wildlife is another problem. Wildlife is a unique African heritage; its conservation depends upon the understanding of the people as a whole, an understanding which is growing, but needs to be widespread and must be supported by effective enforcement of rational and humane regulations.

There are other dangers to the Kenyan environment: pollution of the coasts and destruction of the life of the coral reefs, and there are problems of pollution of fresh water courses from toxic chemical pesticides, particularly serious in Kenya because so many rivers drain into lakes from which there are no outlets.

Another area which needs urgent attention in Kenya, indeed in almost all other developing countries as we saw at HABITAT, is human settlements. UNEP considers human settlements to be an important and integral part of the human environment; and it is for this reason that this is one of our priority areas for action. The rapidly increasing population in Kenya has meant rising pressures on the urban sector (whose population is increasing, if I am not mistaken, by more than *seven* per cent per year) and also in the countryside. In the urban areas, it is shortage of housing and the necessary facilities in general; while in the countryside lack of the traditional building materials is causing severe problems. Programmes aimed at developing new human settlements technologies are urgently needed. We plan to cooperate with the Government of Kenya and the Nairobi City Council in demonstrating some of these technologies, including new methods for securing energy, for waste disposal, for building and for food supply in the Dandora project. Our activities in that project will be part of a global UNEP effort already underway in this field.

Major development projects, such as that envisioned for the Tana River, promise to relieve the poverty of many by enabling a more intensive and productive agriculture as well as the generation of power for industry, and thus an increase in industrial employment. But this promise, too, can be realised fully only if the environmental aspects of water management are taken fully into account. Dams, ponds and irrigation canals create conditons which facilitate the spread of schistosomiasis (bilharzia) a destructive and debilitating disease prevalent in the tropics and sub-tropics wherever conditions are favourable. In the valley of the Volta River in Ghana, schistosomiasis has long been endemic; but after a large dam was constructed, its occurrence reached epidemic proportions. Ninety per cent of the school children living on the western shore of the new reservoir were found to be infected. Schistosomiasis can be prevented and controlled, but in situations involving major water development schemes the effectiveness of control measures is largely dependant on careful study and proper planning before construction begins, to prevent the creation of new habitats for the snails that are the prime vector of the disease and upon which its prevalence largely depends. The Government of Kenya has recognised this problems and at its request UNEP is providing support for the necessary studies.

I have indicated a few environmental problems that I believe to be of significance to Kenya, because I wanted to illustrate, in terms that would be familiar to all of you, the circumstances that threaten the satisfaction of basic human needs all over the world on a continuing basis.

The Kenyan response to these circumstances is declaredly positive and offers great hope. Only a few weeks ago, His Excellency President Kenyatta, speaking on Kenyatta Day, referred to his continuing concern, and I quote: "to ensure proper use of our natural resources, our forests, rivers, the soil, our entire environment must be carefully utilised, protected and conserved. To be able to do this," His Excellency continued, "I am directing that all Government Ministries or departments should in future coordinate their planning activities more effectively to ensure that our developmental efforts do not unnecessarily destroy the natural resources, or the environment on which our future lifelihood depends. I am directing also, that the existing environmental protection and conservation laws should be vigorously enforced, and new laws prepared where they do not exist."

I believe that the concept of environmental management that I outlined earlier provides the framework within which Government executives and administrators can respond effectively to clear statements of political will such as I have just quoted.

Some Environmental Problems

Let us move beyond the borders of Kenya and consider a few of the environmental problems of other countries. I will refer first to the spread of deserts, which is most pronounced in the area known as the Sahel, and is not irrelevant to the future of Kenya.

In the Sahel, as in other dry lands, rainfall is scanty and highly variable. For as long as we know, nomads have pastured their herds in this arid grassland rimming the southern edge of the Sahara desert. The Sahel has seemed suitable for little else, since nomadism takes advantage of the fact that the rain, skimpy as it is, will fall somewhere. Even so, the pastoralists of the Sahel live in the constant risk that the rains, such as they are, will fail, and the land will be affected by drought. Drought struck the Sahel in 1910 – 1913 and again in 1940.

In 1968, it happened again. At Rosso in western Mauritania, which receives an average (1935 – 72) of 284 mm of rain a year, only 122 mm fell in 1968. At first this seemed a mere quirk in the as yet unpredictable weather patterns, since rainfall returned to normal in 1969. But in 1970, the rains failed again; again in 1971 and worst of all in 1972. By 1973, the situation in the Sahel was catastrophic. It provided a spectacle of death, disease and migration that served as the immediate stimulus for the call by the United Nations General Assembly in 1974 for international cooperation to combat desertification, including a world conference on desertification to approve a plan of action.

What had happened to the Sahel by 1973, the fifth year of drought? Lake Chad had shrunk to one-third its normal size. In the preceding winter, the great Niger and Senegal rivers had failed to flood leaving much of the best cropland in five countries (Niger, Mali, Upper Volta, Senegal and Mauritania) cracked and barren. The water table dropped, drying up wells throughout the Sahel's five million square kilometres and placing the nomadic pastoralists in deadly peril. After they had consumed the last shreds of dried-up vegetation, famished herds were sold, slaughtered or driven southward in a fruitless search for pasture. Behind them a stripped landscape, baking in the sun, lay flecked with patches of newly created desert which seemed to link up and spread, producing an impression that the great Sahara desert was "marching southward".

Also by 1973, the last year of the drought, a large programme of international assistance had been mounted for the distressed countries of the Sahel. Contributions in cash, but mainly in food, by Governments, the United Nations system and private individuals approached a value of $200 million in 1974. This was emergency relief, primarily intended to prevent starvation. It could do nothing to prevent the destruction of the agricultural base of five countries (Mauritania, Mali, Upper Volta, Niger and Chad), already among the poorest nations in the world, and severe damage to the agricultural base of two others (Senegal and Gambia). For many of these countries, this meant a loss of their tax base and a situation close to bankruptcy. In the absence of reliable statistics, especially difficult to obtain among nomadic peoples, it is difficult to say how many people died as a direct result of the drought, but estimates have gone as high as 250,000. That the toll of death was not as high as it was in the great Sahelian drought of 1913 could be attributed to the relief programme and to improved comunications in the region. The amount of drought-induced disease is also impossible to calculate precisely. Malnutrition was rife among children, especially among the nomads, and an outbreak of measles took on epidemic proportions. The destruction of livestock was appalling, with estimates reaching as high as 90 per cent in Mali. Even after favourable conditions return to Sahel, at least a decade will be required to restock and a much longer time for the ravaged land to return to what it was.

By 1974, when normal rainfall returned, climatologists were asking if the prolonged drought in the Sahel signified a permanent climatic shift to more arid conditions in an immense territory that had been supporting 25 million people. Yet a review of past climatic fluctuations led to general agreement that the drought, however severe it was, could probably be regarded as part of the "normal" order, something to be expected at long intervals, perhaps two or three times a century, however unexpected the drought may have seemed to the Sahelians themselves and to the rest of the world.

Beyond the tragedies produced by a "normal" event, the great drought in the Sahel gave rise to a number of other questions. Can such occurrences be predicted so that people can prepare for them? What should be done to see people through such successions of lean years in terms of both emergency relief and long-range policy? What are the best rehabilitative measures to be applied after such an occurrence? Finally, what is the relation between drought, a temporary phenomenon, and the longer-term, more insidious process of desertification?

We do not know the practical answers to all these questions, but we are developing an understanding of a number of relevant ecological factors that will help the United Nations Conference on Desertification to adopt the best possible plan to action to combat desertification. This, we hope, will be a concrete example of how to apply proper environmental management.

Action Plan for the Mediterranean

An excellent example of environmental management in practice is provided by what has recently been done by the Mediterranean countries. For some years the beaches and waters of the Mediterranean have been becoming increasingly fouled; the productivity of fish stocks reduced; the quality of life significantly impaired. If the process is not soon halted and reversed, it will have a disastrous impact on the many communities dependent upon tourism and fishing; it will detract even more from the quality of life of the people living in the region; and, to put the matter on an ethical plane, it will demonstrate appalling contempt on the part of modern man towards an area which has played a central role in his cultural evolution.

Concern about the state of the Mediterranean has been expressed for a number of years, and the establishment of UNEP provided an opportunity for this concern to find expression in co-ordinated action. At a meeting convened by UNEP in January 1975, the Governments of the Mediterranean region agreed upon an action plan for the protection of the marine environment. So far most attention has been paid to establishing a huge network of research and monitoring institutes throughout the region and to getting international agreement on conventions to control pollution; this state reached its culmination at a plenipotentiary conference in Barcelona this year when an unprecedented ratio of the participating states signed the convention and protocols.

The next stage of implementation of the action plan will give prominence to the so-called Mediterranean "Blue Plan". The term "Blue Plan" is a misnomer; it is not a plan but a process. It is a long term exercize involving a series of studies by national research institutions to identify likely trends over the rest of the century in such sectors as urbanization, industry, agriculture, transport, offshore operations and energy production and use. It is intended that each study be interrelated with the others so that an aggregate picture of future conditions will result. This will help national planners and decision-makers to adopt the techniques of environmental management. An intergovernmental meeting will take place in early 1977 in Yugoslavia to finalize arrangements for the Blue Plan.

The success of the Mediterranean programme — all the more remarkable in view of the political tensions of the region — has encouraged other countries to approach UNEP for similar assistance in securing international cooperation for the protection of threatened marine environments. One such group of countries comprises those along the west African coast of the Atlantic, concerned at the dangers pollution poses for sustained development of the coastal region. In response to their request, UNEP organized a mission of experts in early 1976 to examine the problems and make proposals for the consideration of Governments. Compared to the Mediterranean, developments on the west African coast are still at an early stage, but it is already clear that there is a need for the environmental management approach to the development of this region.

Conclusion

Let me put in another way, by way of summary, the essence of my attempts to define and illustrate environmental management.

Concern for the environment is an indispensable aspect of concern for humanity. If we are concerned about humanity, the greatest challenge we face today is to design development that satisfies basic human needs, and is at the same time sustainable and environmentally realistic, respecting the planet's outer limits of biological tolerance.

We believe that challenge can best be met through environmental management, which is based on the following principles:

1. economic and social development must be pursued to meet the basic human needs of all people and secure better prospects for them;

2. environmental processes must be thoroughly and widely understood;

3. the productive capacity of the environment must be maintained and resources must be used rationally.

UNEP plans all its activities with these principles in mind. From the almost unlimited demands for support that it receives, UNEP tries to select those projects that will contribute most significantly to better techniques and better understanding of environmental management on a global basis and in all the regions of the world. Given its relatively small resources of funds and manpower, that is why UNEP cannot respond to every problem that is brought before it — even some of those on its very doorstep.

UNEP was conceived by the United Nations, not as an operational agency like FAO, WHO or UNICEF, but as a planner, programmer and stimulator —

a catalyst — a focal point for the development and coordination of environmental activities carried out by the United Nations and its specialised agencies, or by groups of states. The Environment Fund is to be used to help implement the Environment Programme — the world's environmental activities — but by acting as a catalyst and a stimulator, not simply as another source of funds for operational activities.

I can say without being immodest, because many people and many organisations have contributed to the process, that what we have achieved so far in developing and testing the concept of environmental management has been the most effective contribution we could make in light of the unique role placed upon us by the community of nations. I can say as well that we have a great deal more to do in refining and re-testing the concept; and I hope that in doing so in the years ahead I can count on the active help of many of you here.

8

WATER AND THE ENVIRONMENT

Address at the United Nations Water Conference

Mar Del Plata, Argentina, March 1977

THE pre-Socratic scientific philosophers of ancient Greece put water among the four basic elements of which all things are composed, the other three being earth (we might say land), air, and fire (we would probably say energy). Thus they actually hit upon the four basic elements that enter into all our concerns for the human environment.

Water Management

The water-related problems we face pervade so many of our environmental concerns. This has been evidenced since the time of the Stockholm Conference. Water was an important element in the discussion of the world population concerns at Bucharest, of world food concerns[1] at Rome, and of human settlements concerns[2] at Vancouver. HABITAT, in fact, recommended that all Governments "adopt programmes with realistic standards for quality and quantity to provide water for urban and rural areas by 1990, if possible".

You have and will be told many times and in many ways of the seriousness and complexity of the water-related problems facing the world. But the aspect of your Conference that brings me here to address you briefly is quite specific. Since it was recognized that environmental considerations must enter into all

---

[1] For the statement to the World Food Conference, see p. 1.
[2] For the statement to the UN Conference on Human Settlements, see p. 6.

developmental activities including their planning, what was felt to be needed at the time of Stockholm was not a world organization to manage the environment in isolation from other areas of concern, but a focal point of environmental concerns within the United Nations. UNEP serves as an advisor, a source of information, a co-ordinator, sometimes an initiator and helper to get things started in areas where such help is needed, but above all as a catalyst of action to be taken by others. In our view, environmental concerns must be an inherent element in all development policies and planning — and that is the main theme of my remarks today.

For what is the environment? And what is development? I suggest that the environment may be looked upon as the totality of conditions, physical and societal, within which alone are to be found the means for sustaining and enriching human life. And development comprises all those activities through which individuals and societies seek to meet human needs and to better the quality of life. We have come to realize that, for present as well as for future generations, what we must have is benign development, beneficient development, development without destruction.

With water, as with air, land and energy, we cannot achieve rational development without seeking to make the best use of environmental resources, and to take full account of environmental and social consequences, both known and suspected, as well as economic factors. For our concern is for man and not for the environment as such. One common philosophy must underlie all areas of environmental management and it may be summed up as follows:

1. Economic and social development must be pursued to meet the basic human needs of all people, and to secure better prospects for them.
2. Environmental processes must be thoroughly and widely understood.
3. The productive capacity of the environment must be maintained and resources used rationally.

We have come far from the time when the environmental problem was considered simply a matter of pollution abatement. Environmental problems of developing countries are often the result of extreme poverty, and the lack of economic and social development. Moreover, it is in the developing countries that the quality of water — and often the quantity — is lowest, sanitation and nutrition the worst, and disease the most prevalent.

Like any other kind of development, water resources development may have a host of interrelated effects within nations, within regions, or on an even wider international scale. There are, for example, often particularly significant and complex impacts from the construction of large dams on human health, human communities, ecosystems, fish and wildlife. All the effects on human life, and on ecosystems and environmental processes generally, need to be thoroughly understood, and the long-term real costs and benefits of such environmental alterations carefully weighed.

An orderly and rational approach to water resources development demands, first and foremost, a comprehensive assessment of the region concerned, which takes account of its social, economic and ecological characteristics. An action plan for environmental research and monitoring may be required in most cases. Alternative patterns of development should also be studied. The support of an informed public is also essential and programmes of education, information, and sometimes technical assistance and training.

I would lay particular stress on the importance of assessment, environmental research and monitoring. I believe that a prior assessment of probable environmental impacts should be a mandatory element in the planning of all river basin and water development projects. I should like to focus briefly on some of the areas of impact I have already mentioned.

1. There are the impacts on human health. There are proven correlations between, on the one hand, the physical characteristics of water bodies, the quality of water supply, and waste disposal and, on the other hand, the incidence of waterborne diseases. Schistosomiasis, malaria and onchocerciasis are all more prevalent when the characteristics of water bodies favour the abundance of their alternate hosts, snails, mosquitoes and simuliid flies. Careless waste water disposal can contaminate both surface water and groundwater, and the death rate from gastroenteritis is higher in areas with unsafe water supplies.
2. There are impacts on land. Inefficient management and use of water can cause waterlogging and salinity which destroys arable land.
3. There are impacts on human communities, as people must be resettled from areas where reservoir construction is taking place. The disturbance of established cultural and social systems makes for insecurity, especially when people from different ethnic origins are thrown together in resettlement.
4. There are also, of course, marked impacts of water development upon ecosystems, including fish and wildlife populations. The construction of dams may be destructive or beneficial in this respect. Additional ranges for wildlife may be opened up. Yet the flooding of wetlands can also have serious repercussions for wildlife. Planning for wildlife rescue and rehabilitation programmes should be an integral part of dam construction projects.

Management of Shared Water Resources

The management of shared water resources at the regional and international levels has long attracted the attention of the international community. The major issues were clearly identified at Stockholm, and found expression in the Declaration on the Human Environment.[1]

[1] For the Stockholm Declaration, see "In Defence of the Earth," Executive Series 1, UNEP, Nairobi, 1981.

Principle 2 states that water must be safeguarded for the benefit of present and future generations through careful planning of management as appropriate. Differences in the interpretation of this principle still remain, concerning the standard of care a state is to exercize. Principle 23 cautions that, in defining international standards of care, there must be flexibility since account must be taken of the economic circumstances of poor countries. Transfrontier pollution of shared water resources remains a difficult question, for states may wish to use rivers passing through their territories in different ways.

The Stockholm declaration outlines steps towards solutions in such cases, but the details remain to be worked out. Principle 21, for example, applied to water, recognises the sovereign right of States under the United Nations Charter to use their water resources as they wish, but it goes on to impose a responsibility on States to avoid damaging the environment outside their own territories.

International environmental law is still being developed, and the more generally applicable principles of law for regulating transfrontier pollution have yet to be worked out. But this whole question is under the active consideration of organizations like the International Law Commission and the OECD, as well as UNEP. It might be useful to accelerate the study of international treaties, principles of international law, and international decisions widely accepted as binding, to help clarify the extent to which states may be prepared to accept principles that may put new obligations upon them.

I would stress again that action at the international level to improve the effectiveness of water management will be wasteful and of little use unless it is properly coordinated. In the UNEP view, coordination at the global level can be adequately and economically carried out with little change in the present institutional arrangements. At the regional level which, in our view, is the level at which the most important work needs to be done, existing institutional arrangements, centred on the regional commissions, are of the right sort but need considerable strengthening.

Issues relating to the management of river basins shared by two or more states are, as I have mentioned earlier, of vital importance, and must be resolved in a manner that takes environmental considerations into account. If this cannot yet be done on the basis of internationally agreed principles and guidelines, it must for the moment be tackled on a case-by-case basis.

To conclude, I wish to say that we in UNEP believe that the most urgent challenge facing the international community today is the satisfaction of basic human needs, for those billions of our fellow inhabitants of this "only one earth" who live far below the level of subsistence. We identify these needs as food, shelter, clothing, health, education, and productive work. None of these needs can be satisfied without a major role played by water — its quality and its quantity. This is the level of importance we are faced with in this World Conference.

9

HUMAN NEEDS SATISFACTION:

Some Policy Issues of Environmental Sustainability

Address at the University of Houston

Houston, Texas, USA., June 1977

I AM especially pleased to note, that during its fiftieth anniversary year the University has seen fit to address one of the most pressing issues facing the world community at this time, that of basic human needs, and that it has agreed to host a symposium on this question. This initiative will, I am sure, contribute significantly to the debate now taking place throughout the United Nations family; a debate that will soon, we hope, be taken up in national councils as well. A region such as this with its considerable resources, technical vitality and intellectual energy, can hardly avoid becoming involved, in one way or another, in the global discussion of human needs satisfaction.

If I emphasise the need for involvement by all sectors of society in the examination of this issue, it is because I believe it lies at the heart of a problem of the greatest magnitude: the problem of absolute poverty, which is still on the increase even in a world of unprecedented overall affluence. There are hundreds of millions of people today whose basic needs for adequate food, shelter, clothing, health care, education and production employment are not being met. This is no short-term emergency which might be handled through a crash programme of international assistance. The challenge is to meet the basic human needs of all the world's poor on a basis that is sustainable as far ahead as we can see, and that means without encroachment on the equilibrium of the biosphere, and without irreparably damaging the resource base on which we all depend. This is a many-faceted problem. Its solution demands reliable quantitative and qualitative estimates of needs and legitimate demands, of resources and capacities. New expressions of political commitment and new measures of cooperation among nations and among conflicting sectors within nations will be required if the needed modifications of social and political structures are to be peacefully achieved.

This is not just a task for the United Nations Environment Programme, although UNEP has special responsibilities in this regard that need to be understood. UNEP came into being as the United Nations response to the global concern for the quality of the human environment expressed at Stockholm in 1972. This concern was not simply about pollution abatement and conservation. Nor was it an issue of environment versus growth. It was, rather, a concern about the direction growth and development had been taking.

The issue, I may add, spilled over national boundaries. The emergence of the environment issue as a global problem has inevitably, though not immediately, caused the satisfaction of human needs to be seen as a global problem. The new environmental awareness has been linked with a growing trend toward international thinking in many sectors previously considered exclusively to be matters of national prerogative and jurisdiction. At the same time, concern for the welfare of people, particularly at the lower economic strata, has been quietly growing within nations of a variety of political persuasions over many decades, particularly since the Second World War. As Harlan Cleveland points out; "In this respect the differences among governments calling themselves communist, socialist, capitalist, social democratic, Christian democratic or democratic republican have been a matter of degree, not doctrine; all have moved toward welfare-conscious governance."

And so, eradication of poverty has become a global political issue, and a driving force behind the demands for a New International Economic Order. Perhaps at this point I should expand a little on the relationship between the problem of poverty and global environmental concerns.

It has become more and more obvious that socio-economic factors lie at the root of many serious environmental degradation problems. The developed countries are now well aware of the many environmental problems attendant upon heedless development. But serious environmental problems can also be caused by lack of development.

I have said that there are today hundreds of millions of people without the basic human necessities. This is not only an intolerable situation in human terms, but it also has serious environmental consequences. The relentless pressures that arise where, through poverty, basic human needs are not met can be devastating, and can even erase the resource base from which man must inevitably gain his sustenance.

The destruction of forests, the loss of arable land, the loss of human productivity through disease and malnutrition, and the increasing pressures on fragile ecosystems, all of which result from poverty, are today typically problems of developing countries, most acutely amplified in the poorer sectors. These are as significant environmentally as the pollution of air and soil by industry and agriculture, and over-consumption and waste by the affluent. In turn they have led to the recognition that environment poses a challenge to both rich and poor alike. It is an all-encompassing concept with organic and complementary relationships between the quality of man's physical environment, the growth of populations, the patterns of nature's resources and space use, and such factors as societal goals, value systems, socio-economic structures and institutions of production and consumption, life styles and income distribution.

Basic Human Needs

There has thus been a significant shift in patterns of international thought and a growing acknowledgement that the ultimate purpose of both development and environmental policies is to improve the quality of life for all. If we look upon the environment as a stock of physical and social resources available at a given time for the satisfaction of human needs, and upon development as a process pursued by all societies aimed at increasing human well-being and maintaining it over the long term, we will see the inescapable logic of management and development along environmentally appropriate lines. It was considerations such as these that shaped UNEP's philosophy and fashioned the principles that underline all its operation, namely:

1. that the starting point for the world community must be to meet basic human needs;

2. that the immediate purpose of development should be to satisfy those needs;

3. that the process of development itself can and should improve the environment. Deleterious effects often result when development activities are haphazard and unmanaged and do not take account of ecological constraints. When this happens, the natural resource base upon which continued development depends is placed in jeopardy;

4. that we must monitor the impact of development processes and identify any threats they may pose to the life-supporting system of the biosphere, and consequently to human well-being; and

5. that in order to meet the objective of sustainable development without destruction to the natural resource base, we shall need to promote alternative patterns of development and life styles in both rich and poor countries.

These are the guiding principles of UNEP's strategies in environmental management and assessment. They are also highly relevant to the work being done in the Centre for Integrative Studies on Basic Human needs. Let me review briefly what management and assessment mean in the UNEP context.

It is not, of course, the environment itself that is to be managed, but rather those human activities which have a significant impact on the environment. Environmental management thus comprehends a whole system of complex interrelationships. Causes and effects of environmental degradation are often widely separated in space and time. Resultant problems transcend jurisdictional and open national boundaries. Environmental management brings two new dimensions to the development process; it calls for environmental quality to be taken fully into account, and it extends the time frame — development must be sustainable over the long term. When it is examined this concept commends itself to reason, but it has been overlooked in the past and is still difficult to apply fully because Governments and others whose activities can affect the environment have sometimes lacked the necessary information, and, in certain cases, lacked political will or the necessary resources.

We must admit, however, that the most crippling constraint to the application of proper environmental management is the lack of reliable information on conditions and trends which can only be obtained through the environmental assessment process. Assessment, as we all know, is the weighing of costs and benefits and for this we must have suitable information systems. Our global environmental assessment programme has been given the name Earthwatch. Earthwatch is an integrated dynamic process by which relevant environmental issues are identified, and necessary data are gathered and evaluated. It involves monitoring, research, information exchange, review and evaluation. From its inception UNEP began to develop and apply these concepts in practical terms. The most marked progress has been made in the field of monitoring and information exchange. A Global Environmental Monitoring System (GEMS), an International Referral System (INFOTERRA) and an International Register of Potentially Toxic Chemicals (IRPTC) have been established.

The Earthwatch programme must also provide early warnings of any global threats to human welfare, or even survival, brought about through man's activities. Thus UNEP has developed a programme on outer limits which deals in the physical side with threats to the ozone layer and problems of climatic change and weather modifications as well as with the opportunities of increasing bioproductivity.

We are, however, equally concerned with social outer limits — and by that I mean, basically, the limits of human tolerance of stress, deprivation, and change within the social milieu. We believe there are two closely related, but conceptually distinct, ways of looking at what we call "social outer limits" in relation to the environment. First, there is a limit to the rate at which society can adapt itself to change without social disrupion. Secondly, there is a limit to the rate at which society can modify its values and practices in response to environmental imperatives. It was in this context that we commissioned the study of basic human needs, so that UNEP might have available the kind of information it required for examining both sides of the resources and needs equation — and for promoting rational alternative patterns or production and consumption. I am confident that your conclusions this week will not only strengthen the Earthwatch programme in this respect but will supplement it, particularly in connection with our monitoring of critical social issues.

To sum up, if basic human needs are to be satisfied, we must have a reliable assessment of the gaps, wherever they exist; as assessment, that is, of non-satisfaction of basic needs. We must have an assessment of the resources needed to fill the gaps. We also need to know what will be the impact on the environment if we continue to harvest and to use such resources according to present patterns. These are the kinds of information policy-makers need as a basis for decisions on proper management of the environment, and for ensuring the satisfaction of human needs on a sustainable basis. I know there are many problems associated with the assessment for needs, since needs not only vary geographically and climatically, but also different social systems may accord different orders of priority in human needs. Moreover, though a degree of quantification is required, the setting of levels to represent a reasonable minimum is inevitably a somewhat arbitrary act, quite often shaped by political and other extraneous considerations. It is also obvious that the satisfaction of basic needs is immediately linked with the alleviation of acute poverty — a problem which cannot be diverted from degradation of the human environment.

Rational Environmental Management

In the last twenty years developments in technology have led to spectacular increases of affluence, particularly in the industrialized countries. But this affluence is a result of the exploitation, and in many cases the destruction, of natural resources on a scale unparalleled in human history. No wonder that, over the past decade, concern has been mounting about the use of natural resources. Wise resource management on a worldwide scale has become an urgent need. To achieve it we need to examine the symptoms of poor management, understand the causes, and take effective, remedial action.

Assuming that the goal of global society is development which emphasizes the satisfaction of basic human needs, the main symptoms of the current crisis in resource management are irrationality and wastefulness. The use of natural resources is "rational" when resources known to be available are used in the best possible known ways to further the aims which a society has set for itself, and when account is taken of the social, economic and environmental effects likely to follow from the choices we make. Irrational use of resources occurs when unwise policies are followed; wastefulness is the particular form of irrationality that uses more resources than necessary for any purpose.

Irrationality and wastefulness have two effects — exhaustion and encroachment. These are most pronounced in the case of non-renewable resources, but occur also when plant or animal species are exterminated. The seriousness of resource exhaustion cannot be over-emphasised.

Encroachment occurs when one resource-using activity interferes with others through the changes it causes in the social and physical setting in which such activities take place. For example, air pollution from factories may require higher expenditures on health; pollution of water by the wastes of a resource-using plant may increase the costs of downstream water treatment, and inhibit the use of the water for agricultural or other purposes.

A principal factor in the rationality of resource use is the composition and level of the global output of goods. Output depends on the preferences of people with purchasing power, and on the prices of the goods and services desired. People's preferences are a function of lifestyles, which are often manipulated by processors of natural resources.

Public policy must ensure that the rational use of resources is not inhibited by private considerations. Up to now the prices of goods and services have largely failed to take account of the social costs of encroachment effects.

Income inequality distorts the composition of global output towards the lifestyles of the rich, usually profligate in the use of resources. The global resource base clearly cannot support adoption of such lifestyles by an ever-increasing number of people. Effective means must be found to promote environmentally appropriate ways of living in all countries.

The methods of production and delivery of goods and services can also be rational or irrational in their effects upon resource use. This is largely a matter of choice of technology, for different technologies lead to different patterns of resource use, and have different external effects. Many technologies, now in common use and attracting the interest of developing countries, were developed before the magnitude of their exhaustion and encroachment effects were realised. Most take little or no account of the importance of recycling. We should be giving a good deal of attention to the development and adoption of environmentally sound technologies. For this we will require the continuing support of scientists and technologists.

I have said that global output is determined by the structure of economic demand for goods and services, and that this determines resource use. But economic demand is generated mainly in the rich countries, and it coincides neither with the global distribution of known resources, nor with the distribution of human populations. Economic demand in itself, therefore, does not always correspond with the satisfaction of basic human needs. Thus, problems of resource use at the global level give rise to various types of conflict: conflict over rights to use particular resources; conflict between producers (often developing countries) and consumers (often developed countries) of a particular resource; and conflict over the prices at which resources are to be bought and sold.

Such conflicts are likely to become more intense as human populations increase and the supply of non-renewable resourses diminishes. The crucial question is, can the nations of the world continue along the same technological trajectory as has been apparent in the past twenty years? Or, are we now obliged to take a very hard look at the technologies at our disposal, and see how we might adapt and apply them to meet the mounting problem of satisfying basic human needs? If we come up with the wrong answers, or if we try to meet the problem by transferring environmentally degrading technology, we all lose.

It is my firm belief that we can and must strive for a more rational use of natural resources by attempting to change preferences, prices and income distribution patterns. We can and must develop resource-conserving, low-waste, non-encroaching technologies. We can and must switch, in many areas, to the use of renewable resources, and change production patterns to make recycling the common practice. But to do these things we must have the help of people like yourselves, the world over.

Above all, our human priorities must be clear. Perhaps there should be a reaffirmation of the 1948 Declaration of Human Rights, so far as it applies to human needs. Or perhaps an expansion of Article 25 of that historic declaration to spell out in more detail the basic human needs challenge. This challenge is, I believe, more urgent than ever before. It is interrelated with all the major concerns faced today by the community of nations. Peace, a healthy world environment, and social economic justice — these things, surely, are indivisible.

In many quarters in this continent today, there is a rebirth of the state of nature pioneers. A nineteenth century writer, Francis Parkman, gave this impression of early America: "A boundless vision grows upon us; an untamed continent; vast wastes of forest verdure; mountains silent in primeval sleep; river, lake and glimmering pool; wilderness oceans mingling with the sky."

Some go as far as labelling the past years of industrial society as a time of unbridled greed and materialism, not typical in the history of man. What we have witnessed may be more of a concern with satisfying basic human *greeds* than basic human *needs*.

Of course we should not turn our back on industry and technology and urbanism — to head back to the caves, or the log cabins. But the trend will be to ensure that the industrial system functions within the limits of goals agreed to by and for human beings through the political process. The aim will be to create a new harmony, a better quality of life.

The formerly free goods, the birthright of clean air and water and open spaces, are no longer seen as so free or abundant. Their values rise accordingly. Government decision-makers know that fundamental changes are taking place in the rules of the game. The new rules are not clear — changes in value systems, changes in the process of decision-making, changes in social structures, changes in the economy. Value shifts seem to be going on, that effect the kinds of trade-offs that society will entertain in the demands made on the environment. Quality of life is being redefined. There are new attitudes towards affluence, industrialism, consumerism, urbanism. There is concern about the lack of community in modern life — about the lonely man in the congested urban scene.

Some of this is readily understandable. Once mass production and consumption have been attained — and in the West you have gone a long way towards that happy state — concern turns towards the scarcity of other good things — environmental goods. When needs like hunger, clothing and shelter are met, other needs — social, aesthetic, spiritual — assume a greater importance, and life is truly impoverished if this level of human needs is neglected.

10

DESERTIFICATION CAN BE ARRESTED

Opening Adress to the United Nations Conference on Desertification

Nairobi, Kenya, August 1977

WE find ourselves in an appropriate setting for the subject of this conference. It was the African drought of 1968 to 1973, stretching across the width of the continent, that so dramatically focussed world attention on desertification, the subject of our present deliberations. Further, desertification is one of the major global environmental problems, and this city is the seat of the United Nations Environment Programme, and hence the focal point for international concern with the environment.

Global conferences such as this, held under the aegis of the United Nations, are the pre-eminent occasions when men and women of thought make contact with those in a position to act in the quest for resolutions to mankind's most pressing problems. This is familiar to those in political life, who are accustomed to seeking expert opinion. It is the scientists and technicians who formulate the problems with precision, describe their characteristics, specify their dimensions, and, most important, tell us what *should* be done about them. It is those in political life who tell us what *can* be done about them, and then, most important, take action in terms of their sense of human, political and economic possibilities. In this order of events, science dominates the opening scenes of our quest; the climax is played out in the realm of practical affairs.

A similar interaction — between scientists and the United Nations system — characterized the preparations for this conference. Enormous demands were made on specialists by a secretariat which the United Nations General Assembly had directed to assess available data and information on desertification and its consequences. This was at once a reasonable instruction and one difficult to carry out, for the subject of desertification, fragmented among a great variety of disciplines, lacked structure and coherence. Indeed, the very word itself, a neologism that has not yet found its way into the dictionaries, lacked — and still lacks — a definition that satisfies everyone. Precise standards are yet to be formulated for measuring desertification and gauging its advance.

In seeking to carry out the General Assembly's mandate, the conference secretariat was guided by the directives of the Governing Council of UNEP in its capacity as the Intergovernmental Preparatory Body for the conference. The secretariat sought advice from hundreds of internationally recognized experts in a large number of disciplines. These men and women supplied order and structure to the subject in question and reached a number of important understandings, providing a sound foundation for action. Such consultations work in both directions, and our requests, or so we would like to think, stimulated the scientific community to refine its views on the subject of desertification. During this past week, here in Nairobi, an international group of scientific societies conducted a seminar in which some of us were privileged to participate and which, among other things, outlined a project for specifying the standards needed to measure the process of desertification.

The structure of the subject, as our scientific colleagues conceived it, is evident in the documents placed before the conference. They saw the subject as falling naturally into four components — climate, ecological change, human and social aspects, and desert technology — and these components were made the subject of four scientific reviews.[1] The four reviews were summarised in one document, entitled *Desertification: An Overview*.

Contained in these documents are the results of the extensive surveys and scientific investigations carried out by individual scientists and by members of the Inter-Agency Task Force on Desertification and of the Panel of Senior Advisers to the Conference Secretary General. This huge input of the scientific community led to a clear identification of the principal points on which our scientific colleagues found themselves in agreement, and which constitute the heart of the problem. These are:

1. The problem of desertification is a serious threat to the welfare of mankind. Although degradation of the land has always characterized man's systematic use of it, the process has accelerated in recent decades, precisely at a time when population growth and rising expectations began to demand enormous increases in food production. It is estimated that between 50,000 and 70,000 square kilometres of useful land are going out of production every year, and the most important cause of this appalling loss is desertification.

---

[1]Secretariat, UN Conference on Desertification, "Desertification: Its Causes, and Consequences", Pergamon Press, Oxford, 1977.

2. The problem is one of overwhelming urgency. As land suffers degradation, the costs of reclaiming it, modest at first, rise steeply until a threshold is passed beyond which reclamation becomes economically impractical.

3. The causes of desertification are known, and in particular, the reasons for its recent acceleration. A change to a more arid climate could be a cause, but no firm evidence is available that climate is so changing. Such evidence, for example, was not provided by the recent African drought, since that was the third such catastrophe to have occurred in Africa in this century. Although their onset cannot yet be predicted, droughts are recurrent and inevitable, and they are characteristic of arid, semi-arid and sub-humid climates. The culprit, therefore, cannot be found in the shifting play of climate. Rather it is man himself who must be viewed as the agent of desertification. It is man's action that degrades the land by misuse or overuse as he seeks to wrest a living from fragile ecosystems under unpredictable and often harsh climatic conditions, and under a variety of social and economic pressures. Too frequently man acts in this way because no better alternatives are apparent to him.

4. Man has now in his possession both the wealth of knowledge and adequate technical means to bring desertification to a halt and, in many instances, to reverse the process and restore degraded land to productive use. Since such land degradation could be manifest in several forms including soil erosion, salinisation, waterlogging and loss of fertility, the key to combative measures is to be found in proper land use. This applies not only to agriculture, forestry and grazing, but to all other land uses — tourism, recreation, mining, industry and human settlements. When we say that man has now the knowledge to cope with desertification, we do not overlook the fact that each separate situation will require its own assessment as well as action specifically tailored to the situation as evaluated. It remains true that whatever the situation may be, the techniques and technologies for dealing with it are now known.

5. Desertification must be seen as a human problem rather than one concerned solely with the deterioration of ecosystems. If man is its agent, he is also its victim. The degradation of land is invariably accompanied by the degradation of human well-being and social prospects. All efforts to combat desertification must therefore centre on the welfare of man and must contribute to the development and prosperity of the communities affected. From the human perspective, international action might well assign priority to the most vulnerable nations and national action might well focus on the

most vulnerable peoples rather than on the most vulnerable land, although of course, these categories often coincide.

Those are some of the major points on which our scientific advisers were agreed. Although they depict a menacing situation, their views provide grounds for optimism. For, according to what they say, mankind is not in the grip of a danger beyond control, and the advance of desertification can be brought to a halt.

Their assertions find support and illustration in a set of case studies carried out as part of the conference preparations. Six such studies, financed by the United Nations Development Programme, were carried out by the Governments concerned with the full co-operation and technical support of UNESCO.[1] The settings for these studies were carefully selected: Chile and Tunisia provided arid conditions with cool season rainfall; India and Niger, arid land with warm season rainfall; Iraq and Pakistan, irrigation projects affected by waterlogging and salinisation. In addition, six Governments voluntarily contributed associated case studies — Australia, Iran, Israel and the United States contributed one each, the Soviet Union two, and China three.[2] These have enriched the exercize and expanded its scope.

The secretariat was directed by the General Assembly to prepare a world map of areas affected and likely to be affected by desertification. Such a map was prepared by FAO and UNESCO with the assistance of UNEP and the World Meteorological Organisation.[3] At a scale of one to 25 million, this map presents a global panorama which clearly portrays the enormous dimensions of the desertification threat. There are two experimental and more detailed maps of desertification at a scale of one to 5 million — one of Africa north of the Equator, prepared by FAO, and one of South America prepared by the National Institute for Arid Zone Research in Mendoza, Argentina. Since they concern matters diffcult to identify, these maps have been subjected to comment and refinement and are still considered in need of perfecting. We expect they will receive further modification as a result of your reactions to them here. Synoptic maps of desertification hazards at a much larger scale accompany the six case studies and give a better presentation of the processes and causes of desertification. Because of the difficulties of mapping desertification, we have encouraged distinguished researchers to pursue the problem from angles of their own choosing. This has resulted in three additional world maps — one showing the status of desertification in the hot arid regions, another a climate aridity index. The third is an experimental

---

[1] J. A. Mabbutt and C. Floret, "Case Studies on Desertification prepared by UNESCO/UNEP/UNDP", National Resources Research XVIII, UNESCO, Paris, 1980.
[2] Margaret R. Biswas and Asit K. Biswas, "Desertification: Associated Case Studies Prepared for the UN Conference on Desertification", Pergamon Press, Oxford, 1980.
[3] FAO, UNESCO and WHO, "World Map of Desertification at a scale of 1:25,000,000", UN Conference on Desertification, A/CONF, 14/2, Nairobi, Kenya, 1977.

world scheme of aridity and drought probability — all these are available to participants as background documents.

By displaying the vast extent of the lands vulnerable to desertification, the world map illustrates the urgency as well as the huge dimensions of a problem ultimately threatening 30 per cent of the earth's land surface and the livelihood of one-sixth of its people. Of these, 50 million people are immediately menaced.

Desertification often transcends national boundaires, and its arrest may well involve joint action by two or more countries. In an effort to see if transnational action was feasible, we proposed six experimental projects which could be central to the campaign against desertification. These projects involve 29 countries. They concern:

1. the establishment of coherent greenbelts, not to be regarded as walls of trees against desert advance, but rather as mosaics of productive land use and conservation measures, one along the northern edge of the Sahara desert, another along that desert's southern rim;

2. the monitoring of desertification and related natural resources, one in arid regions of South America, another in south-west Asia;

3. the stratification of livestock in pastoral lands south of the Sahara; and the management of deep-water aquifers in north-east Africa and the Arabian Peninsula.

To carry out these major projects, a total of 40 agreements are required, since some countries are involved in two of them, some even three. Eighteen of these agreements have already been obtained, and there is every prospect that Governments will agree to all of the actions suggested. This is a gratifying response, and one of a number of indications of how seriously the problems of desertification are already regarded by Governments.

Another indication is, of course, this conference, convened by the United Nations General Assembly — which is to say, by Governments represented here. But perhaps the most important indication is the great array of measures to combat desertification already initiated by national Governments. Some of these measures are described in the case studies. Others were presented at the regional preparatory meetings in the form of country papers and I am sure more will be presented here. Altogether, they constitute a rich archive of techniques and experience in which we found and will continue to find guidance.

Plan of Action

To coordinate our separate actions, to agree on the further steps to be taken, and to put all this into a comprehensive global programme that will end this menace to human welfare and the world's food supply — these are the purposes for which we are here today. Indeed, we were directed to assess what is known about desertification for one over-riding purpose, and that is to provide a scientific basis for the *actions* we will take, and to guarantee that those actions have the most favourable prospects for success. Thus, our scientific studies and consultations led directly to the draft Plan of Action to Combat Desertification[1] earlier drafts of which received detailed scrutiny and careful refinement at the hands of Governments, of the United Nations organs and specialised agencies, of concerned individuals and of delegates at the regional preparatory meetings. We submit this draft Plan of Action to you for your thoughtful consideration and careful judgement, confident that it will emerge from your deliberations as an effective guide to action.

The Plan of Action calls for the assessment and monitoring of desertification processes. There would be little point to these activities if the information we have gained should fail to be applied to remedial measures. Assessment and monitoring are thus coupled closely in the Plan to the formulation of rational and comprehensive land use policies and plans which will serve as concrete guides to action. With this in mind the Plan of Action states the principles that guide proper land use and outlines the measures that conform to good practice.

While the Plan foresees that most measures against desertification will be initiated by Governments, it proposes regional and international activity in support of national actions. But, since national actions will be central in the global campaign against desertification, crucial importance attaches to strengthening national capacities in science and technology, an objective that was underlined by the General Assembly which convened this conference. Despite a lack of scientific and technological capability in many developing countries affected by desertification, a lack that constitutes a serious obstacle to successful campaigns against this problem, it is interesting to note that there are few developmental activities in which countries, even the poorest, are already as well equipped as they are for the struggle against desertification. Their present capacities undoubtedly reflect their past concerns about a matter as fundamental as the quality of their land. This means that on this subject countries can describe their scientific and technological needs and deficiencies in precise detail. We anticipate that filling these needs will require national institutions to be established or strengthened, and regional centres to be set up which can serve countries sharing similar ecological settings.

During the preparations for the conference, the secretariat asked for assistance from a number of institutions in developng countries. The relationships established and the quality of the assistance we received from those institutions augurs well for the future development of the global campaign against desertification. This interchange provides an example of

---

[1]For the final Plan of Action, see "United Nations Conference on Desertification: Round-up, Plan of Action and Resolutions," United Nations, New York, 1978.

how the international community is coming more and more to rely on distinguished institutions in the developing world.

The Plan of Action places strong emphasis on popular participation in measures to combat desertification. The recommendations proposed affect lives as well as land, and experience has shown that action will not succeed without the willing collaboration of those most closely involved. In the last analysis, land use depends on the land user, and good land use will come from users who are informed, capable and, above all, willing to apply sound practices. This view conforms to the principles of self help which have become part of development doctrine. It is an extension of the concept of strengthening national capacities in science and technology so that developing countries can attack their own problems. In the educational and community efforts through which popular participation is stimulated, technological capacities are extended to the grass roots.

Although it does not describe many specific projects and programmes, the Plan of Action specifies the kinds of measures that should be undertaken and provides comprehensive guidelines for the design of specific projects. Programme design will, after all, be determined by the specific situation to be remedied as well as by national plans and policies.

The six feasibility studies illustrate the sorts of action that the Plan is intended to stimulate. Although transnational in scope, these programmes are fundamentally amalgams of national action integrated into a comprehensive effort in which the actions of different countries support one another, and are reinforced by regional and international cooperation. They are also designed to strengthen local and national capacities in science and technology. As a modest but successful start, the feasibility studies might set the stage for additional transnational projects that may emerge from our deliberations. As a consequence, you may wish to consider strengthening the provisions of the Plan of Action that encourage such activities.

Arrangements now in progress for financing the transnational projects arising from the feasibility studies suggest patterns for future action. While the six studies have not yet been worked out in completed financial detail, it is estimated that the total cost of the regional components of the six projects will amount to about $195 million. Two of the studies, elaborated in detail, provide examples of co-operative financial arrangements. The cost of establishing the North African Green Belt will be largely covered by on-going national programmes. The cost of the regional cooperative exercise may be slightly more than $9 million over the seven-year period, 1978 to 1984. Government representatives have agreed that of this amount, 30 per cent is to be contributed by the Governments concerned, and the remaining 70 per cent will need to come from international and Arab organizations. Again, the regional component of the project to monitor desertification in south-west Asia will cost slightly more than $6 million over the seven-year period. Representatives of the Governments concerned have agreed that national contributions will amount to not less than 20 per cent of the total.

Desertification is a process that can feed on itself once it starts; degradation establishes the conditions for further degradation. With man as the agent, the result is the creation of desertified areas in regions where, from a strictly climatic point of view, such degradation simply should not take place. Because it is self-accelerating, desertifiction calls for the application of urgent remedies. Measures to meet pressing needs are embodied in the draft plan of Action as a short-term programme, running through the year 1984. This short-term programme is integrated in the Plan with long-term actions extending to the end of the century. It is our conviction that desertification on this planet can be halted by the year 2000. The draft Plan of Action was formulated with this goal in mind. The delegations may wish to retain this perspective as they review the Plan of Action.

In whatever terms this conference perceives that the Plan of Action should be formulated, our efforts will be wasted unless its recommendations are implemented. Because we are concerned that the momentum of the conference be sustained, we have organised an orientation workshop, to be held in the week directly following the conference, and to which Governments have been invited to nominate representatives. While we expect that the workshop will lead to an interesting exchange of experience, its primary purpose is to come to grips with the problem of translating the Plan of Action into the design of specific, practical and effective programmes.

Once approved, projects and programmes need continuing and sustained support. The conclusions of a series of consultations with finance specialists are contained in the document, *Economic and Financial Aspects of the Plan of Action to Combat Desertification*. Since our subject is a new one, our financial consultants lacked an accepted and established body of data, and their conclusions represent their best educated estimates. They were urged to be conservative, and indeed, in consultations held since the document was published, they felt that they were too conservative. Nonetheless, if the published figures be tentatively accepted, they indicate that the reclamation of degraded land is profitable; that is, it is an action thoroughly justified in terms of economic rates of return. It follows that preventive measures, much less expensive than reclamation, have even greater economic justification.

Additional financial resources are needed for the implementation of the Plan of Action. Questions have naturally arisen, particularly in the regional preparatory meetings, as to where the money is to come from, however justified such an expenditure may be. The regional preparatory meeting for Africa inclined to the view that the Plan of Action should be financed from a special anti-desertification fund. The Secretariat, while realising the advantages of such a concept, since it would ensure efficiency in management and allocation of resources, foresees problems arising from the attempt to establish yet another international fund. As explained in the document, a group approach, a "multi-bi" approach or, in some circumstances, a consortium approach seem to represent more acceptable ways of financing action arising from the Plan. This is an important question, and one on which the secretariat may come up with further proposals, but we essentially look to the delegations for ideas and guidance.

On institutional arrangements required to implement the Plan of Action, the regional preparatory meetings were opposed to the proliferation of bureaucratic structures. Thus we propose that implementation be co-ordinated and supervised by institutions already in existence. International actions arising from the Plan will undoubtedly require the cooperative efforts of the United Nations and other international Governmental and Non-Governmental Organisations. As far as the United Nations is concerned, the responsibility is seen to be that of the system as a whole and will affect the programmes of its various components, particularly those of the specialized agencies and the funding and financial institutions. The draft Plan suggests, therefore, that overall supervision and co-ordination of the implementation of the Plan be lodged in the Environment Coordination Board, the inter-agency body which now co-ordinates environmental activities within the United Nations system. Membership of the Board consists of the executive heads of all United Nations bodies and specialized agencies. To carry out this additional responsibility, we foresee that the Environment Coordination Board will have to be serviced by a small number of highly qualified staff situated to best advantage within the United Nations system, from within which key elements could be assembled.

The Plan of Action asks that the United Nations General Assembly call on the governing bodies of the specialized agencies and other appropriate elements of the United Nations system to re-examine their programmes and allocations so as to support international action to combat desertification within the context of the Plan of Action. It further recommends that other governmental and non-governmental organisations concerned with desertification participate fully in the implementation of the Plan with a view to coordinating their activities within a worldwide programme.

As true as it may be that present knowledge is sufficient to arrest desertification, there is no question that carefully directed and coordinated research could make the task more effective. To help assure proper co-ordination of scientific research envisaged in the Plan of Action, and to help assure that research is accurately focussed and that its findings will be disseminated, the draft Plan suggests the establishment of a technical council, committee or group, advisory to the Environment Coordination Board, to be composed principally of representatives of research institutions engaged in investigating desertification phenomena.

These recommendations refer to international support, whereas the core of the campaign against desertification will lie in national action. On the subject of institutional arrangements, our most important suggestion is that national machinery be established, where no such machinery now exists, in countries confronted with desertification problems. Administrative approaches to the problem have sometimes been as fragmented as the subject itself, and it is our conviction that effective national action requires a national body capable of keeping the problem in focus, and of acting with sufficient authority to ensure success. Such a body would ensure that national desertification programmes are coordinated with regional and international action. I would like to express a word of praise to those countries that have established national committees on desertification in response to the recommendation of UNEP's Governing Council.

These are the means by which we believe the actions arising from the Plan can be financed and implemented. The conference may agree with these suggestions, or it may come up with additional, or alternative formulations. I am sure that all delegations agree that concrete proposals for financing and implementation are as crucial to success as an effective and realistic Plan of Action itself.

This conference is the latest, and by no means the last, of a series of world conferences sponsored by the United Nations, each intended to come to grips with one of the major problems facing mankind. Recent conferences have been concerned with population, food,[1] the rights of women, trade and development, human settlements[2] and water.[3] It is recognised that all these problems are interrelated, and that the resolution of any one of them would have a marked and beneficial impact on all the others. In this sense, each conference may be thought of as concerned with one aspect of a complexity of problems.

This is no less true with regard to the subject of our deliberations here. The connections between the problem of desertification and the findings of the Water Conference are obvious, and the two secretariats have worked in close collaboration. Equally obvious is the relation between our subject and problems of population, food and human settlements. Perhaps not so obvious, but certainly clear upon reflection, is the beneficial effect that arresting desertification would have on problems of trade and development and the transfer of technology. The transfer of technology is a subject that demands close collaboration between those working on desertification and the secretariats of the upcoming United Nations Conferences on Technical Co-operation among Developing Countries[4] and on Science and Technology for Development.[5]

Action against desertification cannot yield results unless Governments perceive it as an integral part of their established plans for social and economic development and as part of their collective effort to meet the requirements of the New International Economic Order. A powerful current of contemporary thought views a firm and self-reliant agricultural base as an essential prerequisite to national development. From this perspective productive lands

---

[1] For the statement to the World Food Conference, see p. 1.
[2] For the statement to the UN Conference on Human Settlements, see p. 6.
[3] For the statement to the UN Water Conference, see p. 59.
[4] For the statement to the UN Conference on Technical Cooperation Among Developing Countries, see p. 93.
[5] For the statement to the UN Conference on Science and Technology for Development, see p. 106.

and waters are seen as the key national resources, renewable assets that will continue to yield wealth when non-renewable resources have been exhausted. This is the goal of our efforts and the subject of our discussions here — to maintain land productivity, to conserve water resources, to reclaim degraded land and to make it productive once again.

In preparing for the conference, we have done our best to comply with the provisions of the General Assembly resolution that convened it. During the process we came to realise that desertification is a human problem both in its origin and in its effects, and that our main concerns lie in human actions as well as in human well-being. We also came to realize that the problem is global, and that its solution will have direct impact on those who suffer from it, as well as unquestionably affecting, both directly and indirectly, those who do not face it. We have been led to the view that this urgent and serious threat to the welfare of mankind can be arrested when man's actions become directed in harmony with the environment. We came to the conclusion that enough is known to combat desertification right now, and indeed we see that Governments have already begun to act, that they are profoundly concerned over the state of their land, and are ready to work together to overcome a problem that affects at least two-thirds of the countries of the world. What is needed to complete the task is a Plan of Action that is both realistic and realizable — that is to say, scientifically feasible and politically acceptable, for both are necessary. Also needed are ways to implement the Plan and an appropriate continuing mechanism to ensure its implementation in the years ahead. These are the essentials that will emerge from this conference, as it begins to summon the political will required to halt desertification, and to lift this threat from the land and its people.

11

ENVIRONMENTAL EDUCATION

Opening Statement to the Inter-Governmental Conference on
Environmental Education[1]

Tbilisi, USSR, October 1977

LET me first explain why the United Nations Environment Programme attaches such a great importance to environmental education. It is because in the long run nothing significant will happen to reduce local and international threats to the environment unless widespread public awareness is aroused concerning the essential links between environmental quality and the continued satisfaction of human needs. What is more, human needs and aspirations the world over can only be satisfied as environmental awareness leads to appropriate action at all levels of society from the smallest local communities to the whole community of nations. Appropriate action requires a solid base of sound information and technical skills. But action also depends upon motivation, which depends upon widespread understanding and that, in turn, depends upon education. What is required is continuing educative action so that all strata of society everywhere become aware of their responsibilities and become willing to do what they can to help.

Environmental problems are marked by variety, complexity, and urgency. For many in today's world, environmental education is really a matter of life and death: for thousands of industrial workers who deal with chemicals; for countless farm workers who deal with pesticides; for the millions of poorer people whose livelihood and health depend upon more enlightened management of the world's water systems; for the millions of people from developed countries who are threatened by environmentally induced cancer; and for the more than 600 million people who live in arid and

---

[1] Organised by UNESCO in cooperation with UNEP.

semi-arid lands threatened by decreasing productivity induced by desertification. We in UNEP see environmental education, therefore, as a global, life-long process involving society as a whole, directed at *all* members of the community, with due regard to their social, economic, cultural and political needs. We also believe that it is the action of man – as planner, builder, farmer, citizen or consumer – which causes environmental degradation. It is therefore on man's attitude that the future of our air, water, soil, forests, and mineral wealth ultimately depends. This is why we feel it is so important that everyone becomes environmentally conscious through proper environmental education.

Environmental education is also essential in integrating the knowledge generated by the important United Nations conferences of the past five years: on the human environment, population, food, human settlements, water and desertification. Environmental education must be accelerated within nations and internationally if the important results of these remarkable global meetings are to be disseminated, and implemented for the satisfaction of basic human needs for all.

Another prime area where a better worldwide understanding of environmental issues, through appropriate forms of environmental education, has become very apparent in recent years, is development itself, and the implementation of the New International Economic Order. The study of environment and development relationships is resulting in a more comprehensive understanding that development objectives must henceforth embrace, among other things, *sustained* improvement of the quality of life, eradication of poverty, and equitable participation of people in the benefits of development. The problem is not how to choose between environmental protection and achievement of developmental goals, but how to direct development so as to ensure maximum human benefits from the environment for both present and *future* generations. Environment and development relationships, indeed, appear to be the key issue, and a wider view of these relationships demand a wider view of environmental education.

Environmental education is a part of the mandate conferred upon UNEP in 1972 by the General Assembly following the Stockholm Conference on the Human Environment.

UNEP's activities, according to this mandate, consist of three major components:

1. environmental assessment;
2. environmental management;
3. supporting measures.

Environmental Assessment

Assessment is a dynamic process by which environmental issues are identified and data generated and evaluated to provide a basis for rational decision-making, especially at the national level. At the global level this activity is known as Earthwatch. We need assessment to locate and define problems, and to estimate their urgency and dimensions.

Environmental Management[1]

Drawing on the best available knowledge and information provided through environmental assessment, the function of environmental management is to ensure that environmental considerations are taken into account in policy formulation and planning of social and economic development, and throughout the decision-making process leading to action. It is only thus that environmentally sound management of human activities can be carried out.

Supporting measures

But effective implementation of environmental management calls for widespread public understanding, the necessary resources and technical capacity, and the public motivation and will to back it up. And so the third component of UNEP's activities consists of supporting measures. These are: information, technical assistance and environmental education and training. To call these activities supporting measures does not mean that they are of secondary importance. Together with environmental assessment and management they are complimentary, inseparable and indispensable parts of action to safeguard the environment.

The fulfilment of our mandate, therefore, requires a truly comprehensive view of environmental education and training. What is required cannot be achieved by small groups of highly specialized experts who spend many years passing through all stages of formal education. The contribution of such experts is certainly valuable but public participation at all levels is equally necessary, and it is for that reason that UNEP attaches great importance to out-of-school informal education. Millions of people living today will never spend an hour in a formal school setting but it is important that they, too, have the opportunity to learn about the environmental factors essential to their own well-being. In addition, many environmental measures in every country call for active citizen participation which will only be effective if based on and linked to education for the general public. Hence the challenge to this conference is to advance the theory and practice of environmental education on the broadest possible front.

The eight major guiding principles for environmental education spelled out in 1975 by the government experts at the Belgrade International Workshop on Environmental Education are excellent rules for education in its totality.

[1] For detailed discussion of environmental management, see p. 45.

But I would emphasise three unique qualities of environmental education:
1. its aim to promote an awareness of linkages between disciplines;
2. its aim to promote greater consciousness of how actions taken now may affect people in the future;
3. its concern with geographical and social linkages.

It is our past failure to think of the environment in broad enough terms that has led humanity into many of our present day environmental and developmental problems. I would like, therefore, to further emphasize the key importance of a better universal understanding of the relationship between environment and development.

Environmental problems in tomorrow's world will be everyone's concern. The world has been made one community by modern travel and communication facilities, by a vast network of economic and trade links, and by a common interest in understanding and respecting the limits in the ability of the planet's life-support systems to absorb the impacts of man's activities. We cannot say that one region's environmental and developmental problems are the concern of that region alone. One nation's problems can quickly become all nations' problems, just as surely as global threats to the environment are the concern of humanity as a whole.

Environmental and development problems are inseparably linked; they have global and international dimensions; they occur in all countries and societies at every stage of economic development and with every kind of social and political orientation.

A few examples will illustrate the global nature of environmental concerns, and the interrelatedness of environment and development. One obvious global problem is the threat to the ozone layer from the release of certain chemicals into the atmosphere with possible far-reaching consequences for terrestrial life forms, including man. There may also be far-reaching effects on the climate of our globe from the impact of other activities of man — particularly his use or misuse of certain energy sources. The exhaustion of petroleum resources has obvious global implications, and so do some of the measures adopted in the development of new energy sources, especially nuclear fission. It is interesting to note in passing that while most environmental concern about energy has concentrated on the nuclear issue, it could be that the consumption of fossil fuels, through its impact on climate by the emission of carbon dioxide, actually has a more significant environmental impact.

We now know that environmental problems can be associated with both inappropriate development and lack of development. Many complex problems have arisen in the past in the developed world from developmental applications of science and technology without full regard to environmental consequences. In developing countries when development projects are ill-conceived, poorly designed, and badly executed, they may be accompanied by resource depletion, environmentally induced diseases, chemical and biological pollution at levels even higher than are now met in developed countries, and cause widespread social disruption. Lack of development, on the other hand, can result in squalid human settlements, loss of productivity through disease and malnutrition, and loss of arable land through destruction of forests and overuse of fragile semi-arid and sub-humid pasture lands.

A major factor that is becoming apparent in the analysis of causes of environmental problems is the great disparity in living standards, not only between rich and poor countries, but also between rich and poor strata within the same country. Extreme inequalities of wealth make it difficult for any society to benefit fully from its natural resources and can lead to environmental damage both through the desperate search by the poor for the means of sustenance and through the wasteful use of resources by the rich. Rich countries or rich sectors of various societies apply wasteful lifestyles which impose arrogant demands on natural resources, particularly energy, minerals and food. It is now apparent that all countries, developed and developing alike, must, in their pursuit of development, take account of the limitations as well as the opportunities the environment affords; and they must seek out and adopt new approaches and patterns of development and lifestyles in which environmental factors are fully taken into account.

UNEP is required by its mandate to play a central role in environmental assessment and management, and also to promote environmental education both within the United Nations systems as a whole and in the world at large. That is the Stockholm/General Assembly mandate for UNEP. I would emphasize that the Environment Programme is not the exclusive creation and prerogative of our small secretariat headquarters in Nairobi; it is a programme designed with the assistance of the entire international community, and to be implemented by that community. Thus UNEP exists to coordinate the preparation of the programme and to catalyze its implementation. Accordingly in promoting environmental education and training UNEP must work in full consultation and cooperation with other organisations.

We in UNEP have enjoyed with a very fruitful relationship with UNESCO since the Interntional Environmental Education Programme was initiated in January 1975. In a sense all the activities of the programme have been preparations for the Tbilisi Conference. One of the first steps was the initiation of a global overview of publications on environmental education. Next a number of important formal and non-formal education topics were studied, and the results were presented as working documents to the Belgrade Workshop. The Workshop also studied UNESCO/UNEP reports on consultants' missions and a preliminary world survey of environmental education needs and priorities.

The Belgrade workshop adopted the "Belgrade Charter: a Global Framework for Environmental Education". After the workshop there was a series of meetings of experts and pilot projects in every region of the world.

Now, here at Tbilisi, we look for guidance from Governments on their priorities, and on what it is they want us to do. You will review two years of study and experimentation, and an enormous collection of information from intergovernmental meetings. In essence, you will be considering and suggesting an Action Plan for promoting and developing environmental education and training, nationally, regionally, and globally.

But, let us make no mistakes, the success of any international undertaking in the field of environmental education and training, most assuredly, depends on action at the local level. Not only are national participation and financial provision essential, but the implementation of the enormous task of changing approaches to education must be done by nationals within each country.

In conclusion, I would emphasize the magnitude and the urgency of the task before you. What, after all, is at stake? Consider what our planet would be like today if previous generations had known and implemented the environmental knowledge we now possess within the framework of more just world economic relationships. Forests would exist where there is now only denuded land, a great deal of the earth's surface which is unproductive would still be yielding rich harvests, and we would be breathing cleaner air, have access to cleaner water and in all probability have a much better picture of the mass poverty which is devastating the lives of millions and millions of our fellow companions on this spaceship earth. We have not yet reached the point of no return, but surely, in facing the colossal environmental problems of today's world both nationally and globally, we are going uphill. Not only that, but we are also surely racing against time. We have to work together now, right now, if we are to avoid the catastrophes foreseen by the doomsday watchers. We have a great challenge and an enormous responsibility to bring about the revolution in human consciousness and behaiour that is imperative in our era. Plato, writing of Attica, lamented so many years ago, "Our land, compared to what it was, is like the skeleton of a body wasted by disease. The plump soft spots have vanished and all that remains is the carcass." By our action or inaction now, we will determine whether the same will be said a few decades from now, not of Attica, but of the world as a whole.

12

DISARMAMENT AND THE ENVIRONMENT

Statement to the United Nations General Assembly
Special Session Devoted to Disarmament

New York, U.S.A., June 1978

DISARMAMENT is one of the central challenges facing humanity today. We realise, of course, that the issues on your agenda cannot be solved by intemperate rhetoric or glib panaceas, since the question of armaments is deeply rooted in our perceptions of security and in the competitiveness of human nature which is often productive, but can also degenerate into senseless conflict.

I am sure we all agree that the process of armaments control and reduction must be moved forward and the opportunitites presented by this session must be used to revise our assumptions regarding the principal threats to national and global security.

Over the ages the nations of the world have been accustomed to thinking and acting as if the principal threats they faced arose from possible aggressive acts of other nations. I do not think we can any longer maintain this without severe qualification. I say this for two reasons.

First, we have come to see, in our generation, that the deterioration of the human environment and the depletion of the productive capacity of the earth's principal biological systems, on which the global economy depends, pose most serious threats not only to the continuing welfare of nations, but to the security of mankind as a whole. I am not suggesting that we must choose betwen giving our attention to questions of international security and environmental problems. It is not an "either-or" choice, and this is the second fact I want to stress. Wars and the arms race are themselves the source of severe threats to the whole human environment. We must see to it that we are not so mesmerized by the threats to our welfare and security posed by armed conflict that the quality of the human environment is allowed to degenerate to the point where there is nothing much left worth fighting for.

From the outset the international environmental movement has voiced its concern that the human environment should not be endangered by the development and use of armaments. It was largely environmental concerns that have led to existing arms control agreements. The use of any weapon has an environmental impact and the development, testing, and use of weapons of mass destruction represents man's deliberate destruction of all forms of life. Even conventional high explosives, chemical agents and incendiaries can have an enormous ecological impact, as has recently been abundantly demonstrated.

The declaration of the Nations of the World at the United Nations Conference of the Human Environment[1] in Stockholm in 1972 stated unambiguously that man and his environment must be spared the effects of nuclear weapons and all other means of mass destruction. It called upon states to try to reach prompt agreement, through the relevant international organs, on the elimination and complete destruction of such weapons. The Governing Council of UNEP which concluded its 6th session less than two weeks ago, considered "that the environmental consequences of the arms race, including weapons with harmful impacts for present and future generations and irreversible deterioration of the environment should be brought to the attention of the General Assembly, and acknowledged the intention of the Executive Director to address the General Assembly at its special session.". It is heartening to see these types of weapons figuring so highly on the proposed priorities in disarmament negotiations that you are now considering. It would be redundant to reiterate here all environmental consequences of the arms race. They are known to all of you. Suffice it to say that development, testing, transport and use of weapons, not only those of mass destruction, but also of conventional ones, have varying but sure deleterious effects on man's health as well as health of the environment, be it soil, water, air or any of the various ecosystems around us, let alone the irrational use of our scarce natural resources and the irrational use of the much needed human and financial resources.

I am well aware that you have already started the process of arms reduction and control, and the record is impressive. We have the Partial Test Ban Treaty; the Non-Proliferation Treaty; the Convention on Biological and Bacteriological Weapons; the Treaty prohibiting the emplacement of nuclear weapons and other weapons of mass destruction on the sea bed and ocean floors; the Treaty concerning the peaceful uses of outer space and the recent Convention on Environmental Modification as a Weapon of War. The General Assembly at its last session called upon the Secretary-General to prepare a study on weapons of mass destruction and their effects upon the environment, particularly their role in inducing desertification.

---

[1] For the declaration, see "In Defence of the Earth," Executive Series 1, UNEP, Nairobi, 1981.

These are all commendable steps, but it must be admitted that the process has been sluggish. This Special Session presents a most valuable opportunity to accelerate the process and move it forward. It represents an opportunity that must not be passed by and the links between disarmament and environment must be taken fully into account, because the stresses and strains related to the arms race are increasing.

I know the reports before you stress the linkages between disarmament and development and propose excellent guidelines for an in-depth study on the subject. What I want to stress on this occasion is that peace, environment and development are inseparable. Peace is the only road to a better quality of life, and a healthy, productive environment is essential to the development which so many nations badly need, and which the release of resources through disarmament would help to accelerate.

We in UNEP, are firmly convinced that development, proper development, can only be achieved through peace and disarmament. We simply add that what we should be always talking about is environmentally sound development, sustained development, development without destruction.

I am sure you all know more facts about arms race than I do. I am also sure the reports before you and the statement made here and at the General Debate referred to a large body of such facts. But, still, let us look again at some of these facts. The development needs of the Third World countries are urgent, yet global arms trade with them amounts to about three quarters of the total trade. Moreover, much sophisticated weaponry is going into areas of high tension with consequent dangers to man and the environment.

If we consider skilled manpower, which is so badly needed for development in both developed and developing countries, as you know, some 500,000 of the world's best scientists and engineers are engaged in military research and development, which cost almost as much as all other global research and development activities. The total number of men and women now engaged full time in arms factories and research, and in the armed forces of the nations is estimated by several sources to be between 60 and 70 million.

The total quantity of raw materials consumed for military purposes on a worldwide basis is staggering, yet there are shortages of non-renewable resources in both developed and developing countries.

Take the question of costs. Military expenditures have increased thirty-fold during this century. The figure in U.S. dollars during 1975 amounted to an astronomical $371 thousand million, and is now probably over $400 thousand million and is still rising. To put it more simply, world expenditures for military purposes eat up close to $40 million per hour. A good deal of such expenditure can be channelled into environmentally sound development everywhere, in both developed and developing countries. If only one-third of the world's military expenditures could be directed to an international fund for such development, developing countries would be able to meet their urgent needs and build the necessary economic and social infrastructure for a good life.

Another fact: According to the best available estimates, the world total of arms transfers has increased from an average of $9,500 million annually in the 1973-75 period to $13,300 million in 1976. If a tax at the rate of 5 per cent on actual transfers were levied, this should yield, based on 1976 estimates, more than $650 million per year. If levied on arms transfer agreements the figure would become almost $1,500 million. More important, a tax of this rate would have the effect of reducing the volume of sales until hopefully they are completely stopped.

In the next few years the focus of attention will be on the planning of a New International Development Strategy. Such a forward step requires an easing of international tensions, a growth in co-operative endeavours, and a continuing review of the linkages between disarmament, environment and development.

In section A, paragraph 5, of the International Development Strategy, the General Assembly stated that "the success of international development activities will depend in large measures on improvement in the general international situation, particularly on concrete progress towards general and complete disarmament under effective international control". It further stated that "progress towards general and complete disarmament should release substantial additional resources which could be utilized for the purpose of economic and social development, in particular that of developing countries."

Despite the magnitude and complexities of the challenge inherent in any demilitarization on the world's economy, the United Nations cannot falter here if it is to fulfil the expectations that the world continues to invest in it and to discharge its responsibilities for peace and human well-being to this and succeeding operations.

We are indeed at a crossroads with an increasingly impatient world quick to remind us that, and here I quote from the Cocoyoc Declaration[1] adopted at Mexico in October 1974 and presented to the General Assembly at its 29th Session: "30 years have passed since the UN launched the effort to establish a new international order. Today that order has reached a critical turning point. The hope of creating a better life for the whole human family has been largely frustated. It has proved impossible up till now to meet the inner limits of satisfying fundamental human needs. On the contrary more people are hungry, sick, shelterless and illiterate today than when the United Nations was first set up . . ." Four years after Cocoyoc, one cannot claim that the situation has changed.

Today the call is for equity and a New International Economic Order premised on principles of environmentally sound and sustainable development and geared to the satisfaction of basic human needs. None of this is possible, however, without a fundamental restructuring of international economic

---

[1] For the full text of the Cocoyoc Declaration see "In Defence of the Earth," Executive Series 1, UNEP, Nairobi, 1981.

relations, a re-ordering of global priorities, and a redevelopment of our shrinking resources toward the urgent developmental and environmental problems facing mankind and vital to our collective security and survival.

13

ENVIRONMENT IN THE TECHNICAL COOPERATION AMONG DEVELOPING COUNTRIES

Statement to the United Nations Conference on
Technical Cooperation Among Developing Countries

Buenos Aires, Argentina, September 1978

THIS conference's preparations have made it abundantly clear that Technical Cooperation among Developing Countries (TCDC) represents a new and vitally important dimension for international co-operation.

In today's world, new dimensions of cooperation, both between industrialized and developing countries, and among the developing countries themselves, are required. Indeed, I believe that greater cooperation among the developing countries will give them a firmer basis for their cooperation with the industrialized world. The healthy functioning of our interdependent technological society requires the full participation and active cooperation of the two-thirds of the world's population living in the developing countries, and this dictates that we heed their demands for a more just and equitable share of the benefits which this technological civilization makes possible. This constitutes an essential element in the drive of the developing countries for a New International Economic Order.

In our thinking, Technical Cooperation among Developing Countries is linked with one of the major world environmental concerns, namely, the important interrelationship between environment and development.

Although the problem of environmental degradation, with the menace it poses to development and human well-being, is of a global nature, affecting both developed and developing countries, the countries in the developing world particularly must cooperate in sharing their own thinking and experience in all aspects of the environment-development interface. The industrially advanced countries of this world, rich though they may be, face a challenge in reorienting their development, which has left their resources depleted and their environments polluted. For the developing countries, which stand at a new threshold, the challenge is somewhat different, and their experiences in meeting this challenge must be shared, particularly among countries with similar ecosystems. Both developed and developing countries have made only a start in their approaches to local environment management problems, and it cannot be said that the experience gained by one group is very much greater than that of the other. For these reasons Technical Cooperation among Developing Countries is particularly relevant to environmental concerns.

It is recognized today that the conventional patterns of development of the past have not fully met the requirements of mankind, and in particular have failed the poorer countries in their aspiration for development that meets the needs of their people without repeating the mistakes of certain past patterns of development. There can be no doubt that it is of the highest importance to the international community today to devise and to support alternative patterns of development. Whatever the patterns chosen by particular countries, and whatever the routes followed in applying these patterns, the ultimate objectives must be to provide at least for the minimal human needs of their people, and to meet their aspirations for higher standards of living and a better quality of life in a sustainable manner, while protecting and safeguarding the environment which is the basis for the achievement of such objectives. It is through the development process that man acts upon and interacts with the natural environment. Water, air, soil, minerals, plant and animal life constitute the very resources which development itself seeks to exploit. Good management of the environment is thus, in our view, essentially a matter of making the best use of nature's resource endowment without wasting scarce materials or destroying the ecological basis on which sustained development depends.

This is among the great challenges of our time and will determine the viability of our planet Earth for future generations.

In this context, we should be aware that technologies transplanted from industrialized countries may not meet the real needs of developing countries for good management of their environment. What is needed is not a simple transfer of existing technologies, but the development of new technologies and institutions that are relevant to the socio-economic conditions of the receiving countries, that take advantage of and utilize effectively local manpower and readily available raw materials, and that are in harmony with the environments of these countries. In addition there must be adequate infrastructure in the form of trained manpower and information systems, among other things, to identify these needs, establish priorities and define operational and maintenance requirements before particular technologies are decided upon.

One can therefore say that the technologies devised or adapted by developing countries themselves may, in many cases, be better suited to their economic and environmental settings than transplanted or unadapted imported ones. Concrete examples could be easily taken from the field of energy or the conservation of soil. The development of technologies by the developing counties for the use of some new and renewable sources of energy is a case in mind. On the other hand, heavy agricultural machinery has sometimes been introduced into places where ecological conditions are totally different from the countries where they were originally developed and successfully used. This has often led to deterioration of the agricultural potential in the receiving country, or undermined the sustainability of such production. Failures in technology are most often failures in choices of technology. I should also add in this respect that old and tried techniques have been set aside simply because they were old and out of fashion.

In developing their own technologies, or adapting imported ones to their own needs, developing countries must put special emphasis on the exchange of information among themselves. Right here lies one of the most serious constraints limiting TCDC, even where opportunities already exist for such co-operation. I refer to the information gap about technologies, institutions, equipment, development approaches, institutional arrangements or other relevant infrastructures which some developing countries have tested and firmly established. The initiative taken by UNEP to prepare an inventory of developing countries' capacities represents an important step towards a more meaningful system of information exchange. UNEP is being assisted in this by the various specialized agencies who are themselves also developing relevant sectoral directories as part of their own information systems.

The UNEP International Referral System (INFOTERRA), designed to put "users" in touch with "sources" of environmental information, can also be used to identify sources of information on TCDC activities. It is therefore highly relevant to the recommendations contained in the draft plan of action before you. I strongly urge developing countries to consider whether specific data, based on their own experience in devising processes and technologies, could not be put into INFOTERRA. Furthermore, the Global Environmental Monitoring System (GEMS) and the International Register of Potentially Toxic Chemicals (IRPTC), both being developed by UNEP, are extremely useful as "switchboards", in transmitting and receiving relevant information among developing countries. I appeal therefore to all the developing countries to make full use of these systems as a means of promoting TCDC.

Technical Cooperation among countries through bilateral and/or multilateral arrangements to deal with environmental issues was emphasized in the Principles and Recommendations of the Stockholm Conference,[1] together with the General Assembly in its resolution 2997 (XXVII), which established UNEP. The Governing Council of UNEP in its six sessions, and the Economic and Social Council and the General Assembly in their deliberations on reports of these sessions, repeatedly indicated a concern with the special problems of developing countries, and emphasised that these must receive attention in the design of the Environmental Programme and be given

---

[1]For the text, see "In Defence of the Earth," Executive Series 1, UNEP, Nairobi, 1981.

priority in its implementation.

UNEP is also establishing a network of project-oriented institutions to develop and introduce appropriate technologies, with particular emphasis on local technologies. This action is in accordance with recommendations contained in the draft plan of action before you.

Desertification is a major economic and environmental problem, of the greatest particular concern to developing countries. The United Nations Conference on Desertification last year, of which I had the privilege to be the Secretary-General, proposed, and the General Assembly adopted, a Plan of Action to Combat Desertification.[1] The implementation of the Plan will be a major venture in the exchange of relevant expert knowledge and cooperation among the developing countries affected by the advance of deserts, a first example being the six transnational projects in the developing world, which are aimed at monitoring and combating the desertification process. Thus implementation of the Plan will be a major test of the success of the principles of TCDC.

The results of the United Nations Water Conference were an important input to the United Nations Conference on Desertification, and I hope that the results of the Desertification Conference will assist you in your endeavours, and will be seen by you as a fundamental example of an area where co-operation among the developing countries is essential to success. Desertification is thus an area where the Plan of Action you adopt here will meet an important practical test. You may wish to give thought to the steps required to make the test a success.

---

[1] See "United Nations Conference on Desertification: Round-up, Plan of Action and Resolutions", United Nations, New York, 1978.

14

CLIMATE, ENVIRONMENT AND SOCIETY

Statement to the World Climate Conference

Geneva, Switzerland, February 1979

UNEP's goal is the protection and enhancement of the environment for present and future generations. To achieve this goal environmental assessment and environmental management are essential. We must first study the environment, its mechanisms and interrelationships and the changes, taking place in it, and determine whether these changes are natural, man-made or a combination of both. It is only after such assessment that we can go on to the next step — environmental management.

Since its inception, UNEP has been heavily involved in various activities related to world climate, in cooperation with United Nations agencies and especially WMO and UNESCO. The Earthwatch programme is our main framework of environmental assessment, and it is within this programme that most of our climate-related activities are undertaken. Earthwatch comprises the Global Environmental Monitoring System (GEMS), and research, evaluation and exchange of information, in addition to the Outer Limits programme. The latter includes climatic changes, weather modification, and risks to the ozone layer, among other concerns. Within these areas UNEP has undertaken a number of projects related to climate, in cooperation with WMO and other bodies.

The major concerns of UNEP with regard to climate can be summed up in two phrases:

1. the impact of the climate on man;
2. the influence that man has on the climate.

Impact of Climate on Man

Mankind since the beginning of his relatively brief history on this earth has always been preoccupied by the climate. While the race was small in numbers man had perforce to adapt to climatic variability by changing his mode of living. If conditions became too harsh, he might migrate to climatically more favourable areas. Hardship and suffering due to natural climatic fluctuations were constantly present. Nevertheless his problems were relatively insignificant compared to the major tragedies that could happen at this point in time if only a small global climatic change occurs. Humanity has become increasingly vulnerable to climatic variations, the effects of which may be magnified severalfold due to the precarious balance now existing between a large and rapidly increasing population on the one hand, and global food production on the other. The recent remarkably stable climatic conditions, combined with improved farming technology, gave a consistent and high yield of agricultural products, which perhaps lulled the peoples of the world into a sense of complacency in the years between the mid 1950's and the early 1970's. Now, however, we would appear to have moved into a period of more marked climatic fluctuations with great consequent fluctuations in agricultural production. In recent years we have witnessed a number of tragedies caused by climatic anomalies: the Sahel drought as seen by in desertification brought disaster to many parts of Africa; floods in many parts of the world have inflicted tremendous damage and suffering; excessively cold winters and summer droughts have caused shortages in food supplies even in countries with great potential for agricultural production.

Man's Impact on Climate

The scientific community is now well aware that man's industrial, agricultural and land use practices can induce alterations in the climate on local, regional or global scales. Depending on the scale of activity, urbanization, deforestation, overgrazing, water management practices in dams and irrigation can all have effects on the climate, though difficult to quantify. Additionally, the atmosphere's chemical composition is changing because of man's activities, and this in turn may have produced climatic changes.

One area of concern is the well-documented increase in atmospheric carbon dioxide, resulting from the increased use of fossil fuels, coupled with a continued disappearance of the earth's forest cover. I know that concrete figures on deforestation are not available. Even the most quoted figure of 20 hectares per minute is challenged by some. FAO and UNEP are assessing world tropical forest cover and degradation rates. The findings will be ready late next year, but preliminary results may be available earlier. Whatever the results of the study, there seems to be no doubt about the increase in atmospheric carbon dioxide.

The world is concerned over warnings from scientists that there is a risk of global warming due to the so-called greenhouse effect of carbon dioxide. There is no proof as yet that global warming is taking place and, as stated in the documents presented to this conference, it may take twenty years before we can know for sure. But by then it could be too late to do anything about it, and climatic changes could have already occurred with significant environmental impacts, such as alteration of precipitation and evaporation regimes; or melting of Arctic ice which could disturb the pattern of oceanic circulation and hence that of atmospheric circulation.

Some scientists postulate that there may be some beneficial effects of an increase of carbon dioxide in the atmosphere, such as the possible enhancement of food productivity. We should not forget, however, that we know too little about chloroplast architecture and genetics, and about the genetic basic of optimisation of photosynthetic activity, to accept such a hypothesis without reservation.

The CO_2 problem is serious because of its global nature; it is urgent because it may prove difficult for us to shift from fossil fuels to other forms of energy should this be required; it is also complex because of the multiplicity of factors that influence the carbon cycle, especially the oceans, forests and vegetation. In order to help clarify these issues UNEP has cooperated with SCOPE (Scientific Committee on Problems of the Environment) in formulating a study aimed at evaluating existing knowledge of the biogeochemical cycle of carbon.

It has been well said that humanity is in the process of carrying out an uncontrolled experiment on the earth's atmosphere. The scientific answers to the uncertainties concerning the results of man-induced changes in the atmosphere may not come within the next decade, yet it would appear that it is within this time scale that the difficult decisions on global energy options will have to be taken. Because of this, this conference may wish to consider the need for developing a world plan of action for dealing with the carbon dioxide problem along lines similar to those developed to deal with the issue of the ozone layer. UNEP is ready to carry out its role in the important area of assessing the environmental impacts of increased levels of carbon dioxide in the atmosphere.

Simple solutions do not exist for such complex global problems, but world concern is mounting and deserves a reponse at the international level. Because climate is man's primary shared natural resource, it is imperative that concerted action be undertaken by all nations and by national and international organisations. An interdisciplinary approach is also a necessity. The problem must be addressed not only by meteorologists and climatologists but also by social scientists, economists and others.

The formulation of the World Climate Programme, and action plans on such major issues as ozone and carbon dioxide are undoubtedly important contributions, but their implementation will require considerable determination and great resources. A solemn responsibility lies upon all nations of the world, and I feel confident that they will discharge this responsibility in a timely and effective manner.

15

RURAL DEVELOPMENT AND ENVIRONMENT

Statement to the World Conference on Agrarian Reform
and Rural Development

Rome, Italy, July 1979

THE decade of the seventies has seen the international community move to a new dimension in its perceptions of the interrelated nature of the problems of poverty and of development, of natural resources and of the environment. Such perceptions have emerged very largely from a series of world conferences held in this decade, of which the Stockholm conference on the Human Environment was the first, and the present conference among the latest. This conference is the logical next step following the related debates in previous international conferences, those on environment, world food problems,[1] human settlements,[2] desertification,[3] water,[4] and technical cooperation among developing countries.[5] The results of your deliberations will be an important input to the World Conference on Science and Technology for Development next month.[6] What is even more important is that this conference is extremely relevant to the preparations for the next international development strategy for the 1980's and beyond. Agrarian reform and rural development in a number of developing countries already have a long history of discussion, research and policy intervention and experimentation. This conference offers an opportunity to exchange experiences and ideas, and to

---

[1] For statement to the World Food Conference, see p. 1.
[2] For statement to the UN Conference on Human Settlements, see p. 6.
[3] For statement to the UN Conference on Desertification, see p. 71.
[4] For statement to the UN Water Conference, see p. 59.
[5] For statement to the UN Conference on Technical Cooperation between Developing Countries, see p. 93.
[6] For statement to the UN Conference on Science and Technology for Development, see p. 106.

make a critical examination of past efforts by the countries directly involved. It is crucial that a dispassionate assessment be made of the reasons why certain policies have failed to lead to the desired results; what steps can be taken to improve the effectiveness of past approaches; and what new alternatives or avenues need to be explored.

There can be no doubt about the complexity of the matters before you, and the magnitude of your task. Rural peoples comprise about half of the world population but degradation of rural areas is not a matter of concern only to the rural inhabitants. It is not even solely a matter of national concern, for as the Declaration of Philadelphia put it, "poverty anywhere is a threat to prosperity everywhere". The urban problems which characterize our increasingly urbanised civilization cannot be resolved if there is a continuing diminution of the food and other biological resources (particularly wood and fibre) that can only come from the land. The world is one, and all nations have become interdependant today as never before. Agrarian reform and rural development are truly matters of pressing general concern.

Rural development and agrarian reform should thus be seen as an integral part of a larger complex of problems: eliminating abject poverty; ensuring more prudent and more productive management of natural resources while keeping the well-being of future generations in mind; expanding productive employment; promoting distributive justice; and achieving real improvements in the quality of life. These are the major concerns of the world community as it strives to bring about a New International Economic Order and prepare a new international development strategy.

From the point of view of the United Nations Environment Programme we consider that rural areas can only develop if:

1. there is a perceived satisfaction of the needs of the inhabitants (material and non-material);

2. if there is confidence in the ability of the local people to sustain such development;

3. if the development is based on ecological considerations which put a premium on long-term sustainability rather than on growth *per se*.

This latter concept is no new invention. It is merely a lesson we have drawn from the past. For UNEP, the essence of rural development is the environmentally prudent use and management on the widest possible scale of soils, forests, water supplies and other natural resources of the earth, so that development is not only promoted and accelerated but managed in such a way as to be sustainable. Reform means change for the better; and agrarian reform must mean drastic changes in patterns of ownership, management practices, and distribution of products for the betterment of those who depend upon the land.

If we strive for a balanced growth of urban and rural areas, we soon realize that the constraints on location of industries and settlements development in excessively large metropolises offer opportunities to stimulate growth of small towns whose growth is organically linked in mutually reinforcing ways to a number of surrounding villages. There are already a number of well-known examples of successful decentralisation of industries.

Excessive pressures of population and consumption on fragile ecosystems should be turned into opportunities for well thought-out programmes of transmigration, resettlement and area development. Opportunities offered by unused natural resources must be seized, so that benefits of development are shared by all. And in the face of mounting demand for energy, which cannot be satisfied from the dwindling traditional sources, more attention will have to be paid to the generation and provision of energy for rural development based on solar potential and local sources, such as planned fuelwood plantations, use of organic wastes for biogas, wind power, and small-scale hydropower projects.

Planning must ensure broadly based access to amenities of sanitation, community safe water supply, and facilities for disposal of domestic and community wastes. Already there is under way "minimum access" physical planning in some developing countries. In this task cooperation between governmental bodies at various levels and voluntary organizations is essential. Success in these areas can have a marked impact on disease and debility control, labour productivity, pollution control and inland waters, and fisheries improvement.

Food production is of prime importance, and much has been said on how rural communities can achieve self-sufficiency in food supplies. Special attention must be directed to land use planning to ensure soil conservation. More use should be made of farming practices that prevent soil degradation and erosion. Rural areas offer excellent opportunities for an integration of the use of organic compost, with carefully planned application of chemical fertilizers and microbiological nitrogen fixation. Efficient use must be made of pesticides and microbiological approaches to pest control. Irrigation must be planned to minimize health risks and loss of soil productivity from salinisation.

There is also the great problems of food loss in storage and transportation. Not only is there loss of food material itself, at a time when we are all crying for more food production, but there are great health hazards in improper food storage, through aflatoxins and mycotoxins. Provision of weather-proof storage and transportation reduces health hazards associated with badly stored grain, and at the same time improves the bargaining capacity of the small farmer to obtain a better price for his produce.

Careless planning to promote rural development can lead to the undermining of life-supporting systems. Where the landless poor are condemned to cultivate environments that are marginal, they set in motion a chain of irreversible environmental degradation. Two of the major negative manifestations of this environmental degradation are tropical deforestation and desertification. Such environmental degradation, of course, further undermines prospects of rural development.

The "forest farmers" are the rural inhabitants who eke out their living by scratching the soil around their habitat. These include not only traditional farmers of the shifting cultivator type, but all manner of squatter-type peasantry, and are now believed to total some 250 – 400 million persons. They rank as the number one factor in deforestation in tropical lands. They themselves recognize that at the rate their numbers are now growing, they are making such extensive and intensive use of forest environments that local ecosystems can no longer recover. In other words, because of their growing numbers, and because of their increasingly limited access to forest areas, their forest farming is not a sustainable way of life as it was under traditional patterns, but is a once and for all conversion of tropical forests into degraded scrubland.

In arid and semi-arid areas, land tenure practices which for centuries had permitted users to live and maintain resources in ecological balance, have failed to do so in recent decades. The two main reasons for this are population density beyond what the land can support, and irrational use of resources, through lack of understanding or to maximise gains. This has resulted not only in desertification in various forms, but in other serious economic and social problems, including the spread of disease and increased malnutrition.

In many countries, rangelands which were traditionally "owned" by local populations, and which were properly managed through the application of long-standing traditions, were subjected to overstocking as a result of changes in ownership. Further loss of rangelands has sometimes resulted from extension of dry farming and irrigation schemes. Moreover, the provision by governments of boreholes essentially meant to supply drinking water for livestock and people, have tended to encourage pastoralists to settle in the surrounding area, with subsequent overgrazing, trampling and ultimately desertification.

Studies on the question of land ownership in these areas were presented at the United Nations Conference on Desertification. It would appear that zoning, or a formal distribution of grazing usufruct to well-defined population groups might avoid major concentrations. Such solutions would, however, also entail Government responsibility in providing, on an egalitarian basis, social services, including provision of water, and medical and educational facilities.

The lack of specific land holding arrangements in forest areas may lead to over-exploitation of wood resources, whereas a formal ownership or usufruct grant can result in planned and managed cropping combined with replanting. Government responsibility would include the provision of nurseries and forestry extension services to all land holders or usufructuaries. Where deforestation has already created an ecologically unacceptable pressure on existing resources, access would have to be provided to alternative fuel and building materials, and large-scale afforestation programmes would have to be mounted.

Considerable work has been done on the relationship between institution reforms to improve land ownership and resource use patterns, on the one hand, and rural productivity and incomes on the other. However, it needs to be appreciated that careful formulation and effective implementation of agrarian reforms is not only a matter of distributive justice, but has a rationale rooted in sound environmental management as well. The distributional and the environmental *raison d'être* for agrarian reform do not always work in the same direction, but they do so frequently. Planning and implementation of agrarian reform should carefully take into account this connection. Extreme inequalities in patterns of land holding can cause soil degradation not only through commercial monocropping on excessively large holdings, but through progressive fragmentation and excessive cultivation of holdings by small farmers and sharecroppers, leading to soil erosion. Such trends, of course, can also lead to environmental degradation in urban areas as landless labourers and marginalized farmers move to the cities. Thus distributive justice and broadly based participation in the benefits of development have to be viewed from the standpoint of sustaining productivity levels and broadly based participation in the long-term.

Certainly, one of the important functions of this Conference would be to make recommendations on how to tackle this issue in the future.

16

SCIENCE, TECHNOLOGY, ENVIRONMENT AND DEVELOPMENT:
The Emerging Synthesis

Statement to the United Nations Conference on
Science and Technology for Development

Vienna, Austria, August 1979

TECHNOLOGY is an essential instrument for the achievement of sustainable and environmentally sound development. But it is also through the application of such technology that man has most impact on the environment.

For instance, a substantial increase in food and agricultural production, through innovative techniques and technologies, is a major objective on the international agenda. A plan to increase production must, nevertheless, take into account the total environmental impact of that increase on the agricultural resource base. I welcome, in this connection, the declaration by the Director-General of FAO that the Third Agricultural Revolution is to be more environmentally sound, based on renewable inputs such as natural nitrogen-fixation, better photosynthetic abilities, plant and animal breeding and the association of crops with forestry and aqualculture — a timely move from the green revolution based as it was on abundant and cheap energy.

If we turn to the other great productive activity of man, industrialization, we immediately see that the prolific advances of modern technology in the developed countries have led to spectacular increases in affluence, which have not necessarily resulted in an environment more conducive to the physical and mental well-being of man. Misguided industrial development has caused serious health hazards, accelerated destruction of natural resources and harmful effects on life-sustaining ecological systems.

The environmental effects of modern technology were expected to be less serious in developing countries, which are not as heavily industrialized. However, this expectation is not borne out in fact. This is because industrialization of most developing countries has been based on the import of improperly chosen, highly capital- and energy-intensive technology. Urban concentrations of such technology in developing countries have often resulted in levels of environmental degradation as high as those in developed countries or even higher. Further, the haphazardly planned introduction of these technologies has led, among other things, to the well known rural impoverishment through mass migration to cities and resultant festering slums and marginal settlements.

Science and technology have not so far been adequately applied to other sectors of human and societal needs. Existing patterns of human settlements indicate clear misuse or waste of resources.

Energy is needed for countless essentials of man and society. But it is becoming increasingly expensive. In addition, the burning of fossil fuels, coupled possibly with deforestation, is a major factor in the increased carbon dioxide content of the atmosphere, with possible resultant changes in temperature and rainfall patterns which could have highly important implications on agriculture. If this is proved, which is likely to happen, it will have a tremendous impact on energy policies. Furthermore the environmental impacts of nuclear energy are already influencing these policies. All these developments call for committing adequate resources — human and financial — for the serious development of alternative sources of energy which are multi-purpose, renewable and less polluting.

A residual, but no less important, challenge to our scientific capability persists in the fight to protect human health. We have not yet laid to rest many of the ancient scourges (malaria, schistosomiasis and other vector-borne parasitic diseases in developing countries) while we are beset with the new ones spawned by modern civilization.

Requirements for Action

The perceptions I have described, lead to certain broad conclusions and requirements for action.

1. The interdependence of life-sustaining fragile ecosystems, demands international solidarity and the implanting of a sense of belonging to mankind as a whole. Poor nations and poor sectors of nations cannot continue to destroy renewable resources without ultimately reducing the carrying capacity of the ecosystems and threatening human survival. Rich nations and richer sectors in developing countries cannot likewise continue to indulge in over-consumption and over-development, without leading to accelerated depletion of non-renewable resources, and ultimately reaching the outer limits of biospheric tolerance, threatening again human survival. There is an urgent need to reconcile patterns of developments and styles of life with the dictates of the world's resource constraints.

2. There is an urgent need for immense additional resources. Money and scientific skills to launch a massive research and development effort to establish new non-waste or low-waste technologies based on conservation and recycling of resources and on less energy utilization. In this context there is a need for rich countries to seriously consider subsidizing, at least partially, technologies geared to meeting some of the requirements of developing countries such as those relating to the development of renewable energy sources for small rural communities.

3. There is an urgent need for developing countries to make a determined effort to implement the agreed principle that development and utilization of indigenous abilities in science and technology, particularly skilled manpower, are and must continue to be, one of the most effective means for sound development.

4. There is an urgent need for information and know-how to flow to the poor countries, at reasonable charges within their means. In this connection we emphasize examination of:

    (a) The effect of international patents systems on the pace of industrial development in developing countries.

    (b) The feasibility of declaring some of the new scientific and technological advances, for example those meant for more food production, a common heritage of mankind to be transferred to the developing countries without encumbrances.

UNEP has attempted to assist in meeting the need for information exchange by creating INFOTERRA, which puts the seeker in touch with the provider of information. The spectrum of scientific and technical information supplied by INFOTERRA covers such diverse areas as questions, nature conservation, technology, desertification, human settlements, and of course, pollution. UNEP's Industry and Environment Office in Paris has recently established a computerized information system on the subject which is ready for use and is growing fast.

Environmentally Sound and Appropriate Technologies

We in UNEP emphasize the concept of environmentally sound and appropriate technologies. This concept is of somewhat recent origin.

The word "appropriate" acquires meaning only when related to "what or to whom?". Too often, the sole concern is with appropriateness in relation to the capital and labour endowments of a region or a country, but this purely economic view is narrow and one-dimensional. The assessment of appropriateness from the standpoint of development objectives necessitates a three-dimensional view in which environmental and social dimensions are no less important than the economic one.

The case for environmentally sound and appropriate technologies, particularly for developing countries, is not built upon a rejection of industry and industrialization. On the contrary, a great deal is to be learnt from the industrialization process of the developed countries, including both successes and failures. But development does not have to consist of a slavish imitation of the type of industrialization followed by the developed countries.

Environmentally sound and appropriate technology does not reject "modern" technology of the developed countries. It calls for a careful scrutiny of the economic, social and environmental implications of such technology.

Environmentally sound and appropriate technologies should not be taken as a plea for a return to traditional technologies of ancient peoples. The plea is quite different. Traditional technologies have undergone a selection process over centuries of empirical testing, hence they are very likely to represent optimum solutions. But they are optimum only for the particular conditions, constraints, materials and needs under which they were developed. With the emergence of new conditions, constraints, materials and needs, their applicability is likely to be eroded and the technology rendered invalid. Nevertheless, it is quite possible that these traditional technologies can still be improved and rendered useful. We urge that modern science and engineering be used to understand and clarify the rational core of ancient practices.

Development and Resources

A major obstacle in the way of application of science and technology to development relates to the resources, natural, financial and human, which could be made available for the purposes of affording science and technology to developing countries. In discussing the availability of such resources, one cannot escape the agony of the arms race. The arms race is a flagrant misuse of scarce natural resources for purposes devoted to the destruction of human beings. The arms race is claiming colossal financial resources, US$ 40 million an hour, which could be effectively utilized to mobilize scientific and technological "breakthroughs" to solve development problems. The arms race is a drain on available human resources: half a million of highly trained scientists and technicians and more than 70 million others are used to produce means of destruction rather than means of production.[1] These highly qualified and trained people are alienated from the real values and needs of their society. The international community should seriously search for and urgently agree

---

[1] See also the statement to the Special Session devoted to Disarmament, General Assembly, United Nations, p. 88.

on means of releasing these resources or at least parts of them. These, if ensured, as additional resources with automatic flow could bring a major change of perspective in the development of new scientific and technological solutions to persistent and potentially explosive problems of development.

Conclusion

This conference comes at the time of active preparation of a New International Development Strategy. Positions between North and South are hardening and there are frustrations on both sides. An impartial consideration and a global vision of the benefits of ensuring the application of the best available science and technology to development could assist in bridging the existing gap. I pledge UNEP's full cooperation in your endeavour and in the implementation and follow-up of your decisions and recommendations.

17
THE STATE OF THE EARTH:
The Coming Decade of Danger and Opportunity

Address to the Club of Rome Conference
West Berlin, Federal Republic of Germany, October 1979

CONFERENCES and studies sponsored by the Club of Rome have played a crucial role in shaking up attitudes of complacency towards the state of the earth, specifically in relation to the future of mankind. We do not have the final answers to the present predicament of mankind — nor, indeed, do we know with certainty the true prognosis of this predicament. But there is no doubt that the debate on the implications of the present and future interactions among people, resources, environment and development that the Club of Rome has initiated — directly or indirectly — during recent times has been of great significance to policy-makers, planners and people everywhere.

The theme of the present conference, I believe, strikes the right note of wise realism — a realism that balances the possible risks, uncertainties and dangers that threaten human well-being in the years to come, with the possibility of — and opportunities for — steering the course of events in such ways that human well-being can be enhanced. Integration of environmental considerations as a parameter of economic growth and development — and an element of public policy in general — provides precisely such a balanced perspective. On the one hand, it requires that the decision-maker should learn from the negative experiences of past practices and policies. On the other hand, it requires him to identify and harness possible opportunities, which need to be adequately explored and efficiently integrated in actions aiming at enhancement of human well-being.

The subject I shall present this afternoon is "the State of the Earth". That is quite an assignment given to me by my good friend Aurelio Peccei. Moreover, he has asked me to make it in about thirty minutes! There are, of course, outer limits to what one may cover within thirty minutes. For a conference like this, and after the masterly introduction of Aurelio Peccei, one should focus on some critical areas of "danger and opportunity" not in the abstract, but insofar as something can be done about them. One cannot be comprehensive; I shall therefore touch briefly upon a few major environmental problems facing our planet and prospects to resolve some of them. In doing do I will by necessity repeat some of the views and facts reviewed by Peccei.

Perhaps I should first speak of the outer limits of the global life-supporting systems. We live on only one earth, but our knowledge of the basic processes that underlie its global ecology is very limited. It is evident that multi-disciplinary scientific research involving international cooperation is absolutely necessary to bring forth data, analyses and insights which could guide our policies. For example, a better comprehension of the workings of biogeochemical cycles of carbon, nitrogen, sulphur and other elements is essential if we are to understand ways in which resources of soil, vegetation, water and atmosphere can be better utilized and their utility sustained.

Mankind exerts major influences on these cycles. For instance, the flow of carbon dioxide to the atmosphere is intensified through burning of fossil fuels, clearing of forests and cultivation of land. The World Climate Conference[1] held in early 1979 pointed out that, as a consequence of such activities, the amount of carbon dioxide in the atmosphere is increasing, probably by about 4 per cent every ten years. Should this trend accelerate, or even continue, a gradual warming of the lower atmosphere might occur which could lead to serious changes in temperature and rainfall patterns and hence have serious impacts on agriculture.

Chemical fertilizers are applied to increase agricultural production as part of the attempt to meet our food needs. The nitrogen and phosphorus cycles are of special significance in this respct. Industrial production of nitrogen in fertilizers may eventually exceed the quantities produced by natural biological nitrogen fixation. This can have signifcant effect on global nitrogen cycles. For example, nitrogen oxides, of which nitrogen fertilizers are one source, may be an important factor affecting the stability of the stratospheric ozone layer. Yet the rates of production, transfer and destruction of nitrogen oxides on the global scale are at present known only in broad outline.

Let us consider food production further. The world has the potential capacity to produce enough food for the world population even if it reaches the highest levels projected by the year 2000. But this bright prospect is of little more than academic interest. There are constraints that undermine this potential capacity. The target of 4 per cent average annual increase in the agricultural production of developing countries, which was envisaged by the World Food Conference[2], would require that food production of these

---

[1] For the statement to the World Climate Conference, see p. 97.
[2] For the statement to the World Food Conference, see p. 1.

countries be doubled during less than 20 years. This is no simple undertaking, and even that rate would probably not suffice to meet minimum nutritional needs throughout the developing world.

The task is made still more difficult by the fact that the resource base in the regions where the need for augmenting food production is most urgent, namely Asia, the Middle East and Africa, is being eroded by desertification and deforestation.

The rates at which tropical forests are being depleted are greatly accelerating, with far-reaching consequences. The effects of clear felling in mountain areas are equally severe, especially in the Himalayas, the Andes and the East African Highlands.

In South Asia, South-east Asia, and the South Pacific, the area under forests is being depleted at a rate of 2 per cent per annum. In certain areas, for example Malaysia, Nepal and Thailand, there are some indications that if the present logging, farming and other practices continue, there could be a virtual disappearance of closed forests within the next 25 years. The environmental consequences of such large-scale destruction of tropical forests in terms of erosion, salinisation, desertification, flooding, waterlogging, silting up of reservoirs and streams, clogging up of irrigation networks, and unfavourable changes in local micro-climatic patterns are bound to be very grievous.

Loss of arable land is an escalating environmental problem. Nearly 44 per cent of the land resources of Africa, and 43 per cent of those in south Asia, are subject to drought. Moreover, 47 per cent of the soil resources in South America and 59 per cent in south-east Asia are subject to nutritional deficiencies or the impact of toxic substances.

Barely 15 to 18 per cent of the soils in South America, Africa and Asia may be described as having no serious limitations for agricultural use. As much as 95 per cent of the total land area in the arid and semi-arid zones is subject to the risk of desertification. And desertification is not confined to the dry areas. Its hazard can reach large proportions even in the sub-humid zones. Nearly 35 per cent of the world's land is subject to moderate-to-very high desertification hazard: 55 per cent of Africa, 34 per cent in Asia and 20 per cent in South America.

Another potential global problem in this area of food production is fisheries. Collapses of ocean fisheries have in recent years become increasingly common. If sea fisheries are to continue to supply significant amounts of high-quality protein foods a much more rigorous management of fishing and human activities around and in the ocean will be needed, regionally and nationally. This management must be based on sounder ecological considerations than hitherto.

These various pointers to danger are the result of dynamic and complex interactions among social, economic and physical factors. In a given ecological and socio-economic setting, a process that seems eminently rational at the micro level for adequate satisfaction of household needs can lead to devastating consequences when aggregated over extensive terrain and cumulated over a period of time. Moreover, there are tradeoffs among development goals which have to be carefully evaluated for their long-term effects. Examples are substitution of commercial monocropping for subsistence agriculture aimed at earning essential foreign exchange, resorting to multipurpose dams for large-scale irrigation and hydroelectric power generation, in place of a number of small-scale projects, and depletion of cropland in the interest of industrial development.

I share the views of Aurelio Peccei that we should not be unduly pessimistic, however. The situation can still be remedied, if the proper action is taken. Man's constant alteration of the surface of the earth has in many cases been for the better, and has even evolved pleasing, productive and highly diversified ecosystems. Whenever the transformation and adaptation have been based on scientific understanding of natural ecosystems and their evolution, and creatively aimed at improving upon nature, they have contributed to furthering human well-being in sustainable ways.

There are vast opportunities for achieving sustainable improvements in soil productivities through biological fixation of atmospheric nitrogen.

The great advances made by international research institutes in genetic improvement should be turned into concrete and extensive applications in the field. The technology for effective and integrated management of pests needs to be disseminated on a much broader front, and there is significant scope for introduction of pest-resistant crop varieties and agricultural practices that may reduce pest outbreak.

There are significant opportunities for augmenting food availability per head by effecting simple improvements in storage and transportation. Losses on account of organic degradation, chemical contamination, and pests and rodents are reported to be as high as 20 per cent in some countries. Such losses have to, and could, be stopped. In China and Ghana, notable successes have been reported in this respect, through the construction on a decentralized basis, with raw materials mainly of mud and straw, and using simple construction technologies, of environmentally sound silos.

In the short space of 25 years, systematic and comprehensive conversion of rural wastes into organic fertilizer and bio-energy has enabled China to more than double its food production, introduce and sustain economic dynamism in rural areas, and make environmental sanitation available to the rural population. This can be repeated.

Turning now to the issues of safe water supply, facilities of waste disposal and sanitation, and eradication of environmental diseases, one can say that they represent areas where the role of education, innovation, pragmatic wisdom, and real involvement of people, cannot be exaggerated. In rural areas, as well as in some large cities of developing countries, as many as 40 per cent of deaths are considered to be related to deficiencies in water supply and waste disposal. Fewer than 500 million of the 2,400 million people living in developing countries have adequate access to safe water or waste disposal facilities, and this number is estimated to be growing at 70 million every year.

This magnitude is so immense that it is doubtful whether the international goal envisaged by the United Nations HABITAT Conference,[1] provision of safe water supply and sanitation to everyone by 1990, can be realized unless priorities and approaches are radically readjusted.

Another health problem that is being flagged lately is the possible contamination of human milk by chlorinated hydrocarbons on a global scale. No comprehensive, adequately controlled survey of levels of chlorinated hydrocarbons in mother's milk is available. However, there are some indications of elevated levels resulting in possible intakes by suckling children of amounts higher than those internationally regarded as acceptable. Under such conditions it would be irresponsible on my side to sound any alarm. What we need now is to improve the data, broaden the coverage, and establish trends, so that a better assessment of levels can be made, while at the same time intensifying work on our understanding of possible effects on children.

Another major area of environmental stress and opportunity today is industrialization. There is no question that the developing countries have to industrialize rapidly so as to diversify the bases of their production, alleviate poverty and provide productive employment to their large and rapidly growing labour forces. Developing countries, excluding the centrally planned ones, will by 1990 barely account for 20 per cent of gross world production though they will contain 57 per cent of world population. On the other hand, the industrialized countries of the West, with less than 14 per cent of the world's population, will account by 1990 for 62 per cent of gross world production. Even using ambitious projections, the share of industry in gross national product in low-income Africa and Asia will be less than 20 and 30 per cent respectively in 1990.

The urbanization which accompanies industrialization has led to certain problems of environmental degradation, relating to lack of basic shelter, water supply, sanitation and waste disposal, transportation and, in general, denial of an environment to live in dignity as human beings. Today, about 250 million of a total of 840 million urban dwellers in developing countries lack reasonable access to minimal nutrition, safe water, basic sanitation, education and shelter. Unless serious steps are taken to alter the present trends, these numbers will grow at a rate of 15 to 18 million people every year, and by the year 2000, 600 million people will be living in such degraded conditions in the developing countries.

The question that needs to be addressed by a highly qualified forum like this is what better alternatives are available or could be developed.

Much has been said since the Stockholm Conference about the dangers to human health, and to plant and animal life, of chemical pollution in its various forms. It is a matter of concern that available knowledge, including comprehensive analyses of such large-scale disasters as the outbreaks of Minamata disease or Itai-Itai disease, or the Seveso accident, is not

---

[1] For the statement to the UN Conference on Human Settlements, see p. 6.

purposefully used the world over to prevent, or minimize, environmental health risks associated with chemical pollution.

Industrial effluents are discharged practically unprocessed into the atmosphere, rivers and seas. Sulphur dioxide emission has been responsible for causing acid rains in upstate New York, and is believed to have destroyed the fish life in hundreds of lakes in the Adirondack mountains. If the emissions are not effectively controlled, they might even threaten fish life in the thousands of lakes in Canada. Acid rains, as is well known, can also pollute forests and poison soils. There are recent reports of alarmingly high levels of toxic mercury, lead and cadmium in fish, milk and vegetables in the surroundings of Bombay, resulting from effluents released by various industries into the river systems. However, not all the signs are negative. There is a clear realization of these dangers, and a determined effort is being made to develop low-waste or no-waste technologies. This is an opportunity which we should not miss.

Energy is a crucial factor in ensuring development and better quality of life. But there are indications that by the year 2000 energy supplies may not be sufficient to meet demands. Further, potential human and environmental health hazards of available sources of energy are beginning to weigh heavy on everybody's mind and become the subject of very hot debates in various quarters. These hazards include damaging oil spills, essentially through transportation and offshore drilling; increasing amounts of SO_2 emmissions; possible serious effects of increasing amounts of CO_2 in the atmosphere; serious hazards of radioactivity in nuclear energy production and use especially milling, fuel wastes and possibilities of serious reactor accidents.

Major transfer of resources, human and financial, are required to make real breakthroughs in the production and use of renewable sources of energy. However, given the fact that there is no way of meeting energy demand up to the year 2000 from these sources alone, two immediate actions are needed:

1. Conservation of energy which will require in-depth studies and concrete recommendations. Such conservation is certainly possible. Electricity usage patterns now average 6,000 kwh/cap/year in industrialized countries with 10,000 for the United States of America; 300 for developing countries, with figures as low as 100 for Kenya, 10 for Yemen and 7 for Burundi.

2. More accurate assessment of the comparative environmental impacts of the various sources of energy to allow policy makers in the individual countries to identify appropriate mixes of available sources of energy that would be most suitable for their special situations.

The energy consumption figures I have just mentioned, are but one quantitative reflection of the fact that the present state of the earth is marred by the vast disparities in levels of living between developed and developing countries, as well as within developing countries themselves. The magnitudes of these disparities are very well known. Such disparities between overconsumption and deprivation constitute a great danger not only because of the unrest and violence that they engender, but also because, by their dynamic "demonstration effects", they entice the world to join the "revolution of rising expectations", with progressively harmful consequences of environmental degradation, resource depletion, erosion of quality of life, and most importantly, denial of the opportunity to the young, the poor and the not-yet-born to improve their quality of life and sustain that improvement. For example, it is estimated that if the world consumed minerals at the current rate of United States consumption, known recoverable resources of copper would be exhausted in 9 years, bauxite in 18 years, zinc in six months, lead in 4 years, petroleum in 7 years and natural gas in 5 years.

Given the present vast disparities, it is not very helpful to warn that mankind is in great danger of transgressing environmental outer limits, nor to say complacently that mankind has the capacity to push back the outer limits of the environment. It is essential to institute mechanisms and processes which will ensure that this capacity is expanded to embrace the day-to-day lives of those who suffer.

One of the real obstacles to alleviating environmental hazards on the one hand, and to making rational use of resources on the other hand, is the arms race. If the world is serious in this respect, it must immediately divert part if not all the resources used for producing destructive weapons into constructive development processes. The colossal natural resources, the $40 million every hour, the more than half a million highly qualified scientists and technicians can surely be better used than to produce devastating weapons. Nuclear arms constitute a direct threat to the human environment and to human survival. Diversion of scarce national resources to building up, and deployment, of arms has had very adverse consequences for development in several countries. Wars and strife have devastated the environment in several developing countries. The recovery from such devastation is an arduous, costly and time-consuming task.

There is no doubt that the entire world stands to benefit from a more rational mobilization and use of the world's physical and human resources. The developing countries need more purposeful and augmented development assistance to learn from past environmental mistakes of industrialized countries, and to realize the environmental opportunities that they have. Availability of environmentally prudent and developmentally satisfactory technology is not enough to improve the state of the earth. In order that the dangers are kept at bay, and promising opportunities are actually made use of, economic and institutional reforms in international relations have to be brought into existence. If only a real relaxation of tension between the East and the West, and a genuine belief in interdependence between developed and developing countries, can be achieved, there will be a world of a change in the prospects for improving the quality of life everywhere.

18

ENVIRONMENTAL PROTECTION AND ECONOMIC DEVELOPMENT:
Interdependent and Mutually Supportive

Lecture at Qing Hua University

Beijing, China, October 1979

RIGHT from the time it came into existence, it has been UNEP's view that programmes and measures of environmental protection and improvement, on the one hand, and those of economic and social development, on the other, have to be formulated and implemented in harmony with each other in order to ensure a sustainable enhancement of human well-being. China has always been, and I am sure will continue to be, among the avant-garde, in advocating and implementing these concepts.

When environmental problems first came to be discussed internationally some ten years ago, they were prone to be quickly identified, in popular perception, with the problems of pollution control, conservation of wildlife and aesthetically motivated protection of nature. Certain misgivings were expressed by developing countries: they considered that concern about their environment was unnecessary, uncalled for, and would jeopardize their efforts to industrialize rapidly and to diversify and modernise their economies. More recently, misgivings have been expressed in certain developed countries as well. The use of increasingly significant proportions of national expenditure for environmental protection and improvement is seen by them to induce adverse implications in terms of inflation, unemployment and economic growth.

Environmentally Sound Development Policies

It has been clear to UNEP from the outset that environmentally sound development policies and measures should have major aims:

1. minimization of waste in the use of natural resources;

2. maximization of productive use of residues of all kinds;

3. respect for the integrity of ecosystems. Modifications in them should be introduced only after careful evaluation of their likely consequences;

4. minimization of the degradation of the environment, and maximum abatement of such degradation when it has been unavoidable;

5. harnessing, to the maximum extent possible the complementarities between environmental improvement and socio-economic development.

Now that it is generally seen, and accepted, that environmental and developmental objectives can be pursued in mutual support and, infact, that they are interdependent, the next issue that must be faced is how such a complex relationship can be given an operational content. There are no general or universal solutions. But it seems to me that in order to succeed in our goal of harmonizing the two sets of objectives, four prerequisites have to be fulfilled.

One, concrete alternatives in respect of technologies, processes, practices and products have to be identified, in production as well as in consumption. These should result in economies in the use of scarce natural resources and cause minimum environmental degradation. They also should maximize the chances of simultaneous attainment of development objectives, such as increased production, expanded employment and eradication of poverty, and environmental objectives such as improvement of environmental sanitation and health, prevention and control of deforestation, desertification and soil erosion. Obviously, implementation of such alternatives may entail, in some situations, definite and far-reaching changes in the lifestyles and consumption patterns of the people. Present forms of lifestyles based on over-consumption and irrational use of resources cannot simply be sustained.

A second prerequisite is that there have to be appropriate methodological frameworks within which various alternatives can be evaluated to determine both their developmental and environmental benefits and the associated costs. Again, such methodological frameworks cannot be uniform or rigidly applicable in all countries. But there is no doubt that uncritical reliance on a narrowly conceived economic calculus of financial rates of return is inappropriate, if the goal is to reach environmentally prudent and socially satisfactory solutions. It may, perhaps, interest you to know that UNEP is currently engaged in an evaluation and analysis of case studies, received from member states, of the application of broad-based cost-benefit analyses to measures of environmental protection and improvement. The exercize is in its experimental stage and its purpose is to help develop a set of more appropriate methodological frameworks for such analyses.

A third prerequisite is that there is a need for appropriate institutional frameworks which facilitate decision-making and action in respect of the choice of alternatives catering to the best interests of the people. Such institutional machinery encompasses environmental legislation as well as systems of incentives and disincentives such as taxes and subsidies.

The institutional set-up also includes the government machinery at various levels which would deliberate and decide on matters relating to environmental and developmental policies and activities, as well as the machinery for people's participation in this exercise. The search for environmentally prudent alternatives in development must permeate all sectors. Thus, forums for decision-making on matters of environment and development therefore need to be multi-disciplinary in composition and representative of various sectoral interests.

A fourth prerequisite for making environmentally sound development a reality lies in the attitudes, perceptions, information and knowledge of the people themselves, in respect of what is environmentally prudent and in their best interests, and what is not. Dissemination of environment-related information and environmental education and training must play a valuable role in bringing about an alliance between popular and technical evaluations of various alternatives for development.

The Present State of the Earth

Let me turn now to the second point in this lecture, some of my perceptions of the present state of the earth. The world today is experiencing several acute environmental problems, and there is no sign yet of these problems being effectively alleviated. Loss of productive soil, desertification, tropical deforestation, depletion of essential raw materials, energy problems, the spread of diseases as a result of environmental mismanagement, pollution and health hazards caused by industrial effluents and deployment of toxic chemicals, malnutrition, urban congestion and spread of environmentally degraded human settlements, and the outer limits of the global life-supporting systems, are all daunting problems, in need of urgent and purposeful attention at all levels. For various and obvious reasons, countries which are relative latecomers to modern economic development suffer large numbers of these problems more severely.

Conditions of widespread poverty have caused serious environmental deterioration in several developing countries. On the one hand, these countries suffer poverty-induced degradation patterns of their natural resources of land, water and forests. On the other hand, to achieve rapid improvements in the levels of living of their people, they have to launch ambitious, quickly conceived, economic development programmes, with an inherent capacity for environmental degradation.

Let us take a few examples. Widespread malnutrition makes a rapid and substantial increase in food production imperative and urgent in many poor countries. The world has the potential capacity to produce enough food for the world population even if it reaches the highest levels projected by the year 2000. But this bright prospect is of little more than academic interest. There are constraints that undermine this potential capacity. The target of 4 per cent average annual increase in the agricultural production of developing countries, which was envisaged by the World Food Conference,[1] would require that food production of these countries be doubled during less than 20 years. This is no simple undertaking, and even that rate would probably not suffice to meet minimum nutritional needs throughout the developing world.

The task is made still more difficult by the fact that the resource base in the regions where the need for augmenting food production is most urgent, namely Asia, the Middle East and Africa, is being eroded on account of desertification, soil erosion, salinization, deforestation and simply by the pressures of settlements development.

The rates at which tropical forests are being depleted are so much accelerating with far-reaching consequences. The effects of clear felling in mountain areas are equally severe, especially in the Himalayas, the Andes and the East African Highlands. There is, for example, a report of a large island, about 50,000 square kilometres in area, being formed in the Indian Ocean as a result of soils washed away from the Himalayan slopes and the proximate watersheds.

By 1975, closed forest area was only 0.2 hectares per person in Asia and 0.5 hectares per person in Africa, as compared to 2.0 hectares per person in North America and 2.7 hectares per person in the USSR. In south Asia, south-east Asia, and the South Pacific, the areas under forests is being depleted at a rate of 2 per cent per annum. In certain countries, for example, Malaysia, Nepal and Thailand, there are some indications that if the present logging, farming and other practices continued, there could be a virtual disappearance of closed forests within the next 25 years. The environmental consequences of such large-scale destruction of tropical forests in terms of erosion, salinization, desertification, flooding, waterlogging, silting up of reservoirs and streams, clogging up of irrigation networks, and unfavourable changes in local micro-climatic patterns are bound to be very grievious. The destruction of tropical forests is considered by scientists to be linked to the observed increase in CO_2 concentration in the atmosphere caused by burning fossil fuel. The present rate of increase is estimated as you know, at 4 per cent every 10 years. If this rate is accelerated or even maintained the lower layers of the atmosphere will most probably warm up with consequent influences on rainfall patterns in the world and hence serious impacts on agriculture. In February, 1980, UNEP, in co-operation with FAO, UNESCO and other interested organisations, will convene an interntional expert meeting in Libreville, Gabon, to examine in depth the urgent question of conservation and wise utilization of tropical

---

[1]For statement to the World Food Conference, see p. 1.

forests. During the same month we will hold a meeting with WMO and ICSU to work out a plan of action to study the possible changes in CO_2 concentrations and the actions needed to mitigate the impacts of such changes.

Loss of arable land is an escalating environmental problem. Nearly 44 per cent of the land resources of Africa and 43 per cent of those in south Asia, are subject to drought. Moreover, 27 per cent of the soil resources in South America and 59 per cent in south-east Asia are subject to nutritional deficiencies or the impact of toxic substances.

Barely 15 to 18 per cent of the soils in South America, Africa and Asia may be described as having no serious limitations for agricultural use. As much as 95 per cent of the total land area in the arid and semi-arid zones is subject to the risk of desertification. And desertification is not confined to the dry areas. Its hazard can reach large proportions even in the sub-humid zones. Nearly 35 per cent of world land is subject to moderate-to-very high desertification hazard: 55 per cent in Africa, 34 per cent in Asia and 20 per cent in South America. UNEP has been endowed with the responsibility of coordinating the implementation of a world plan of action to combat desertification which emerged from the UNCOD and was endorsed by the United Nations General Assembly in 1977.

Industrialization is another major area which, increasingly of late, has been posing difficult problems of choice of alternatives and planning to low-income countries. The poor countries of the world, in their efforts to improve levels of living of their people, have to industrialize rapidly, diversify their production and build up economic infrastructures to increase national self-reliance. The world community has, for example, in the Lima Declaration, specified that the share of the developing countries in world industrial production should increase by the year 2000 to 25 per cent, from the present level of little over 7 per cent.

But this quest for industrialization has to contend with several environmental considerations. For instance, because of irrational and wasteful production and consumption, industrial raw materials are no longer available inexpensively and without risks of environmental degradation as they used to be. Further, the developing countries are faced with the responsibility of screening carefully industrial investments coming from abroad and modifying them to suit their own needs, as some of these may embody environmentally harmful technologies and products. The cost of petroleum which had been a cheap source of energy for industrial and other development for so long, has escalated rapidly over a short span of time, and imposes constraints on industrial and agricultural production, in several developing countries. Other forms of fossil fuel like coal, oilshale, tarsand as well as nuclear energy are coming under heavy debate in every corner of the world, because of their possible health and environmental hazards. This is a real problem. We cannot meet all our needs from renewable sources alone by the year 2000. Thus we need three urgent actions:

1. develop renewable sources quickly;

2. identify hazards of present sources of energy to establish most sound mixes;

3. conserve energy.

Average electricity use per capita per year in 1979 in developed countries was 6,670 kw (10,670 kw in the United States) and 360 kw in market-economy developing countries (113 kw in Kenya, 12 kw in Yemen and 8 kw in Burundi).

Industrial pollution is a major problem in both developed and developing countries. However late starters in industrialization have the advantage of learning from the environmental mistakes made in the process of industrial growth in developed countries. Yet, these late starters face some negative aspects. The cost of introducing control and abatement measures is an additional claim on the meagre financial resources they can allocate to industrial development, and critical trade-offs have to be made. Moreover, the international patents system may restrict their access to known technologies of pollution abatement and control, or increase the cost of such access.

In several developing countries, the urbanization accompanying industrialization has also led to severe problems of congestion, lack of housing, inadequate access to sanitation, water supply and waste disposal and, generally, a degraded quality of life in large cities. At times, the technologies and scales, as well as the choices of location of industrial production have been such that they have neither helped sizeable employment expansion and broadly based distribution of benefits of development, nor promoted a healthy balance, and mutual support, between rural and urban development. This is another field where, I believe, the development experience of your country has a great deal to offer to other countries. I understand that all industrial units in China have a standing instruction to take environmental considerations into account at the three stages of design, construction and actual operation. Judicious planning of agricultural development with related industrial development over large parts of the country has not only sustained a broadly based dynamism of economic growth, but also promoted balanced rural and urban development. Careful choices as regards technologies and scales of production in industry, and its well-planned spatial spread throughout the countryside, have dramatically helped transform Chinese agriculture, as well as industry over a relatively short span of time.

Environmentally Sound and Appropriate Technologies

One major key to sustainable and socially satisfactory development is the adoption of environmentally sound and appropriate technologies in all fields. This concept has sometimes led to uncalled for apprehensions and unintended interpretations. So it is important that it is correctly understood.

The word *appropriate* acquires meaning only when one specifies appropriate to what or to whom. Too often, the sole concern is with appropriateness in relation to the capital and labour endowments of a region or country, but this purely economic view is narrow, restricted and one-dimensional. The assessment of appropriateness from the standpoint of development objectives necessitates a three-dimensional view in which the environmental and social dimensions are no less important than the economic one.

It has sometimes been assumed that the case for environmentally sound and appropriate technologies, particularly in developing countries, is built upon a rejection of industry and industrialization. This is not true. A great deal will have to be learnt from the industrialization process of the developed countries. But that process includes both successes and failures, with corresponding lessons. Hence, development does not have to consist of a slavish imitation of the type of industrialization followed by the developed countries.

It has often been assumed that the proponents of environmentally sound and appropriate technology demand a total rejection of the modern technology of the developed countries. In fact, what is demanded is a careful scrutiny of the economic, social and environmental implications of such technology.

In some quarters, the argument for environmentally sound and appropriate technologies has been misunderstood as a plea for a return to, and total dependence on, the traditional technologies of ancient peoples. In fact, the plea is quite different. Traditional technologies have undergone a selection process over centuries of empirical testing, hence they are very likely to represent optimum solutions. But they are optimum only for the particular conditions, constraints, materials and needs in response to which they were developed. With the emergence of new conditions, constraints, materials and needs, it is likely that their applicability will have been eroded and the technology rendered invalid. Nevertheless, it is quite possible that these traditional technologies can undergo qualitative changes through minor modifications. These improvements can be brought about by the use of modern science and engineering to clarify the rational core of ancient practices.

The dynamic nature of the concepts of environmental soundness and appropriateness follows inevitably from the continuously changing nature of a country's physical environment and the structure of its development goals. Thus, what is environmentally sound and appropriate at one juncture of history may not be so at another. The concepts of environmental soundness and appropriateness are not static; they must evolve with the state of the environment and with the nature of development tasks.

Although a determined effort on the part of the Government and the people could achieve much, global international cooperation is also essential to facilitate environmentally sound development. International cooperation is urgently needed if we are to better understand the outer limits of the global life-supporting systems. We live on only one earth, but our knowledge of the basic processes that underlie its global ecology is very limited. It is evident that multi-disciplinary scientific research involving international cooperation and large financial resources is absolutely necessary to bring forth data, analyses and insights which could guide our policies. For example, a better comprehension of the workings of the biogeochemical cycles of carbon, nitrogen, sulphur and other elements is essential if we are to understand ways in which the resources of soils, vegetation, water and atmosphere can be better utilized and their utility sustained. Several environmental problems related to development activities transcend national jurisdiction. This is the case not only in respect of shared natural resources, such as rivers, forests and seas, or the global commons (e.g. the oceans or the atmosphere). It is also true of scarce natural resources which are subject to international trade and of the imperative preservation of the natural heritage of mankind, such as wildlife.

All this points to the vital importance of the formulation by the United Nations of a New International Development Strategy. The United Nations General Assembly has resolved that the strategy should reflect, in an appropriate manner, the need for the protection of the environment, and for taking environmental considerations into account, in accordance with the development plans and priorities of developing countries. We should all take advantage of the opportunities offered by the formulation of the new strategy to advance the concepts of environmentally sound development: Development without Destruction.

I would like to conclude, by reiterating here what I said at the opening of the annual conference of the Club of Rome[1] that the present state of the earth is marred by the vast disparities in levels between developed and developing countries, as well as within developing countries themselves. Such disparities between over-consumption and deprivation constitute a great danger not only because of the unrest and violence that they engender; but also because, by their dynamic "demonstration effects", they entice the world to join the "revolution of rising expectations", with progressively harmful consequences of environmental degradation, resource depletion, denial of the opportunity to the young, the poor and the not-yet-born to improve their quality of life and sustain that improvement. For example, it is estimated that if the world consumed minerals at the current rate of United States consumption, known recoverable resources of copper would be exhausted in 9 years, bauxite in 18 years, zinc in six months, lead in 4 years, petroleum in 7 years and natural gas in 5 years.

Given the present vast disparities, it is not very helpful to warn that mankind is in great danger of transgressing environmental outer limits, nor to say complacently that mankind has the capacity to push back the outer limits

[1] For the statement to the Club of Rome, see p. 111

of the environment. It is essential to institute mechanisms and processes which will ensure that this capacity is expanded to embrace the day-to-day lives of those who suffer.

There is no doubt that the entire world stands to benefit from a more rational mobilization and use of the world's physical and human resources. The developing countries need more purposeful and augmented development assistance to learn from past environmental mistakes of industrialized countries, and to realise the environmental opportunities that they have. Availability of environmentally prudent and developmentally satisfactory technology is not enough to improve the state of the earth. In order that the dangers are kept at bay, and promising opportunities are actually made use of, economic and institutional reforms in international relations have to be brought into existence. If only a real relaxation of tension between the East and the West, and a genuine belief in self-reliance and in interdependence between developed and developing countries, can be achieved, there will be a world of a change in the prospects for improving the quality of life everywhere.

19

ALTERNATIVE PATTERNS OF DEVELOPMENT AND LIFESTYLES

Opening Statement to the Regional Seminar on Alternative Patterns of Development and Lifestyles[1]

Santiago, Chile, November 1979

THE period since the establishment of the United Nations has seen the emergence of many countries from colonial dependence in physical terms, and with it a new responsiveness and commitment to ensuring a more equitable world for all peoples. The striving for political independence has been increasingly merged into a quest for economic development, and yet the model for this quest has frequently been seen as one established by the developed countries of the industrialized North. The questions we must pose ourselves are:

1. Can developing countries imitate the development patterns of the North?
2. Even if they could, would this be desirable?
3. Can the countries of the North themselves continue with the same patterns of resource-intensive consumption-oriented development?

Imitation of present patterns

In regard to the first question, let us look for instance at the national resource base for food and agriculture, recalling the World Food Conference[2] call for a doubling of production in developing countries in twenty years.

[1] Sponsored by UNEP and ECLA.
[2] For statement to the World Food Conference, see p. 1.

Barely 15 to 18 per cent of the soils in South America, Africa and Asia may be described as having no serious limitations for agricultural use. As much as 95 per cent of the total land area in the arid and semi-arid zones is subject to the risk of desertification. And desertification is not confined to the dry areas. Its hazard can reach large proportions even in th sub-humid zones. Nearly 35 per cent of the world land is subject to moderate-to-very-high desertification hazard: 55 per cent in Africa; 34 per cent in Asia and 20 per cent in South America.

In south Asia, south-east Asia, and the South Pacific, the area under forests is being depleted at a rate of 2 per cent per annum. In certain areas, for example Malaysia, Nepal, and Thailand, there are some indications that if the present logging, farming and other practices continued, there could be a virtual disappearance of closed forests within the next 25 years. The environmental consequences of such large-scale destruction of tropical forests in terms of erosion, salinization, desertification, flooding, waterlogging, silting up of reservoirs and streams, clogging up of irrigation networks, and unfavourable changes in local micro-climatic patterns are bound to be very grievous.

Another potential global problem in this area of food production is fisheries. Collapses of ocean fisheries have in recent years become increasingly common. If sea fisheries are to continue to supply significant amounts of high-quality protein foods a much more rigorous management of fishing and human activities around and in the ocean will be needed, regionally and nationally. This management must be based on sounder ecological considerations than hitherto.

These are all cases where the sustainability and applicability of certain development patterns is a major issue. If we add such dimensions as the energy intensive nature of much of modern agriculture, or the capacity of land to provide employment under certain development patterns, or the pollution of water from agricultural residues, or the increased resistance of agricultural pests, the questions multiply. And, as you are aware, similar questions arise when the resource base for industrial development is considered. Were developing countries to succeed in consuming minerals at the current rate of United States consumption, known recoverable resources of copper would be exhausted in 9 years, bauxite in 18 years, zinc in six months, lead in 4 years, petroleum in 7 years and natural gas in 5 years.

The desirability of present patterns

Look at the patterns, for example, in the context of the present and urgent problems of urbanization in Latin America. Empirical evidence clearly indicates that levels of per capita wealth of countries and their levels of urbanization are closely associated. There is no doubt that along with industrialization and diversification of economic structure and social development in general, urbanization will continue to gather momentum in developing countries.

The present, daunting urban problems of congestion in settlements and transport, squalour, poor hygiene, noise, unemployment, mass poverty and social unrest which are experienced by developing countries today were also experienced by the large cities of London and Paris during the 18th and 19th centuries.

But the important difference is that the magnitudes of these problems, and the rates at which they are getting aggravated today in developing countries, are quite different. If the populations of the early cities increased at about 0.5 per cent per year, the populations of several large cities in the developing world are increasing today six times as fast, at 3 per cent per year, in certain cases even more. Whereas urban societies and policy-makers had to contend with annual population increases of tens of thousands, today in the developing countries, they have to provide the basic requirements of shelter, sanitation and water supply for annual additions of hundreds of thousands of people. It is estimated that merely the increment in the urban population of Latin America over the period 1975-2000 will exceed 200 million people. The relative extent of urbanization in Latin America is thus expected to exceed that in southern Europe by the year 2000, constituting more than 75 per cent of the population. Concrete, realistic and feasible plans to stop the trend of tremendous increases in large cities populations have to be urgently formulated and implemented.

One aspect of the undesirability of imitation is the use of resources in military expenditure. Certainly there is no worse constraint to much needed development than wars and armed conflicts. In themselves they induce tremendous hazards and disastrous impacts on the human environment. Through their claim on resources, they jeopardize opportunities for development. The figures are startling. World military spending today is over $1,000 million every day. If half of the funds spent on armaments throughout the world from 1970-1975 has been invested in the civilian sector, annual output at the end of the period could have been perhaps $200 thousand million larger than it was — more than the aggregate GNP of Southern Asia and the mid-African region, two large regions of acute poverty with a total population over 1,000 million. It was estimated that for the world as a whole 60 million people are engaged in military related occupations. This corresponds to the entire labour force in manufacturing in Europe outside the USSR. About 25 per cent of the world's scientific personnel are engaged in military related pursuits. The world's armed forces are major consumers of a wide range of non-renewable resources, both energy and raw material reserves. It has been estimated that world military consumption of liquid hydrocarbons is about 700-750 million barrels annually — twice the annual consumption for the whole of Africa. There is still a widespread belief that disarmament or discontinuation of some specific weapons programme would swell the ranks of the jobless, particularly when unemployment is already high. There is evidence to the contrary. The U.S. Government estimates have indicated that while $1,000 million of military expenditure creates 76,000 jobs, the same amount released in tax cuts would create 112,000 plus. Let us face facts squarely. We will not achieve much in terms of development and environmental protection through searching only for more appropriate patterns of developments and life styles. The world must be serious in dealing with the issue of the arms race if it really wants to shoulder its responsibility to establish better quality of life for all.

Present patterns in the North

Can the countries of the North continue with present patterns? Aside from the questions of international equity, illustrated by the example of the American child consuming more than six times as much grain as the Indian child, and of the deepening international crisis with increased potential for conflict as competition over scarce resources intensifies, questions relating to the internal social strains in the countries of the North are now becoming apparent. The consumption society has not solved the problems of its poor or of employment or even of health, as the statistics for cancer show. Problems of societal stress are on the increase, as shown by figures for crime or drug abuse. The present energy-intensive production and consumption patterns are seriously questioned as to their viability in the wake of what is being termed of late the energy crisis triggered by issues of availability and prices of oil. The potential environmental risks of burning more coal and the possible serious impacts of proliferation of nuclear energy are creating heated even emotional debates everywhere. Cries for energy conservation and for quick development of safer and more readily available renewable sources of energy are being heard in almost every corner of the globe. Adjustments in development and consumption patterns in the North are very much on the way with genuine efforts to base them on concepts of social justice, sustainability and conservation, and quality of life.

The Growing Consciousness

A wide-ranging discussion of the nature, meaning and purpose of development goals and objectives is occurring. This discussion may be said to stem from disillusion due to failure to achieve targeted economic growth rates during the last two decades. Not only disillusionment but near despair is particularly marked when considering the following issues:
1. eradication of poverty; material deprivation;
2. unequal distribution of economic growth among different countries; among geographical areas and among population groups;
3. furtherance of national self-reliance and cultural identity;
4. protection and enhancement of the environment while sustaining and improving the quality of life.

Concern about appropriate alternatives to economic growth is not confined to developing countries. The positive and negative effects of development is universal, encompasses all countries. Questions continue to be raised about the composition, distribution and the motive force of economic growth, and the impact of that growth on social and personal well-being. These concerns also include issues of national self-reliance or minimization of external dependency, particularly in the wake of marked increases in the international prices of oil. They also include what countries should or should not do in their growth and life styles to reduce the negative impacts of present production and consumption patterns.

It is increasingly recognized that there can be no full comprehension of today's world if the intricate interrelationship between economic and other systems is neglected. Physical planning of socio-economic development at all levels must reflect an appreciation of the complex and integral relationships between environment, development, resources and population. In selecting development alternatives — whether in terms of policies, programmes or projects — environmental objectives cannot be considered in isolation from other considerations, such as income growth, expansion of employment, alleviation of poverty and a more equitable distribution of income and wealth. All these goals have to be integrated in a viable pattern of development, whether defined at the national or international level and we must make the total interrelated system work in an optimal manner to reach the goals.

Before the Stockholm Conference in 1972, environmental problems were popularly identified as issues for the rich and elite: pollution control, the conservation of wildlife, and aesthetic preservation of landscape. These perceptions evoked some reservations and misgivings in developing countries; it was considered that such concern about the environment was uncalled for in terms of their own threshold situations and would gravely jeopardize their efforts to industrialize rapidly and their economies. But the Stockholm Conference marked a watershed in environmental thinking. Economists, ecologists and physical scientists and representatives of the world's people came together, emerging with new view of interactions and caused relationships that exist between socio-economic activities and physical phenomena. The nature of the efforts of UNEP in regard to the assessment, monitoring and management of the environment, reflects the progress achieved since 1972 and reflects also the inherent difficulties in the evaluation of the economic and social, no less than the environmental, consequences of development.

Notwithstanding the extensive literature and commentary on the need for appropriate development alternatives, it is regrettable to note that there has been little evidence, so far, of any significant breakthrough in consumption patterns and lifestyles, in public policies or in the structure and content of international co-operation for development. On the contrary, it would seem that the problems are becoming increasingly intractable. The reasons for this situation are not far to seek. It is my belief that they lie in the difficulty faced by policy-makers to take account fully in their considerations of the integral nature of the relationship between population, resources, environment and development.

Environment-Development Relationships should induce a Systemic Approach

Environment, when correctly understood in its relation to development, serves as a unifying, or integrating force with the capacity to facilitate the efficient utilization of resources and the efficient attainment of many contemporary and pressing objectives of development. Concern with the environment with today's quality of life, with the future well-being of the young, and with inter-generation ethics, should be natural concerns of human beings everywhere.

An examination of the environment-development relationship which has emerged in recent years affords a number of insights:

1. Environmental problems in development often transcend national jurisdiction and, consequently, international cooperation is essential to find lasting solutions to them. This is true, not only for the use and management of shared natural resources and for global commons, but also for international trade in scarce natural resources, and the preservation of the heritage of mankind in respect of endangered tropical and equatorial forests and wildlife.

2. Extremes in consumption levels and wide disparities in access to resources often lead to environmental degradation and resource depletion. There is, thus, significant common ground between broadly based distribution of the benefits of development and environmental improvement.

3. There is no built-in conflict between output growth or growth of resource productivity and environmental protection and improvement. This is apparent in the successful recycling of wastes for greater output and employment and for improvement of environmental sanitation. It is also shown in programmes of environmental improvement at the community level that have simultaneously expanded employment and enhanced productivity of resources. There is also growing evidence that measures to improve the environment have generated significant economic benefits in developed countries.

4. It is much less costly and much more efficient to integrate environmental considerations, *ex ante,* in decision-making and

planning for development than to react in response to such considerations at a later stage.

5. The relevance and the practical viability of any alternative pattern of development cannot be guaranteed unless there is broadly based and well informed participation in the process of decision-making. It is essential to influence attitudes and perceptions of people. At the same time, there is a residual fund of environmental tradition and wisdom with people themselves concerning adjustments to environmental conditions. Evolution of alternative patterns of development must draw upon such knowledge and modes of adjustment.

6. The question of autonomous determination of desirable lifestyles is crucial to the realization of environmentally sustainable improvements in the quality of life. This is so, not merely because the lifestyles associated with the recent experience of economic growth in developed countries may not be replicable in the poor countries on account of resource limitations, but also, and more importantly, because they may not be desirable in the interest of long-term social well-being.

Technology: Pattern Setter or Instrument?

Technology is the fundamental link between natural and social systems. As it increasingly sets the pattern for the definition of needs and the use of resources, the issue of the choice of technology becomes crucial to the choice between patterns of development. Thus, it is important that the development of technology should not be linear, but it should respond to various criteria set by its supposed beneficiaries.

Currently, technology — which is inappropriate from the social and environmental standpoints — continues to be imported into developing countries without appraisal and accepted uncritically. It is crucial that policy-makers and planners, in their quests for rapid development, concern themselves seriously with the choice of the most appropriate technology. The concept of appropriateness, however, acquires a meaning only when it defines appropriate to whom and for what. It requires a determination of appropriateness in which the environmental and social dimensions are equally as important as the economic ones. Such technology should be optimal to the conditions in each case and may range from being the most advanced technology especially designed for such conditions, or adapted, to being traditional either to the area or in the sense of being in wide use elsewhere. Recently a very high-level meeting of Governments of Europe — East and West — convened in Geneva and adopted, among other important documents, a declaration on low and non-waste technology emphasizing the urgent need for a rational use of natural resources, stressing the potential dangers to the environment of present day technology and setting a programme of action for Europe to develop low- and non-waste technologies and ways and means of reuse and recycling of waste. Addressing that meeting, I pointed to the issue of what I termed "transboundary pollution caused by transfer of hazardous technology". I believe it is a solemn duty of the developing countries to deal with all these issues with utmost precision and efficiency.

The Search and the Strategy

The United Nations will soon deliberate upon an International Development Strategy for the 1980's and, as we are all aware, the General Assembly has decided that the New International Development Strategy will primarily focus on the attainment of the New International Economic Order. In this context, we perceive that some of the environmental problems of developing countries stem from an asymmetric relationship between developed and developing countries; for instance, in the environmental impact of monoculture and cash crops for export, over-exploitation of natural resources (including living marine resources), rapid depletion of minerals and fossil fuels to support resource-intensive consumption and production patterns, and land degradation caused by certain mining and industrial activities of transnational bodies. Moreover, measures taken by developed countries to protect their environment may, in certain circumstances, have a growing impact on development and environment in developing countries. Examples include environmentally motivated import restrictions, redeployment of production capacities on environmental grounds, and increased costs of imports in developing countries on account of the application of stringent environmental standards in developed countries.

There can, of course, be no single rigid, universally acceptable approach to realizing socially satisfactory and sustainable development. At the same time, it is also clear that specific approaches and solutions in particular situations need to be based on an integrated examination of the issues involved. Much can be achieved by way of identifying and adopting concrete and environmentally prudent solutions in particular circumstances. Much more can, perhaps, be achieved by making the methodological apparatus of the evaluation of the costs and benefits of environmental and developmental alternatives more broadly based, so as to embrace considerations of the quality of life of the populations affected. That is why I expect that this Seminar, with its primary focus on the unique and integral relationship between environment and development, will stimulate and catalyse concrete action at national, regional and international levels, and indeed move beyond conceptual clarification to the identification of an operational content of the environment-development relationship.

Role of the Seminar

Latin America occupies a special position when considering what should be done in developing authentic and environmentally sound development patterns. Most of the countries of this region have experienced and experimented with organized economic and social development over long periods. They have a first-hand understanding of social and environmental problems associated with rapid achievement of high levels of industrialization and economic growth. At the same time, they have experienced severe social and environmental problems associated with poverty, marked inequalities in the distribution of assets and income, and regional disparities in levels of living and resource development. High levels of air pollution, soil loss, disappearance of forest cover and colossal environmental problems in urban centres are but a few examples. Many Latin American countries have, with particular severity experienced that economic and environmental problems created, or exacerbated, by weak bargaining powers in international trade and investment markets. Some have also experienced the promise of self-reliant and socially satisfactory development offered by technical and economic cooperation among developing countries themselves. With high levels of literacy and a strong political consciousness, they are also in a favourable position to initiate and sustain broadly-based and forward-looking patterns of development.

The question that needs to be addressed in all earnestness by a highly qualified forum like this is what promising alternatives are available, and how they can be implemented. The solutions, of course, are not likely to be simple or uniform; they will have to be based on diagnoses of problems, and comprehensive assessment of possibilities and potentials in particular situations.

But what I consider of greater importance is the impressive fund of knowledge and experiences of practical development planning that this gathering presents, which will enable you to examine the nature and feasibility of alternative, sustainable and satisfactory patterns of development and ways and means of achieving them.

20
WORLD CONSERVATION STRATEGY

Opening Address for the Launch of World Conservation Strategy

Nairobi, Kenya, March 1980

THERE is a hard realization that the earth's seemingly vast supplies of living resources — of air, water, soil, our plants and forests and woodlands, our oceans, our wildlife, and our genetic resources are not inexhaustible in the face of rising populations, uncontrolled demand, mindless consumption and waste. Growing universal awareness of this situation has resulted in the call for a strategy to help governments make enlightened decisions to achieve sustainable development, development without destruction of the resources on which development, and life itself, depends.

The World Conservation Strategy we are launching today is the answer to this call. As a part of its global responsibility to assist governments to protect and enhance the quality of the environment for present and future generations, UNEP commissioned the International Union for Conservation of Nature and Natural Resources to draw up this strategy. With a membership of more than 450 organizations in over 100 countries it is highly equipped for the tough task. The World Wildlife Fund, the largest international fund raising non-governmental organization in the area of wildlife, came strongly to the financial support of the big endeavour. After nearly five years of intensive consultations with more than 700 scientists, the IUCN finalized the preparation of the Strategy in full co-operation with UNEP and WWF. This Strategy has the full endorsement of FAO and UNESCO. The main thrust of the World Conservation Strategy is to present the case for conservation as a means for sustained development, to describe the main requirements for the achievement of conservation objectives and to set up ways for meeting these requirements.

Why the World Conservation Strategy is Needed?

The Strategy comes at a point in man's development when he must effect measures for the universal conservation and protection of the world's resources in such a manner as to insure their continued use, not their exhaustion. Over-exploitation of living resources by the poor locks them deeper into poverty — often forcing them to destroy their very means of development and livelihood. Over-exploitation and over-consumption by the rich renders development processes less economic and needlessly wasteful of vital resources. Consider a few elements of the present state of our Earth.

1. Nearly half of the world's rain forests have been destroyed. At the current rate, between five and ten million hectares are lost every year.

2. Only about 11 per cent of the world's land area offers no serious limitations to agriculture.

3. Every year we are losing some six million hectares of arable land, going out of agriculture to the process of desertification. Approximately 29 million acres of agricultural lands were converted to non-agricultural uses in the United States in the past ten years. Between 1960 and 1970 Japan lost 7.3 per cent of its agricultural land to buildings and roads. In India 6,000 million tons of soil are lost every year from an area less than quarter of the size of that country. We can realize the magnitude of such a loss if we know that nature takes from 100 to 400 years or more to generate only 1 cm of topsoil.

4. Coastal lands and breeding grounds for over two-thirds of the world's fisheries are being degraded or destroyed.

5. Over 1,000 animal and some 25,000 plant species are today threatened with extinction.

6. Large segments of our atmosphere, our soils, our rivers and our seas are polluted in one way or the other. Agricultural runoffs — hazardous waste dumps — acid rain — toxic chemicals — CO_2 build up in the atmosphere and ozone depletion are all with us. The danger list is endless.

7. The implication for man is serious. If man is to survive on this earth, he will have to manage his resources on a much more rational basis. He must adopted alternative patterns of development and lifestyles which are less arrogant in their need for and less wasteful in their use of natural resources.

Are there obstacles to achieving such goals? Certainly there are many. The tense international climate, the economic problems facing almost all countries, the disquieting inequalities between and within nations, the rigid stands of both developed and developing countries and the continued wasting by the world community of its resources, human, natural and financial in building machinery of destruction — of war — instead of building societies of dignity and sustaining a reasonable quality of life for all. An obvious obstacle that is of specific concern to us today is the failure to integrate conservation with development which often results in a process that is needlessly destructive. Then there is the lack of knowledge and awareness. As a result there is no realization of the damage — often irretrievable — no capacity to conserve, and no popular support for conservation. The World Conservation Strategy has been carefully designed to chart the path towards facing these difficulties.

The Prospects for Success

A prime objective of the worldwide launch today will be the adoption by all governments of the conservation principles outlined in the Strategy and the announcement of new specific actions inspired by the Strategy or the intensification of ongoing activities in response to its recommendations. This will, I am sure, lead to comprehensive conservation programmes that will figure prominently in national development plans. We may be running short of time. But the situation is not in anyway grim. I am optimistic and encouraged about the future. There is definitely a worldwide realization of the importance and urgency of wise utilization of our natural resources, especially the living ones and there is this well thought-out strategy to help us achieve this goal. Signals from a number of governments are already positive. But, I wish to avail myself of this opportunity of launching the Strategy in Nairobi, the host city of the global Headquarters of UNEP, to call on all governments to adopt the principles of the World Conservation Strategy and to apply them in their development activities.

21

UNEP: RETROSPECT AND PROSPECTS

Introductory Statement to the Eighth Session of the Governing Council of UNEP

Nairobi, Kenya, April 1980

I HAVE had the unique privilege of serving UNEP as its Executive Director for almost five years in addition to my two and half years of serving as Deputy. As I approach the end of my present term of office, I would like to share with you some of my thoughts on the difficulties and accomplishments of this formative period in UNEP's development.

One of the most pressing problems that UNEP has had to face in recent years relates to the establishment of a balanced programme reflecting the needs of both developed and developing countries. Although there is a global convergence of long-term interests and objectives, the short-term and medium-term preoccupations of the two groups of countries and their perception of immediate needs and constraints do not often coincide. A divergence of interests was foreseen at Stockholm, and the Plan of Action of the Conference, as well as the programme decision of the first session of the Governing Council in 1973, gave an orientation which sought to make UNEP's programme of activities equally relevant to both worlds. The prescription has not worked entirely satisfactorily.

From the outset, perceptions of various Governments regarding the question of concentration of UNEP activities varied widely. You know, the agencies know, we all know that to tackle too much at the same time is not conducive to efficient utilization of our scarce resources. While trying to work on a wide array of issues which rightly preoccupy the world community, it was necessary to concentrate. Some years back we proposed the formula of "concentration areas". I have proposed the 21 goals for 1982. All this, with one objective: to be efficient in those areas of key importance which require priority attention.

Yet, you will recall that at session after session of this Governing Council, the Economic and Social Council and the General Assembly, I have had to try to reconcile the need for concentration with insistent demands for many diverse activitites to which one or more Governments wanted UNEP to devote its time and attention and its increasingly scarce financial and human resources.

Besides those specific requests which reflect the particular priorities individual Governments attach to certain subjects — a fact which I fully understand and appreciate — there have been other factors which have made it difficult to concentrate time, effort and money on a few areas in which visible and impressive results could be accomplished. I refer now to the proliferation in recent years of concerns and alarms on many subjects related to the environment which have at times created grave concern for the future of our planet. UNEP, because of its very mandate, is itself continuously on the lookout for such concerns which should preoccupy us all. But UNEP must also follow all such developments closely to see whether they are given sufficient attention by Governments, specialized agencies or the international scientific community. If they are not, it is UNEP's task to bring this to your attention.

All this has not made our task of attempting to fashion a viable global programme easy. I have tried to maintain not so much a delicate balance of interests, but, rather, a balanced global programme from which the whole of mankind could benefit. I hope you will agree that, difficult as it may have been, through the collective wisdom of this Council the balanced programme you wanted has been preserved.

I am sure the Council appreciates the complexity not only of the problems to which UNEP is addressing itself, but also of the mechanisms through which UNEP operates. We are not a funding agency supporting activities implemented by others, nor are we an executing agency implementing programmes and projects in a clearly defined sector.

UNEP has the difficult task of attempting to develop a programme meant for implementation not by itself alone, but also by others — Governments, United Nations agencies and bodies and supporting organizations. Such an effort requires time, careful negotiations and the willing cooperation of partners. Views and information need to be sought, and consensus positions reached. It is equally necessary to avoid duplication of effort, create an atmosphere of harmony and dynamic conditions for working together.

There are two essential preconditions for such an exercise. The first is the development of an intellectual input which the other parties involved will consider authoritative enough and persuasive enough to act upon. This is not easy to develop. UNEP, with its small staff, does not have a wide range of specialists at its disposal. Nevertheless, for the period ahead we must of necessity concentrate on strengthening our intellectual leverage in a number of ways.

The second requirement relates to financial resources which would help provide our partners with necessary incentives to undertake tasks of primary interest to us. The resources currently available to the Environment Fund, affected as they are both by inflation and by stagnation, are not of such importance as to offer any but the most minimal inducement to our partners. It has thus become a matter of some urgency to have enough voluntary contributions for the effective implementation of priority activities approved by this Council.

One difficulty faced by UNEP stems from the rapid turnover of staff, particularly in areas of administration, including finance, budget and personnel. As you know the efficiency of substantive staff is a direct function of effective support. But it has proved extremely difficult to attract experienced administrative personnel to work with us. They are in short supply system-wide, and we don't have too much by way of incentives to offer in our small secretariat.

The recruitment of substantive staff has also proved to be problematical over the years. While many international organizations have a clear and well defined area of activity, UNEP's responsibilities cover a wide spectrum of specialization. It therefore does not have a clearly defined and well established professional community from which to recruit its substantive staff.

Member Governments have been active, sometimes over-active, in assisting UNEP in its recruitment efforts. Because of its small size and core character, the quality of every single staff member in UNEP is of crucial importance to its effective functioning. Yet not always the highest calibre of manpower has been offered by Governments as staff or consultants. In several instances, the staff seconded by Governments have been poor and most disappointing. I know that the type of talent we are looking for is not abundant. This is particularly true in developing countries, because of the general scarcity of highly trained expertize. Nevertheless, we can only serve you better if your response to our staff needs is better oriented.

A major problem for the organization in the last two years has been the shortfall in resources compared to the target approved by the Governing Council. Let me put the record straight. I must start by expressing deep gratitude to a number of countries which have come forward with substantially increased contributions for our planning period 1978-1981. Unfortunately they are few, and their example has not been widely followed. A large number of Governments have yet to contribute to the Fund. Even on the basis of pledged contributions regarding which there are major uncertainties, we are still more than $24 million short of the target for the four-year period. Thus, year after year, we have had to exercise the most painful prudence in committing funds for new and important activities which the Council has earlier approved but for which sufficient resources have not been made available. Year after year, our hands have been tied, despite an apparent comfortable "cash carry-over" which has sometimes been used as a justification for not increasing contributions. If approved programmes have not been implemented as effectively as they should have been, it has been due, in large part, to the uncertainty regarding the volume and timing of expected contributions and, more importantly, the substantial shortage of resources available to implement these programmes.

Another problem which has been confronting us for the past three years is the issue of efficient communication and data processing. One way of dealing with this issue has been the establishment by UNEP of a sending/receiving station through the Symphonie Satellite. Our negotiations are very far advanced with the United Nations in New York and Geneva, as well as with the Governments concerned: France, the Federal Republic of Germany and Switzerland. In fact, France and the Federal Republic of Germany have made a very generous offer in this respect. The matter is now in the hands of our host Government, Kenya, and I hope it will respond without further delay to our request to start the operation soon in compliance with the Headquarters Agreement for ensuring the efficient functioning of UNEP.

If I have drawn attention to the problems and difficulties that UNEP has faced during the period of my office, it is not to inject a sense of pessimism in our deliberations. Not all the signs are negative. There certainly have been major achievements. Let me give a few examples:

1. The relationship established with our partners, the members of the United Nations system. After a period of ups and downs, these relationships are now stabilizing on an open, frank and most constructive basis, as you will see from the report of ACC to the Governing Council. We have learned from experience which aspects of our methods of work have irritated our partners. They in turn have learned to accept the legitimacy of our concerns. We look to our partners as repositories of experience and vehicles for action by which the United Nations system can help the world community to meet environmental concerns;

2. Our methods of programme development, first the three-level programmatic process, then the move to joint programming, and now thematic joint programming and the methodology of SWMTEP, are major acomplishments. When occasionally I become impatient with the development of our programming, I reflect on the progress made over-all in the United Nations system, where some of the concepts of our programmatic process remain an objective towards which the system hopes shortly to move, and I feel that UNEP has indeed contributed and is contributing meaningfully to over-all system-wide cooperation concepts;

3. Let me also list for you, without amplification, some of the specific areas where UNEP's efforts have borne fruit:

    (i) The successful regional seas programme;

(ii) The reflection in drafts of the New International Development Strategy of UNEP's views and approaches to the reconciliation of economic and environmental concerns;

(iii) The programme on cost/benefit analysis of environmental protection measures;

(iv) The declaration of principles by multilateral development financing agencies on the incorporation of environmental considerations into their development policies, programmes and projects;

(v) The results of the seminars on alternative patterns of development and lifestyles held in cooperation with the regional Economic Commissions of the United Nations;

(vi) UNEP's positive role in work on interrelationships between resources, environment, population and development;

(vii) The industry seminars and the resulting guidelines;

(viii) The development of environmental impact assessment guidelines;

(ix) The effective INFOTERRA network of focal points and a number of sectoral information systems such as the industry and environment information and data system;

(x) The important work of the Coordinating Committee on the Ozone Layer;

(xi) Our assistance to Governments in establishing priorities among their environmental problems and developing national environmental legislation and environmental legislation and environmental machinery;

(xii) The Plan of Action to Combat Desertification;

(xiii) The development of a global plan for the wise utilization of tropical forests;

(xiv) UNEP's assumption of responsibility for the Climate Impact Studies Programme;

(xv) The state of the environment reports, which are receiving wide publicity and are triggering serious consideration of emerging issues: carbon dioxide, firewood, toxic chemicals, environmental diseases, resistance to pesticides and so on;

(xvi) The Tbilisi Plan of Action and our work on environmental education;

(xvii) Our reports on the environmental impacts of production and use of various sources of energy.

UNEP is only just over seven years old. To have achieved all that we have done has meant a tremendous effort on the part of its very small staff: as I have said on several occasions, only as big as a division in a major organization of the United Nations system. Our "small core" character has been seriously tested. The achievements realized are the work of the staff of UNEP, those present and those who have left us. They are also the work of a whole host of senior advisers, who accepted me as one of them, and were extremely kind to come and give me advice, sometimes at very short notice and in the midst of their very crowded programmes. To all these I pay tribute. And above all, my tribute and profound gratitude goes to you, to your Governments, who have always encouraged and guided us to what we consider our successes.

We are entering this year the new decade of the 1980's. Despite all our efforts to protect and improve the environment, we are entering the new decade with a long list of dangerous situations. Let me give a few examples:

1. Nearly half of the world's rain forests have been destroyed. At the current rate, between five an ten million hectares are lost every year;

2. Only about 11 per cent of the world's land area offers no serious limitations to agriculture;

3. Each year we are losing some six million hectares of arable land to the processes of desertification. Almost 12 million hectares of agricultural lands were converted to non-agricultural uses in the United States of America alone in the past ten years. Between 1960 and 1970, Japan lost 7.3 per cent of its agricultural land to buildings and roads;

4. In India, some 6,000 million tons of soil are lost every year from an area less than one-fourth of the size of the country. We can realize the magnitude of such a loss when we recall that nature takes from 100 to 400 years or more to generate only 1 cm of topsoil;

5. Coastal lands and breeding grounds for over two thirds of the world's fisheries are being degraded or destroyed;

6. Over 1,000 animal and some 25,000 plant species are today threatened with extinction;

7. Large segments of our atmosphere, our soils, our rivers and our seas are polluted in one way or the other. Agricultural runoffs dumping of hazardous wastes, acid rain, toxic chemicals, carbon dioxide build up in the atmosphere and ozone depletion are all with us.

We are also witnessing the emergence of new sets of environmental problems. One set is brought about by the energy problems facing the world. Essentially, it relates to the new developments which are taking place in coal liquefaction and the use of crops for alcohol production to replace oil. The former may lead to a serious build-up of carbon dioxide in the atmosphere, while the latter implies, among other things, serious competition for land between food and fuel production. A second set is what I called at the ECE high level meeting "another form of transboundary pollution". I meant by that the environmental problems induced by transfer of hazardous goods and technologies, as well as toxic wastes, from developed to developing countries. Governmental and non-governmental quarters in some Western countries are protesting against the use of Third World countries as dumping grounds for hazardous wastes. Developing countries are calling for assistance in identifying hazards in products which they import. Yet export of banned chemicals by producing countries continues, as does the transfer of hazardous technologies from developed to developing countries under the pretext that the environmental carrying capacity of the latter is still high. The third set of emerging problems relates to the potential hazards of overfishing and of oil exploration in Antarctica and the Southern Ocean. Overfishing of krill, a tiny shrimp-like creature, can endanger several species of very important marine living resources. In conditions like those of Antarctica, oil operating hazards are very high and thus oil exploration there should be approached with the utmost caution.

These issues may be seen as serious problems. But we should also look at them as opportunities for real, genuine, candid international cooperation. We all know that while the resource base for development is eroding, the resulting environmental hazards are increasing and taking more complex and wide-ranging forms, attacking the symptoms of environmental degradation can only buy a limited pause. The problems must be attacked at the root. While, therefore, we fight the symptoms of environmental degradation, we must expand our knowledge of the basic causal processes, and simultaneously seek and implement solutions which are mutually reinforcing. These solutions must have a positive impact on the whole interrelated system of resources, people, environment and development. Such a holistic approach offers both challenges and opportunities.

An approach of this kind requires new concepts and techniques of management, in which costs of required actions may need to be borne by groups — be they departments of Government or sectors of society — other than those who reap the benefit. Situations may also arise where costs are borne by some nations, but benefits accrue not only to them but also to others. The true justification for such endeavours where costs accrue in a different pattern from benefits is the over-all pattern of benefit for our generation and generations yet to be born.

There are various ways of developing multifaceted solutions which take account of this complex system of interrelationships. Let me mention two possible points of entry. The first relates to spatial planning, where the rational management of land influences the environment, the use of resources, and the distribution to the population. Such spatial planning techniques can increase the carrying capacity of our planet. The second relates to energy, where the pace of change is so dynamic that it affords the leverage needed to affect positively a whole host of problems ranging from the use of materials and the production of hazardous waste, through agricultural practices and transportation structures, to human settlements and societal patterns.

Our problems and our opportunities are different aspects of the same reality. Possibly the central issue is our inability to look to man's long-term welfare, to muster the courage to accept and use change in beneficial ways, instead of being the victims of some juggernaut. We see examples of this inability in industrialized countries, where economic problems have led in certain cases not to forward-looking solutions but to attempts to seek palliatives, and to a move away from concern for the environment. We also see examples in developing countries, where such problems as the advance of deserts and the disappearance of forest are not accorded by the countries concerned the same significance as problems perceived as more immediate. The resources the world expends on the arms race are another symptom of our inability to take hard decisions today to safeguard our tomorrow. The real issue is the lack of commitment to the long term. The leadership of the nations of the world and of the institutions which serve it must show the moral courage badly needed to effect the basic changes required to meet the critical problems of the years ahead.

22

AIR QUALITY MANAGEMENT

Statement at the Opening Ceremony of the Fifth International Clean Air Congress

Buenos Aires, Argentina, October 1980

IT IS the objective of UNEP to coordinate and catalyze activities throughout the United Nations family in an endeavour to develop joint programmes in the various fields of environment. Air pollution is one such field. Our common effort in the United Nations is geared to cover all aspects of air pollution in an integrated manner and to see them in the total environmental context, not just as one of the media.

UNEP also endeavours to encourage the supporting role of the non-governmental organizations, particularly those like the International Union of Air Pollution Prevention Associations, which help to provide a sound scientific and technical basis for understanding the nature of air pollution problems as well as finding technologically feasible, cost-effective solutions.

Our overall aim in UNEP is to help in achieving environmentally sound development. For this, UNEP works not only with Governments and intergovernmental and non-governmental organizations, but also with industry and the multilateral development financing institutions. UNEP has prepared and promulgated a Declaration of Principles on the incorporation of environmental principles in development policies, programmes and projects which has been accepted and signed by nine major development financing agencies including the World Bank, UNDP, EEC, the Inter-American Development Bank, the Organization of American States and others. These institutions, which disburse large funds for projects, considerably in excess of what the Fund of UNEP has at its disposal, have agreed, in effect, to keep environmental concerns centrally in mind when approving projects and programmes.

UNEP will be ten years old in 1982 and we are preparing to take stock of what has happened since 1972. A report on the state of the environment — ten years after Stockholm — is in preparation. In our assessment of the trends during the last decade we look to the work of the scientific and technical community of those actively engaged in pollution control — associations like those whose Congress we are inaugurating today.

I would like at this stage to call attention to a number of the trends which we see have been occurring in the field of air pollution during the last decade and which will continue to be of concern to all of us.

Clearly, any generalizations will, at best, be a simplification and at worst, inaccurate or misleading for specific circumstances. Further, I would like you to consider what I have to say especially since we in UNEP hold the view that

(a) that industrialization is necessary for any real development, and
(b) that it can be achieved in an environmentally sound manner.

This is a pragmatic view that I know is shared by your associations. In general terms, the rate of industrial growth has been more rapid during the last decade in the developing world than in the developed countries. But this growth has been very uneven. In the developed countries, new less polluting industries have tended to replace older, often highly polluting industries, so that there has been a trend to improved physical environmental quality i.e. ambient concentrations of many air pollutants have been falling during the last decade in many cities of the industrialized world and we expect the levels to continue to fall, and for the World Health Organization long-term goals for air quality to be met. Sulphur dioxide and smoke levels are good examples where cities, such as London, Paris and Toyko have shown remarkable improvements in ambient concentrations. Additionally, planning procedures have become stricter in the developed countries, allowing better siting of new industry from an environmental point of view. Improved air modelling techniques are only one of a variety of tools which enable better planning to reduce air pollution impact.

In the rapidly industrializing countries of the developing world, inevitably pollution levels tend to be increasing faster since they were low initially. However, a number of factors aggravate the situation and make it worse than it might otherwise be. First, since environmental protection is not usually a particularly high priority, with other more pressing needs and sometimes also a lack of public awareness, although this is changing, the best available abatement technology might not be considered necessary. Second, industrialization may not be planned and sited so as to minimize the impact of pollution. Third, technically trained manpower may not be adequate to ensure as high a standard of plant operation and maintenance as could be achieved. Finally, many countries have neither adequate enabling legislation for the control of pollution, nor planning procedures incorporating environmental aspects, nor sufficient trained administrators to enforce environmental protection.

Entirely on their own, or with some assistance from the United Nations family, developing countries are already on the proper track to reversing the trend of degradation in air quality. Let me take just two examples from Latin America. First, here in Argentina. The population of this country which is largely urban in domicile and lifestyle lives, in contrast to much of the developing world, in an almost idyllic topography blessed with a temperate climate and abundance of natural resources. Due to the over-concentration of industry and of population, however, the problem of air pollution and indiscriminate discharge of harmful industrial substances both into the air and into the river waters generally is emerging as a matter of concern. This has led to the substantial work done to identify and alleviate pollution problems by the Under Secretariat for Environmental Management in this country and to the adoption of various national legislation in the field of pollution, including legislation for the Preservation of the Environment and Maintenance of Proper Living Conditions in Industrial Promotion. A model action-oriented programme in this country is the cleaning of the air of Buenos Aires through a massive change in the system of incinerating waste and garbage. Marked changes occurred over the past three years.

Another example is the case of Mexico City. Two years ago, UNEP was requested by the Mayor of Mexico City to help the Mexican officials develop a programme of air quality in the Valley of Mexico. A group of the world's leading air pollution experts helped draw up a programme which is now being implemented by the Mexican Government. Already two years later, positive trends of improvement are being observed.

Air pollution was perceived as a major problem in some countries as early as the 1950s, though in others not until the late 1960s. Initially it was seen as a phenomenon consisting of high concentrations of a few well known pollutants such as particulate matter, sulphur oxides, nitrogen oxides and carbon monoxide that were found primarily in urban and industrial areas, and that caused easily identifiable effects, such as ill-health, loss of visibility or detrimental effects on plants and other material.

Extensive studies have recently contributed to our knowledge of the existence of other pollutants in the air, for example, photochemical oxidants, hydrocarbons, etc. Until the early seventies photochemical oxidant air pollution was considered to be a very localized problem associated with a few major urban areas, with high traffic densities, such as Los Angeles, Tokyo and Sydney. This decade, however, has seen a rapid rise in the number and extent of areas affected by the photochemical smog. The OECD in 1975 made the following evaluation:

> "Contrary to previous considerations that only regions with conditions typical of the Los Angeles basin could expect photochemical oxidant air pollution, it is now clear that provided certain meteorological conditions prevail, any region with dense traffic or industry may also be subject to this type of pollution. The meterological conditions which are required for the formation of oxidants are that a stationary high pressure system be

accompanied by adequate sunshine and low early-morning wind speeds. These conditions can occur in most parts of the world."

Response was almost prompt and four years later, in 1979, the OECD reported that regulatory action by several countries has contributed to curbing the increase of such pollutants in the air.

Photochemical oxidant air pollution also has regional impacts with precursor travelling large distances and reacting *in situ* to cause damage far from emission sources. This was already being observed in North America in the early seventies and has subsequently been observed in Europe. In the second half of the seventies knowledge also increased with respect to the transformation and transport of these chemicals in the atmosphere which will hopefully allow better coordinated actions to alleviate such regional impacts.

Another example of regional air quality deterioration is that due to sulphur dioxide and related products. Most major cities of western Europe have been observing falling ambient air concentrations of sulphur dioxide during the decade. This has been attributed to: slower economic growth, a slower rate of growth in energy use, increased energy conservation, greater use of natural gas in some countries, increased use of low sulphur content crude oil, as well as rapid growth in the use of scrubbers and other techniques for the removal of sulphur. The improvement in these urban areas has occurred also partly because of a greater dispersion of sulphur compounds, thus giving rise to problems associated with long-range transport of these compounds. These problems involve increased acidity of precipitation in areas remote from industrial pollution sources with consequent lowering of the pH-value of poorly buffered surface waters. In some cases — particularly in northern Scandinavia and in the northern United States and Canada — this has been followed by spectacular changes in the freshwater ecosystems and the disappearance from the affected waters of fish species of great commercial or recreational value. Long-range transport of pollutants has been measured and quantified during the last few years, first through the OECD measurement programme in western Europe, then, more recently, through the activity under the sponsorship of UNEP, the ECE and the WMO in Europe as a whole. Concern about the increased acidity of precipitation, which may also affect certain soils and therefore, at least indirectly, the vegetation cover, is such that the countries members of the ECE have adopted, less than a year ago, an important "Convention on Long-range Transboundary Air Pollution". Under the Convention member states undertake, among other things, to develop the best policies and strategies, including control measures compatible with balanced development, to make possible a reduction of the amount of pollution that crosses their own borders.

The last decade has further seen a growing realization that air pollution could have impacts on a global scale. The 0.3 per cent annual increase in carbon dioxide concentration in the earth's atmosphere has been known for a long time, but only in the last decade have modelling techniques enabled the scientific community to better realise the possible impact of this increase. It was clear that an increase in CO_2 concentrations as a result of burning of fossil fuels and the possible climatic changes resulting from the so-called greenhouse effect of CO_2 could have major environmental and societal impacts. In spite of our deep concern about such impacts, both in respect of primary and feedback effects, very little is known with certainty about the global geochemical cycles in terms of interrelationships controlling changes in carbon dioxide concentrations. In 1979, the President of SCOPE, Professor Gilbert F. White and myself, in a joint statement, appealed to governments and to the scientific community to exert a highly concerted effort during the next ten years to the subject of biogeochemical cycles to allow better understanding of the possible risks to the environment and the negative impacts of our mishandling of the natural resources of our planet.

As many of you are probably aware, UNEP is sponsoring a programme for the continued assessment of the risk of depletion of the ozone layer due to man's activities and the impact of such depletion on society. The latest assessment issued by the UNEP Coordinating Committee on the Ozone Layer in November 1979 indicated that an ultimate depletion of this layer would be about 15 per cent if chlorofluoromethanes releases continue at the 1979 rate. An up-dated assessment of these risks will be prepared by this Committee next month. A number of countries have already taken action to regulate the release of these chemicals while others have agreed to reduce the use of aerosols by 30 per cent relative to the use in 1976.

Of quite a different character, but also of growing importance during this decade, has been the environmental impact of accidents and accidental emissions. The rise in the number and significance of these accidents is due in a large degree to the increasing size and extent of industrial activities, as well as to their combinations. From an environmental impact point-of-view, recovery has to come sooner or later but the disturbance and its ramifications are quite significant.

This brings me to an important final point I wish to make. Protection of air quality does not depend only on the state of abatement technology. It depends just as much on the proper operation of the industrial plant and equipment, including its maintenance. Air pollution prevention associations which organised this Congress, with their high standard of scientific engineering capabilities, have stimulated the development of improved air pollution abatement techniques as well as new low polluting processes. Members of these associations, whether as pollution control authorities or as environmental managers in industry, exercise a high level of professional competence in ensuring that the plant is well operated and maintained and that feasible levels of air pollution control are attained. It is essential that the experience of these associations is made available to the rapidly industrializing countries of the developing world. As I attend conferences like this one, I am pleased to see an ever growing number of scientists and engineers from developing countries taking a more prominent role. Much still has to be done in expanding the number of trained people at all levels. I believe there is a major task ahead to educate the plant and furnace operator, the operator of small air polluting commercial enterprises, even the motor vehicle user, so that processes, machines and motor vehicles are operated in an efficient way to save scarce resources and protect air quality.

23

WATER SYSTEMS AND THE ENVIRONMENT

Statement to the Diplomatic Conference of the Environmental Protection Agency (EPA) of the United States of America

Washington, USA, October, 1980

THERE have been significant advances in the last decade in our understanding of the integrated relationship between environment and development. The concept has been advanced that environment should be viewed as the stock of physical and social resources available at a given time for the satisfaction of human needs, and development as a process pursued by all societies with the aim of increasing human well-being. Hence this concept advocated that the ultimate purpose of both environmental and development policies is the enhancement of the quality of life, and thus these policies are not only complementary but mutually supportive. This was a daring concept at the beginning of the decade but is now understood and generally accepted. This thinking is reflected in the formulation of new terminologies such as "alternative development", "new styles of development", or "alternative life styles", which suggest a more rational way of looking at the development process, one in which environmental considerations play a central role. A new kind of thinking on the environment-development interrelationship has proved necessary because development must be related, not only to the opportunities offered by the available natural resource base, but also to the constraints imposed by that base upon various human activities. The global community expressed itself clearly along these lines in the New International Development Strategy (NIDS) just agreed upon last month. All the topics discussed during this three-day meeting (Global 2000, desertification, tropical rain forests, World Conservation Strategy (WCS) and several others) are, I assume, meant to clearly underline one particular point: that it is simply self-defeating to pursue development strategies that are not sustainable over a long-term basis due to destruction of the resource base or other serious environmental damages. Development of water systems is no exception to this generalization.

Water, however, is not just simply another resource. The survival of mankind is dependent on water. Approximately 71 per cent of the earth's surface is covered with water. Of the total volume of this water, 97.3 per cent is ocean water. The balance, that is 2.7 per cent, is fresh water. At any given time, 77.2 per cent of fresh water is frozen in the polar ice caps and in glaciers in various parts of the world, and thus, for all practical purposes, is unavailable for use by man. Groundwater and soil moisture constitute 22.4 per cent of global fresh water, but much of this is beyond man's present exploitation as about two-thirds lies at a depth of more than 750 metres. Lakes, the atmosphere and streams contain only 0.04 per cent of fresh water, or about 0.01 per cent of the total volume of water on earth.

I have been asked to address this subject of water-systems within the framework of the role of the United Nations Environment Programme (UNEP), including the Regional Seas programme. This is a rather impossible task because of the vastness of the subject and because several specific topics that come under the major concerns of UNEP in this area are covered, during this meeting, and I am sure more appropriately, by a large number of distinguished speakers. So by necessity, I have to be general, giving in effect some quick snapshots. I hope I will not disappoint you by following such a line.

On the question of the role of UNEP, let me clearly indicate first that UNEP is not an operating agency. UNEP was established in 1972 to be the focal point for environment in the United Nations system and to ensure co-ordination and catalysis of the implementation of a realistic environment programme. UNEP is essentially meant to be the environmental conscience of the world. It has to monitor emerging problems, assess the possible risks of existing and long-standing ones, develop proposals to contain these problems and risks through better management of the environment and promotion of education and information that would raise public awareness as well as that of decision-makers and their supporting complements of technicians. A difficult and challenging task. But we are not doing this alone as a small secretariat. Our role in the Secretariat is to propose — in full consultation with the various agencies and organs of the United Nations system — a programme of action in the three major components of our work: environmental assessment, environmental management, and supporting measures (education, training, information and technical assistance). Our Governing Council gives the final guidance on what the programme should be. We use the Environment Fund — quite small compared to resources available to other UN organs, let alone national Governments — as a catalyst and incentive, to implement the programmes to which our Governing Council give priority. Water and oceans are among these priorities.

Let me first address the issue of fresh-water.

Worldwide, agriculture uses about 80 per cent of all the water consumed.

Between 1900 and 1975, water consumption for agriculture has increased seven times and is estimated to increase by about 20 per cent the present rate of consumption by 1985. Water consumption in industry has increased more than twenty times between 1900 and 1975 — the present high rate is expected to almost double by 1985. I stress that these consumption figures are all estimates. They may drastically change — possibly upwards — by further developments in technology. Spreading use of nuclear reactors for energy production or the use of coal and shale to produce synthetic fuels, as you know, have very high demand on water.

In theory, the global stock of water could meet the increasing human needs. But in practice, this may not be the case. Two important factors should be considered:

1. The sources of water supply are inequitably distributed among people and countries. Some communities live where regular precipitation gives them an ample surplus at present. Others have far more water than they want or need, but not necessarily in the right place or at the right time. Still others have barely enough water for current needs, and drought is perennial through the wide belt of arid lands.

2. Man has affected water in different ways. He has modified the water circulation and quality directly by over-exploitation, waste water disposal, river regulation, etc., and indirectly by modifying vegetation and soil cover in connection with land use activities, thereby causing indirect effects on the hydrological cycle.

In other words, fresh water of adequate quality is becoming more and more scarce. Water quality degradation of rivers and lakes has been observed for a long time. Sewage has long been an important cause. With growing industrialization, a great number of industrial wastes and pollutants find their way to surface and groundwaters. Urban and agricultural runoff constitute major sources of pollution. According to the Environment Protection Agency (EPA) such sources in the USA affect 90 per cent of its drainage basins.

Sulphur oxides and nitrogen oxides emitted from industry and/or burning of fossil fuels are removed from the atmosphere as acid precipitation. The acidity of rain has been especially recorded in wide geographic areas of the eastern USA and Canada and in Scandinavia. The acidification of thousands of lakes and rivers in southern Norway and Sweden during the past two decades has resulted in the decline of various species of fish, adversely alters a variety of other aquatic organisms in the food web, and causes other changes in lake-water chemistry which may represent a major physiological stress for some aquatic organisms.

Water development projects, for example the construction of dams, have environmental impacts — regardless of the dam's geographical location.

Concern has been recently voiced about groundwater pollution which is among the most difficult types of pollution to overcome. Case studies in the USA indicated that the severity and extent of groundwater contamination is determined by a number of complex factors. Groundwater contamination can result from agriculture, industrial wastes, sanitary landfills, municipal wastes, deep-well disposal of wastes, etc. Industrial lagoons and impoundments are the most common sources of contamination in some countries. The United States Environmental Protection Agency, for example, has located about 181,000 such lagoons at industrial and municipal waste disposal sites around the United States.

Public concern about the quality of drinking water supplies has risen sharply since the early 1970s. Water quality in many developing countries falls far short of the WHO safety standards. Over half the peoples of the developing countries — some 80 per cent of which in rural areas — have no access to adequate or safe water supply. Today, 100 million more developing countries' people drink dirty water than in 1975; 80 per cent of these countries' diseases are linked to water. Those numbers could become much higher by the year 2000 unless accelerated efforts are taken to remedy the situation.

All these problems of fresh water availability in the future are clearly basically problems of management (rational exploitation and use) and of protection of water quality.

More emphasis has to be placed on demand management rather than on supply management, as has generally been the case so far.

What is urgently needed, therefore, is the formulation of long-term policies that reflect changing water demand patterns consistent with efficient use and better appreciation of the social and environmental effects, with a view to minimize the adverse impacts. In fact, one can argue that the time has come when the emphasis should shift to comprehensive land and water planning, treating land and water as an integrated and interacting unit, rather than water planning *per se*.

As for water quality, a series of institutional, legal and economic measures are necessary to induce pollution control including standards for effluents and the appropriate techniques of their disposal. Monitoring of water quality should serve as early warning of damage that could occur. However, it is appreciated that monitoring is made difficult by two main conditions. Firstly, the concentration of pollutants in aquatic ecosystems is affected by many external conditions. Secondly, it is uncertain how a given dose of a particular polluting substance will adversely affect humans, fish, benthic and other organisms in the environment. The difficulties of monitoring water quality constitute a challenge to the scientific community to accelerate research efforts to solve these problems.

Role of the United Nations Environment Programme

These are all issues which have been debated during the last decade and the

United Nations Water Conference in 1977[1] which brought forward all the facts and suggested specific actions. The same problems were generally on the minds of the world community when they met in Stockholm in 1972. Several recommendations in the Stockholm Action Plan refer to the importance of proper water resources management and protection from pollution. To translate these recommendations into programmes, our Government Council decided that the main objectives of the water programme of UNEP should be:

1. to develop and promote the application of integrated and environmentally sound management techniques for the conservation and utilization of water resources;

2. to promote the development and application of integrated and environmentally sound water supply and sanitation techniques for rural and urban poor populations;

3. to promote the development and application of methods for assessing water quality; and

4. to promote the development of training, education and public information programmes in the field of water resources management.

An important area of UNEP's work has been, and continues to be the assistance in the elaboration of international standards for the use of shared water resources. The latter constitute an integral part of UNEP's effort to establish principles for the guidance of states in the utilization of shared natural resources.

Water management certainly figures as a key element of the World Plan of Action to Combat Desertification, the follow-up of whose implementation is entrusted essentially to UNEP. The World Conservation Strategy — the result of five years of cooperative work between the International Union for the Conservation of Nature (IUCN), the World Wildlife Fund (WWF) and the United Nations Environment Programme (UNEP) — puts special emphasis on the issue of environmentally sound management of water resources. These are a few examples. Our programme is not static. We report to our Governing Council on what is being done with or without the support of UNEP, essentially by the UN family, but as far as we can, we also include reporting on major actions by governments and non-governmental organizations (NGOs). This reporting allows us to identify areas which need concentration of effort and the Governing Council directs as to what we should be doing next.

---

[1] For the statement to the UN Water Conference, see p. 59.

Oceans

Oceans cover 71 per cent of the world's surface. This vastness has largely contributed to the myth that the oceans have an infinite diluting capacity, and that, therefore, they can be considered as one huge garbage dump for all of man's wastes. This turned out to be wrong and ocean pollution is becoming a serious problem.

Although the impact of pollution on global fisheries is still inconsequential in terms of total world output, there are already signs of serious damage to local fisheries resources which could eventually multiply to significant proportions.

A real challenge to scientists lies in separating out the various fishery and natural environmental effects so that the changes brought by marine pollution and other man-made disturbances can be clearly discerned.

Coastal versus Open Ocean Pollution:

It is estimated that coastal waters to the edge of the continental shelf constitute 10 per cent of the area of the world oceans. But 99 per cent of the world fish catch originates from these coastal waters and from the relatively small oceanic areas of upwelling. Most of the open ocean, lacking in nutrients to sustain life, is a biological desert.

In terms of protection of living marine resources — and this is a rather vital consideration in pollution control — it is obvious that one would have to give prime attention to the coastal region.

The serious problems of coastal pollution first became apparent in those heavily industrialized nations where there are concentrations of people and industry along the coast. The estuaries are some of the first aquatic areas that succumb to the insults of man.

However, the problem of global marine pollution is where international concern must be particularly expressed. This has been quite clear in the minds of the delegates negotiating the Law of the Sea. They are all aware of the state of the marine environment and have included in the Law of the Sea, provisions directed to environmental protection.

Let us look at a few examples of the state of the marine environment:

1. In the Baltic Sea, the input of domestic sewage is about 2.3 million m^3/day (with 40 per cent treatment). In the northern parts the load of liquids from paper and pulp industries is about 400,000 tonnes/year. The input of mercury is about 34 tonnes/y.

2. In the North Sea, the input of sewage is about 7.3 milliom m^3/day and of industrial wastes about 4.9 million m^3/day.

3. A preliminary assessment of the pollution of the Mediterranean showed that the input of phosphorous is about 360 tonne/y, of

nitrogen about 1,000 t/y, of mercury 130 t/y, of lead 4,800 t/y, of chromium 2,800 t/y, of zinc 2,500 t/y and of organochlorines about 90 t/y.

These are only some examples; others could be cited from other regions. However, these and other data are far from complete, and coupled by our inadequate knowledge of marine environment processes and the fate of pollutants, etc., make it difficult to establish quantitive trends on time scales on a global basis.

Marine oil transportation has largely increased. In 1960, about 450 million tonnes of oil were transported from producing to consuming countries by sea. In 1977, the figure increased to 1,700 million tonnes. Although the world tanker fleet generally has a good safety record, the fact that ships today are so much larger than they were 20 years ago means that the consequences of an accident are potentially much greater.

It should be noted that it is not tanker accidents which are the main sources of oil pollution but transportation in general and runoff (urban, river, industries) and coastal areas, estuaries are the main receivers. Although the environmental consequences can be serious, immediately after the spill, it appears that recovery occurs over timescales of months or years in most cases. The chronic oil pollution in many ports may be more important locally in the long term.

Offshore oil and gas production accounts for about 90 per cent of the value of mineral resources recovered from the sea-bed.

The presence of offshore structures, such as platforms, well-heads, pipelines will restrict fishing activities in the vicinity of the site and may also lead to local redistribution of fish resources. Present limited field evidence does not suggest any harmful effects of drilling processes and equipments. Studies on the blowouts in the North Sea in 1977 and in the Gulf of Mexico in 1979 indicate that the acute environmental effects were rather brief and long-term effects were rather small.

Fisheries contribute about 2 per cent of the food calories consumed globally by humans, and directly supply about 14 per cent of the world's animal protein consumed by humans. The coastal ecosystems produce some 99 per cent of the total fish production. The trend in marine fish production has been downwards since the peak year of 1970.

Marine life may be damaged by pollution and the consequences of other activities of man in a number of ways:

1. destruction of habitat;
2. acute poisoning by toxic wastes;
3. adverse alteration of water quality;
4. sublethal effects of pollutants;
5. bacteriological and viral contamination;
6. bioaccumulation of toxic metals and organic substances; and
7. tainting and/or discoloration of the flesh.

The economic effects of pollution and other environmental changes introduced by man on the world fisheries are difficult to assess at the present time. However, the rejection of fish products because of high metals content, for example, can pose a hardship to fishermen, an economic burden on governments which may have to pay compensation to fishermen for their losses, and of course, a loss of protein urgently needed in a hungry world.

The only recourse is mitigation with:

1. intensification of fish propagation by enhancement techniques;
2. transplantation of desirable species into waters suitable for their propagation;
3. aquaculture with protected water quality; and
4. environmental improvement.

Another important area of concern to us is the need for a better understanding of the role of oceans in the carbon cycle with the growing concern over the increasing CO_2 concentration in the atmosphere.

In the light of all the above facts which are normally put before UNEP's Governing Council, the Council decided that our overall objectives in the area of oceans should be:

1. To assess the state of ocean pollution and its impact on marine ecosystems;

2. To promote international and regional conventions leading to the conservation, management and wise utilization of marine living resources and their habitats;

3. To promote research into ocean ecosystems as a whole with increased attention to the interactions between terrestrial ecosystems influenced by man and marine ecosystems;

4. To encourage the restoration of depleted marine populations;

5. To encourage Governments to take legislative and other measures to avoid mass killing of non-target mammals and birds in the course of fishing.

Again, we are supporting a number of activities to achieve these overall goals. However, it has always been the position of our Governing Council to give higher priority in our Oceans Programme to enclosed or semi-enclosed seas, or what we call the Regional Seas Programme. UNEP's work in regional seas is essentially that of establishing negotiating fora, through which interested governments in various regions of the world agree on plans of action to protect and improve the marine and coastal environments of their regions through proper management processes. These Plans of Action include legal conventions and protocols setting the ground rules for working together;

programmes covering the three major components of environmental activities: assessment, management and supporting measures as well as the financial and institutional measures required to implement these programmes and enforce the legal instruments. This has already been done for the Mediterranean and the Kuwait Action Plan regions. We are hoping to conclude similar arrangements in 1981 for the Caribbean, the Gulf of Guinea and the South-East Pacific regions. Work is further in progress for the East Asian Seas, the South-West Pacific and the East Coast of Africa. The overall objectives of the plans of action for each region generally — with various combinations — cover:

1. Assessment of the state, sources and trends of marine pollution and its impact on human health, marine ecosystems, resources and amenities;

2. Coordination of, and support for, environmental management efforts in the protection, development and exploitation of marine and coastal area resources;

3. Assistance to interested governments in the implementation of existing conventions and promotion of regional conventions, guidelines and actions to control marine pollution and protect and manage marine and coastal areas resources; and

4. Support for education and training efforts to enhance the participation of developing countries in the protection, development and management of marine and coastal area resources.

Governments of the Mediterranean region, for example, have agreed on a Convention and two Protocols which already entered into force, and agreed also on a Plan of Action to protect their sea and its coastal areas resources — including the establishment of a Regional Centre for cooperation in cases of implementation. This year they made a major breakthrough by agreeing on a Third Protocol on land-based sources of pollution: a ticklish subject impinging on the economic development plans of those countries. One major component of the Mediterranean Plan of Action is the Mediterranean Pollution Monitoring and Research Programme (MED POL), drawing on existing national research facilities of the region. The programme has, so far, engaged the cooperation of 84 research centres in 16 Mediterranean countries. Ten pilot projects have been developed under this Programme and are yielding significant results to which I referred already.

These exercises in the area of regional seas which are really vast and complex — just touched upon in this cryptic presentation — are vivid evidence that governments are willing to cooperate and work together in protecting their common heritage in the environment, irrespective of their levels of development, social systems or political differences. Environment has certainly proven to be a unifying factor in a world which is, otherwise, exhibiting wide differences over a whole host of other issues. This simple fact, in my view, is the main success of the United Nations Environment Programme and is definitely a very bright spot in international cooperation which should be always highlighted and pursued. We are trying our best to capitalize on this fact.

24

URBANIZATION AND THE ENVIRONMENT

Statement to the Fourth Session of the Commission on Human Settlements

Manila, The Philippines, April 1981

THE task before us remains enormous. A number of critical problems remain, requiring urgent attention, and as is often the case, the resources at the disposal of governments as well as international organizations are not commensurate to the tasks at hand. One of the problems which lingers on is the great disparity in living standards and perceived opportunities between urban and rural human settlements. A high rate of urban population growth of five to six per cent persists in many developing countries. This growth is sustained by massive rural-urban migration, and appears to be taking place in the absence of an urban economic base which sustained growth in a similar social setting in the developed countries some years ago. The economies of many countries show strain as they attempt to provide for a larger and larger proportion of total population in cities. The effort to establish balance in the system of human settlements has not yet borne fruit, as evidenced by the continuing dominance of primate cities in the world.

Another major problem is that developing countries continue to experience a constant reduction in the area of cultivated land, partly because urban development encroaches on fertile soil at an increasing rate.

There are indications that the large cities in Asia, for instance Bangkok, Bombay, Calcutta, Jakarta, Manila and Singapore amongst others, not only face the traditional environmental problems — lack of sanitation, chronic shortage of services, polluted air and water, disappearing open space and recreational areas, traffic-congestion, etc., but more critically face complex environmental problems adversely affecting the capacity of the ecosystem to sustain such giant conurbations at existing levels of growth and consumption patterns.

For example, one of the corollaries of rapid urbanization is the exponential growth in the demand for water, coupled with a dramatic decrease in the quality of surface water and critical lowering of groundwater due to high pumping rates. In many cases, human settlements are provided from catchments even when the water is unsatisfactory. To make water satisfactory, certain halogenorganic compounds are used, suspected to be of carcinogenic nature if they exceed certain limits. There is, therefore, a great need to search for other environmentally sound methods for restoring the quality of drinking water for human settlements.

Another major problem is the chronic one of slums and squatter areas. I am pleased to note that the Commission will deliberate in depth the question of the provision of water and waste management services for slum and squatter areas and rural settlements. Few other interventions can have such dramatic results in improving standards of living of low income peoples as provision of adequate and acceptable water supply and proper sanitation. Today there is no more than a handful of cities or towns in the developing countries where water is always safe to drink and where wastes are disposed of in an environmentally sound and proper manner. In many Third World countries, less than fifteen per cent of the urban population is connected to sewerage services. Lack of safe water and poor sanitation means a billion gastroenteritis cases a year, mostly amongst children. On the occasion of launching the International Drinking Water Supply and Sanitation Decade, WHO estimated that 40,000 children below the age of 5 die in the developing countries every year, mainly from diarrhoeal and other diseases directly related to a lack of safe water and proper sanitation.

Given the severe financial constraints of governments, it is vitally important to redouble our search for alternative, affordable and sustainable systems in order to ensure a healthy and productive life for millions of people living in low income communities. In this regard, the full potential of sanitation systems that use little or no water should be explored, as should the potential for greater salvaging of wastes, increased use of renewable energy sources and maximum utilization of local materials and resources.

Although I hope that human settlements development holds better promise to millions of people in line for shelter, it is clear that the present decade provides less supportive opportunities for development than a decade ago. 800 million people in the world live in absolute poverty. Half of these are to be found in this region. The challenge before all of us remains daunting. Although the need for action is urgent, we recognize that the path is not always crystal clear, but rather presents itself as a complex maze of choices. The price for making these choices can be high but the value of the investment is undeniable.

25

INTERRELATIONSHIPS BETWEEN PEOPLE, RESOURCES, ENVIRONMENT AND DEVELOPMENT

Note to the Ninth Session of the Governing Council of the United Nations Environment Programme (UNEP)

Nairobi, Kenya, May 1981

THE International Development Strategy for the Third United Nations Development Decade, adopted by the General Assembly in resolution 35/56 of 5 December 1980, states that the interrelationships between environment, population, resources and development must be taken into account in the process of development, that research on these interrelationships will be intensified, and that bilateral and multilateral donors will provide assistance, including in the field of training, to develop the endogenous capacity of developing countries to follow methods which take fully into account the existing knowledge of the interrelationships.

In traditional rural societies, socio-economic decision-making was based on deep insights into the complex interactions between social, economic, demographic and physical factors, gained by experience over generations and permeating all facets of social life: socio-economic structures and processes, culture, traditions religions and myths. Environmental management, developed by trial and error over generations, was thus being performed on an empirical basis, with feedbacks taken into account and secondary and tertiary impacts weighed in decision-making. It was self-evident that one generation should not favour itself at the expense of its successors, and the population was kept in balance with the carrying capacity of the land on which it lived. People were managing resources efficiently and rationally, in close cooperation with each other.

In the rapid modernization process, such empirical knowledge of the interrelationships has frequently been disregarded. As a consequence, the interaction of man and environment has tended to produce important unintended dysfunctional consequences (poverty, unemployment, explosive growth of urban slums, environmental degradation and irrational management of natural resources) which, to a large extent, are borne by people who are not in a position to influence the socio-economic decisions that initiate, affirm and reinforce them.

The balance needs to be redressed, and means found to optimize positive systemic consequences. Interrelationships which reinforce negative impacts should be counteracted by coordinated policy action involving relevant sectors. Points of leverage need to be identified for the application of appropriate integrated policies and programmes development. The group in this connexion emphasized the importance of collective and national self-reliance and increased popular participation in decision-making.

The validity of the views on the conceptual framework for interrelationships studies expressed in the report of the Secretary-General to the Economic and Social Council at its second regular session of 1979 should be stressed, and food systems, soil management, energy systems, forest management and water management are important areas where study of the interrelationships should be fruitful and where advice for coordinated policies and programmes was urgently needed.

The interrelationships differed in form and intensity between sectors and countries, and even from area to area within most countries, depending *inter alia* on differences in level of development and on social and cultural considerations. The problems of assessing the interactions and defining integrated policies and programmes for positive systemic impact should thus be tackled largely on a disaggregated national or area basis.

The FAO/UNFPA study on land resources for populations of the future, conducted in conjunction with UNEP and IIASA, developed a clear methodology for examining interrelationships between land use potential, food systems, degradation hazards, soil and water management options, and population pressure. The conclusions of its global assessment indicated *inter alia* that Africa would lose 70 million hectares of its soil resources and that the rest would deteriorate in quality by 35 per cent by the year 2000. The group pointed out that country-level studies could, by being more specific, form a factual basis for the practical implementation of global and regional development strategies, as well as providing important tools for integrated national development planning aimed at promoting increased self-reliance and self-sufficiency in food production.

Consideration of rural ecology and development demonstrates the importance of developing models for answering precise questions. Empirical work on specific variables and the relations between them, to reliable data was stressed as a *sine qua non* for modelling. A balance has to be struck between the risk of overloading the models with too many variables and the importance of reflecting the complexity of the real world. Among the criteria for the selection of variables there is a need to take into account long-term along with short-term perspectives, and to consider uncertainties and risks, as well as the secondary and tertiary effects of socio-economic decisions.

It is concluded that, to provide more knowledge on the interrelationships between development, people, environment and resources, the interrelationships should be mapped through a series of case studies in different regions and countries, priority being given to cases where such knowledge was required in order to analyse negative processes of a very serious nature that have already reached an advanced stage, e.g. deforestation and desertification. Other areas that should be included in a programme of work include those where knowledge of the interrelationships would be of great importance in identifying points of leverage for coordinated policy actions by governments, such as energy, river basins and islands.

26

RENEWABLE ENERGY AND THE ENVIRONMENT

Statement to the United Nations Conference on New and Renewable Sources of Energy

Nairobi, Kenya, August 1981

THE environmental dimension of energy is a quite specific topic. Many of the impacts of energy production and use are not new. Air pollution, for example, was recognized since the discovery of the energy potential of coal in the 14th century. But concern for atmospheric quality — and hence action for pollution abatement — did not materialize until smog episodes affecting the population at large occurred in some countries. One can say the same for land degradation, water pollution, etc. In other words, little got done until a negative and highly visible effect became manifest.

Fortunately, this situation began to change in the 1970s; and it has been realized that environmental protection is a prerequisite for the improvement of the quality of life and that there were no conflicts between environmental objectives and development goals; on the contrary they were mutually supportive.

An environmentally sound energy policy should include three basic elements:

1. conservation, by which I mean restrained and rational use of energy;

2. establishing the most appropriate energy mixes;

3. development of new energy sources, especially renewable ones.

Conservation is presumably expected first and foremost on the part of developed countries. It is known that a 10 per cent reduction in the present level of consumption of these countries would allow an almost doubling of the level of consumption by the developing countries. Market forces alone have already given rise to appreciable energy savings in OECD countries, but more is needed. To achieve further reduction new technologies need to be developed which are less energy intensive than the present ones and there should be a shift to life styles less demanding in their needs of energy than the ones practiced today. This requires both human and financial resources, but above all political will and a real commitment to global interdependence.

Establishing the most appropriate mixes does not only depend on available technical options but more substantially on political, socio-economic and environmental considerations. It is generally accepted that new and renewable sources of energy are less damaging to the environment than conventional sources. The environmental impacts of renewable sources of energy have been brought into focus in UNEP's comprehensive review of the subject which is available to the Conference.[1] I believe the existing state of knowledge is such that it should allow policy makers to build their energy mixes, among other essential considerations, on a prior assessment of the environmental impact of the various energy options open to them.

Development of renewable sources of energy is fully discussed in the documents before the Conference. One of these sources is fuelwood. The last decade brought into focus the magnitude of the problem of fuelwood consumption in the world. Continuing reliance on fuelwood is leading to deforestation, desertification, soil erosion and various other forms of serious environmental degradation. Morever, such sources of energy are not even used in the most efficient way. Other traditional sources of energy share the same fate. And all these inefficiently burned fuels have valuable alternative uses.

Several countries have now embarked on extensive re-afforestation and fuelwood plantation schemes. However, all estimates indicate that the present rate of plantations needs to be increased at least five fold if we are to meet the increasing requirements of the evergrowing populations depending on fuelwood and to save the precious forests. Thus, we urgently need more plantations. We also need major improvement in the efficiency of using fuelwood. Further, some intelligent way must be found to reconcile the following:

1. the need for the use of fuelwood plantations as source of energy to reduce the pressure on forests;

2. the attraction of the offers by certain multinational corporations to buy the future outputs of these plantations for other purposes.

Such income would naturally be used to resolve some of the immediate economic difficulties of the countries concerned.

[1](a) Essam El-Hinnawi, "The Environmental Impacts of Production and Use of Energy," Tycooly International Publishing Ltd., Dublin, 1981.
(b) Essam El-Hinnawi and Asit K. Biswas, "Renewable Sources of Energy and the Environment," Tycooly International Publishing Ltd., Dublin, 1981.

All this again needs financial and human resources, international cooperation and immense political will.

To ease the pressure on the forest resource base, and to reduce the fuelwood consumption, special attention is being given to the development of appropriate technologies to harness alternative locally available sources of energy, especially those that are renewable. UNEP has experimental demonstration centres to harness renewable sources of energy in rural areas of Sri Lanka, the Philippines and Senegal.

The resource base of renewable sources of energy is large with an enormous potential for renewal. But with the present state of knowledge it is difficult to estimate how much of the resource base can be technically and economically exploited. However, with a much more accelerated research and development effort, through the gearing of appropriate human and financial resources, renewable sources of energy could undoubtedly play an important role in meeting future needs, especially in rural areas of the developing countries.

Maintaining the living standard of the rich, improving the quality of life of others, and satisfying the basic requirements for those billions of our fellow inhabitants of this one earth who live far below the level of subsistence cannot be met without the provision of adequate supplies of energy. But, as has been rightly pointed out at the inaugural session of this Conference, a number of the serious environmental problems we are facing today are the result of present forms of production and use of energy. The environmental cost of fossil fuel noted one hundred years ago is now fully recognized in terms of acid rains and potential danger to the climate of increasing concentrations of carbon dioxide. The risks of the only alternative already in an advanced phase of research and development — i.e. nuclear — are clear. Therefore commonsense, both environmental and economic, requires greater effort and real commitment to move faster on the benign, less environmentally damaging renewable front. In this respect UNEP has as priority the following activities identified by its Governing Council and for which it is approving regularly increasing allocations from the Environment Fund:

1. assessment of environmental impacts of production and use of various sources of energy;

2. promotion of activities related to development of renewable sources of energy and energy conservation measures.

There is a need for a dramatic increase in action at the national level and genuine international cooperation in this important area — which is at the heart of future world development.

27

THE HOLISTIC CONCEPT OF THE ENVIRONMENT

Keynote Address to the Meeting of the Arab Towns Organization

Kuwait, December 1981

IT is my hope that the thoughts I will share with you will contribute to a better understanding of the concepts of holism and the environment, and will also lead to practical application of the holistic approach to human settlements planning.

The Underlying Perceptions

All natural phenomena on the earth including all geographical and geochemical phenomena, all forms of life and even all human activity, form part of a single system in the context of the transfer or transformation of energy and matter. This system is partly composed of ecosystems or subsystems in which organisms are the central factor.

Ecologists who study these subsystems tend to divide them into still smaller units for interim study. There is a need however to synthesize the results of these individual studies into an integrated image of the whole system. There is a need to know what kind of interactions link these factors together into a balanced ecosystem. As far as we are aware, no adequate study of this area has yet been made. So in spite of the fact that the word "ecosystem" has been in use for nearly half a century, we have not achieved much progress in synthesizing these studies.

However, as human intervention in natural ecosystems is known to be the main cause of environmental problems, the need to group all the natural, economic and social implications of human activities has come to be emphasized. This is made necessary by the fact that the human component is an integral part of a system in which no single component can have an entirely separate existence and in which each component in some way affects and, in turn, is affected by all the other components.

The system, therefore, must be considered in a comprehensive manner. This idea of "holism" is the concept that the living and non-living components of the system function together as a whole according to physical and biological laws. The basic concept of holism is that as components are added together to create larger functional units, additional attributes come into focus, attributes which are not present or not evident in the behaviour of the components when functioning separately. The attributes of individual trees, for example, are not the same as those of a forest.

When taken in the context of human activities, the holistic concept of the environment requires a still broader definition. It should cover both the natural and socio-economic aspects of man and his activities. His interaction with the natural environment, his use of natural resources and the technology applied in the exploitation of these natural resources should be seen as parts of an integrated system.

Man's environment is of two types; natural and man-made. Human civilization is based upon man's capacity to create his own environment by modifying nature. The traditional concept of man's relationship to the environment was one of struggle against ecological rules and the limitations of nature. In other words, man has tried to build an environment independent of the natural system and its subsystems. This is especially apparent in the area of human settlements where some of the most disastrous problems are clearly linked to man's attempts to revolt against the ecological rules.

Many of the problems of human settlements result from their exceeding their environmental limits. These settlements are not related to a manageable resource basis. They are outstripping the ability of their resources to provide for the needs of their inhabitants. And in the process they are damaging the resources upon which they depend.

The ecologist, E. P. Odum, has stated the problem in this way: "The sociological dilemma can perhaps be summarized by considering two views of the city:

(1) It is the ultimate creation of human civilization where want and strife are unknown and life, leisure and culture can be enjoyed in comfort by men shielded from the harsh elements of the physical environment;

(2) The city is a gross alteration of nature that provides a thousand ways to destroy and cheapen the basic conditions on which human life and dignity depend.

As the ecologist views it, situation (1) will only come about when the city functions as an integral part of the total biosphere ecosystem, and situation (2) is inevitable so long as cities are allowed to grow without negative feedback control or are "managed as something apart from their life-support systems".

Satisfying those basic needs has become increasingly difficult as Third World cities continue expanding at explosive rates. In 1950, just one city — Buenos Aires with four million inhabitants — had a population comparable with the big cities of the industrialized world. Today there are twenty two cities in the developing world with a population of four million or more: at the turn of the century there will very likely be three times that number. And at least ten of those cities in the year 2000 will have to cope with a population of more than ten million.

On average a third of this expanding population lives in the squatter settlements that fringe the inner urban area — a tumbledown orbit of deprivation and despair. At current average rates of growth, the populations of these shanty towns are doubling once every ten years.

And on top of the problems posed by poverty, these developing world cities are confronted with a carbon copy of the pollution problems that have degraded the quality of life in the cities of the North since the time of the Industrial Revolution. Over the previous ten years big cities have discharged in increasing quantities not only effluents to the land and water, but also emitted chemical pollutants and particulates.

One distinct consequence of uncontrolled growth is the accelerating loss of prime farming land, at the rate of 3,000 square kilometres each year to new residential areas, highways, airports etc. In the developing countries, the pressure of population growth demands more production of food, fuel and shelter, leading to further deforestation and loss of agricultural land.

Urban encroached on agricultural land, combined with the need for increased food production for an expanding population causes the continued extension of agriculture to unsuitable land. The cultivation of marginal land and loss of forests in turn causes erosion, desertification and, in the long term, tends to decrease rather than increase the food supplies. Soil forms at the rate of one cubic metre over 125 to 400 years under natural conditions. With good soil management this might be reduced to 12-14 years. This means that when top soil is lost or degraded, its recovery requires a tremendous investment in time and resources, which many nations cannot afford. These and numerous related problems are closely intertwined with ecosystem function and human survival, and are as much problems of human settlements as they are of economic planning.

Development

UNEP's commitment to environment implies an intense concern with development. Putting this concern into a human settlements perspective, I believe that in your deliberations you may wish to bear in mind the following related sequence of principles:

1. in planning and managing human settlements, the top priority must be to meet basic human needs;
2. in so doing, great care must be taken to minimize the impact on resources and environment at large and so ensure the environment's sustained productivity;
3. the purpose of our concern with human settlements, should be the positive improvement of the human environment; this will not come about, though, if our approach is haphazard, uncoordinated or ignores ecological constraints;
4. at every level from the international, where UNEP has a key role to play to the individual city or town, we need to monitor changes in human settlements and be alert to the danger signals of environmental sickness;
5. all this will come about only if we can promote alternative patterns of development, and life styles, in rich and poor countries.

Environment and Human Settlements in the Arab World

Studies of settlement patterns in the Arab World show, in most cases, a concentration of population either in major cities or scattered in overwhelming number of very small settlements. A striking characteristic of this pattern is the scarcity of medium sized settlements.

The Arab world exhibits a great population concentration in towns and cities along four distinct and rapidly urbanizing corridors. The first corridor in northern Africa is parallel to the Mediterranean coast. The second is along the Nile, the third is the north-east corridor which parallels the Mediterranean seashore and the fourth corridor runs along the valley of the Tigris and Euphrates Rivers, including the oil producing corridor.

The latter area represents the first region to undergo urbanization in human history and it is clear that the major pattern of urban civilization owes its form to the experience undergone within this region. Yet today, the urban pattern of the Arab Nation exhibits poorly interrelated components, both in terms of social, economic and physical infrastructure.

The population of the Arab World comprised about 160 million people in 1980 and is projected to reach about 280 million in the year 2000. In 1980, the percentage of urban population varied from as low as 10 per cent of the total population (in Yemen) to as high as 88 per cent (in Kuwait). The annual rate of urban growth in the period 1975-1980 varied between 3.4 per cent to 8.6 per cent which is amongst the highest rates in the world. It is estimated that by 1990 the urban population in the Arab World will increase from the present 80 million or so to maybe over 120 million and by the year 2000 will exceed 150 million. The different countries show wide variation in the degree, level and speed of urbanization. Iraq, with 72 per cent of the population residing in urban centres in 1980; Lebanon, 76 per cent; Saudi Arabia, 67 per cent; and Kuwait with its 88 per cent are the most urbanized countries.

The level of urbanization in the Arab world may not be indicative of the rate of economic development but rather of special local conditions. Urban population growth in Arab countries, which is generally unguided, is the result of high rates of general population growth (3 per cent) and an equally high rate of migration (3 per cent). The two factors have equal weight in explaining the pattern and level of urban growth. Such a level of urbanization is historically unparalleled. Whereas it has taken industrialized countries 150 years to reach the present levels of urbanization, it is only taking 10 to 15 years, for a number of Arab countries to reach the same level of urbanization. The result, besides an excessive overloading of services, is the funneling of a disproportionate share of resources to urban centres. Although the share of gross national product ascribed to urban areas is only two to three times that of the rural, per capita spending in urban areas is four to six times that for the rural population. This has resulted in a great imbalance in development levels between rural and urban areas. Notwithstanding the resources directed to the urban sector, several Arab cities are facing mounting pressures especially in respect to housing and related facilities. It is estimated that 30-50 per cent of urban population in the Arab countries are currently living in sub-standard housing and in slums. Growing ghettos, shanty towns and squatter settlements are typical of many cities in this region. Unless something serious is done to meet these situations the problems will become compounded by the end of the century. A UN estimate shows that the growth patterns of the largest Arab towns will be as follows:

The largest twelve Arab cities (urban centres) in the year 2000*

City	1970	1980	Projected population in 2000
1. Cairo (Greater)	5,600,000	7,464,000	13,058,000
2. Baghdad (Greater)	2,500,000	5,138,000	11,125,000
3. Alexandria	2,030,000	2,929,000	5,500,000
4. Casablanca	1,492,000	2,194,000	4,624,000
5. Algiers	991,000	1,391,000	2,543,000
6. Beirut (Greater)	920,000	2,003,000	4,183,000
7. Damascus	835,000	1,406,000	3,109,000
8. Tunis	800,000	1,046,000	1,994,000
9. Kuwait City	640,000	1,300,000	3,000,000
10. Aleppo	639,000	935,000	2,031,000
11. Khartoum	600,000	1,621,000	5,079,000
12. Riyadh	300,000	1,259,000	3,005,000

*Arranged according to population in 1980.
Compiled from UN Population Reports and UNFPA (1980, 1981).

One very important element in Arab town development, and generally, in discussing the relationships between man-made and natural environment, is the question of water. This is particularly so because most of this region falls within the arid and semi-arid zone with a low precipitation, and thus faces a chronic shortage of water of potable quality. While water consumption in the Arab region is rising exponentially, the water shortage caused amongst other things, by unsound utilization of existing resources, has exacerbated the situation and has increased concern in this area. In many communities in the Arab world — especially along coastal areas — the loss of potable water, through salt water intrusion, is a bothersome problem.

In several large towns where there is supposed to be a water distribution system, not all areas are covered. The "leap frog" patterns of urban development common in Arab towns, means that outlying areas are, in effect, not served by the network. In such cases, privately owned tankers retail water, at very high cost, even when the reliability of the supply is poor.

In some places ground water being pumped at rapidly increasing rates is causing the water table to fall by as much as 2 metres per year. Traces of salt as well as insoluble materials have begun to appear. Wells have had to be sunk deeper and deeper, as much as 1,400 meters, and it is likely that fossil water is being drawn up. Some Arab countries endowed with abundant energy have resorted to desalination. One Kuwait plant for desalination of water is estimated to utilize 62×10^9 BTU's to produce 600 million litres of potable water i.e. 1,000 BTU per litre. Clearly such enormous outlays of energy are not within reach of all towns in the region.

The problems of fresh water availability in the future are basically problems of management (rational exploitation and use) and of protection of water quality. More emphasis has to be placed on demand management rather than on supply management as has generally been the case so far.

What is urgently needed is the formulation of long-term policies that reflect a changing water demand pattern consistent with efficient use and better appreciation of the social and environmental effect, with a view to minimizing the adverse impacts. In fact, one can argue that the time has come when the emphasis should shift to comprehensive land and water planning, treating land and water as an integral and interacting unit, rather than water planning *per se*.

As for water quality, a series of institutional, legal and economic measures are necessary to induce pollution control, including standards for effluents and the appropriate techniques for their disposal.

Worth noting is the fact that there is now a global framework — the *International Drinking Water Supply and Sanitation Decade,* 1981-1990 — through which national and regional action can be orchestrated to solve what has thus far been a somewhat intractable problem, especially in this region.

How in practical terms can "holism" be applied? The following guidelines have been found most useful in preserving and enhancing the relationship between the man-made environment of human settlements and the natural environment. The guidelines were prepared through a UNEP sponsored study which examined the ecosystems approach to human settlements planning.

Planning Guidelines

1. Allocate land use according to its potential: the best agricultural land should be used for food. Watersheds, river basins, groundwater supplied, delicate wetlands, forests and slopes must be protected.

2. Maintain a balanced density: high enough to make efficient use of settlement services and facilitate community cohesion, and low enough to avoid environmental damage and human stress.

3. Plan the settlement according to available water resources, and their efficient use.

4. Plan new settlements which are more self-sustaining, rather than allowing growth of existing settlements by unplanned accretion.

5. Maintain mixed land uses: indigenous vegetation and wildlife, agriculture or urban farming, industrial production, and social uses, where feasible, in all settlements.

6. Decrease transportation distances for both people and goods by decreasing specialization and increasing diversity in the settlement.

7. Promote participation through the direct participation of the people in their own development.

8. Take the contribution of the Islamic tradition into account in the building of human settlements. This is both at the level of town design — particularly as regards the distribution of buildings and the communication grid (relation of mass to empty space and the orientation with respect to sun and wind) — the design of houses themselves (control of climate — heat, humidity, dryness, light, glare). The enormous experience of these countries in water control is worth mentioning both at the level of the settlement (micro-climate, sanitation) and at the broader level (water supply, irrigation).

9. Maintain the health of the population by supplying settlement services to necessary levels of quantity and quality.

10. Deal with all services within the settlement wherever possible in order to minimize unnecessary imports and exports of energy and materials.

Technical Guidelines

Energy

1. Reduce consumption and waste and increase reuse of energy and materials, through conservation, reafforestation, etc.

2. Use all resources as and when they occur naturally and return to the same place and condition, whenever possible.

Water

3. Maintain natural drainage, runoff patterns and vegetation to ensure continuity of supply and avoid erosion and flooding.

4. Recycle water to water table in a suitably uncontaminated form to avoid subsidence and pollution of supply.

5. Utilize all available water sources and encourage small-scale collection, purification and consumption.

6. Encourage rain and storm water collection and storage.

7. Use water at different levels of purity.

8. Protect existing rural ponds used for domestic and farming water supply.

9. Encourage water conservation through efficient use and recycling, design of industrial processes and domestic plumbing and fixture, changes in life-style, legal constraints and incentives, information dissemination and education.

Food processing

10. Maintain and improve existing rural settlements, through improved agricultural production, settlement services and food processing industries.

11. Develop appropriate technologies for improved food conservation and storage especially in rural areas.

12. Develop improved methods for food distribution.

13. Encourage urban farming, in planned integration with living, industrial and recreation land use.

14. Develop detritus-based food technologies for urban areas, integrated with waste management and gas production where possible.

15. Allow for domesticated animals in low-density urban settlements, with suitable controls on erosion and health hazards, for increased protein production, waste consumption and biogas production.

16. Assist urban food production in marginal settlements through technical and financial aid, training, and information dissemination on intensive food production, and allowing for densities low enough for food growing, where possible.

17. Encourage urban food cooperatives for sharing tools, supplies and labour, and for distribution of food.

Waste management

18. Reuse human waste as a soil nutrient through *safe* collection, processing and distribution systems.

19. Place emphasis on aerobic composting in conjunction with organic waste disposal, or on anaerobic processing to produce biogas, as more productive alternatives to the conventional sewage plant.

The character of Arab towns is closely related to the architectural heritage enshrined in Islam. As one Arab scholar puts it "this . . . heritage has been evolved over long periods by trial and error. It took hundreds of years to gradually develop and refine the quality of space and environment."

The dwellings, even of the masses, in the old Islamic towns borrowed concepts of space and form from both mosque and palace. This slow but sure process of evolution produced a solution which made the urban environment humane, spatially distinctive and devoid of any sense of monotony. It provided for a sense of family privacy and enshrined the deeply held percepts of different levels of social interaction, amongst the inner family, amongst men and women, children and adults. There was an environmental *raison d'être* for every juxtaposition of space; an explanation for every shape and form; for every link and nod. Today most of this has changed. Drastic division of functions implants a very coarse grain in the Arab urban pattern. Excessively industrialized building processes lacking in empathy for the cultural, social and religious characteristics of the Arab nation have introduced visual monotony in new town development — and clearly, suppressed the sensitive solution to traditional shelter needs. Work places are now increasingly located in far away areas, forcing people to be on the road for long periods. Over-concentration of buildings and lack of services have made many settlements not only inefficient but also cause strain on the life of occupants.

At no time has it been more crucial to respond to the popular desire for well organized city components and an orderly urban environment, sympathetic to basic needs of the people of the Arab Nations, than it is now. Arab progessional organizations need to rise up to this challenge.

28

THE ENVIRONMENT IN 1982:
The Urgent Need for Recommitment

Statement to the Environment Committee of the European Parliament

Brussels, Belgium, November 1981

IN May 1982, a conference on the environment open to all member states of the United Nations will be held in Nairobi. The outcome of this UNEP conference will have a crucial bearing on the future course of the global environmental movement, because its aim is nothing less than to put the environment back where it belongs: at the top of the international agenda for action.

As all of you are no doubt aware, the occasion for the Session of a Special Character is the tenth anniversary of the Stockholm Conference, which set up the United Nations Environment Programme. The Session, endorsed by the General Assembly, is a manifestation of the concern of UNEP that the sense of urgency and commitment evident at Stockholm should not, now, be allowed to flag.

I make my address to you today in full cognizance of Europe's fine record on the environment. Many of the roots of the environmental movement are to be found here in Europe.

Several hundred years B.C., the Greek philosopher, Plato, complained of the deforestation which was turning his beloved hills of Attica into what he termed a "skeleton of a body wasted by disease"; in the middle ages, we hear of townspeople complaining about pollution from coal fires; and in this century, there has been the concern over the London smogs of the 1930s, the outcry over the Torrey Canyon disaster, the worries over pollution of common waters like the Rhine and the Mediterranean, and the acid rains, which are killing the lakes of Scandinavia.

From UNEP's headquarters in Nairobi, we have been encouraged by the growth of that nebulous commodity, "environmental awareness", in European government circles. The explosion in environmental legislation, the growing political strength of environment ministries, Europe's central role in promoting the conservation conventions, and, indeed, the formation of this Environment Committee — are all signs of the importance Western European nations now attach to the environment.

Conservation is another activity now taken very seriously by most European governments. Just one indication is a recent statement made by Britain's Secretary of State of the Environment, Mr. Michael Heseltine. "... in any individual decision", Heseltine said, "the starting point will be to conserve what matters: those who have a contrary objective must bear the onus of proof". I single this out because it is a perceptive reversal of previous attitudes that conservation had to be justified before action was taken.

Our goal for the 1982 conference is a renewed commitment to the environment cause. What does that mean in practical terms? It means, for example, that governments should make environment considerations a top priority in their bilateral aid programmes; it means more emphasis should be given to national environment legislation; it means that more resources should be directed to monitoring, which enables us to forecast future environmental trends, and, hence, to assist, with more confidence, in planning for proper management of the environment.

However, in making my call today for a renewed commitment to the environment, I am conscious of the financial constraints to action EEC nations now face. Western Europe, on the eve of 1982, is in a very different economic situation from that which prevailed in 1972, the year of the Stockholm conference. It was then assumed that European prosperity would increase with each passing year; but runaway inflation, market saturation, mounting unemployment and slowing rates of economic growth have undermined that assumption.

My own overwhelming concern, and that of UNEP's, as a whole, is that in these circumstances, Governments will be tempted to cut back their support for the environment, at all levels. UNEP does not have all the arguments against retrenchment, by any means, but the indications are that one of the justifications for environmental protection is that it can pay — in hard cash terms.

As the global economic recession deepened towards the end of the 1970s, so governments inevitably became more cost-conscious. A recurrent question in my meetings with Governments over the past few years was whether or not we could support — in practical terms — our assertion that environmental protection is a positive stimulus to development.

In an endeavour to answer this legitimate question, UNEP, two years ago, launched a programme of cost-benefit evaluation of environmental protection measures carried out by certain Governments. We set a realistic target, by concentrating on evaluation of pollution control at plant level. So far, we have analysed several of these government case studies and have attempted to distill and reformulate the experience so that others can share it.

The majority of these case studies came, as expected, from the EEC nations. The results of a French study, on 24 pollutants, for example, revealed that the cost of pollution in 1978 came to approximately four per cent of the GNP, whereas cost-benefit analysis indicated that an investment in environmental protection of, between one and two per cent of the GNP, could have saved those additional costs. Similar studies have produced parallel results in Italy and the United Kingdom.

Further benefits of environmental protection include lower death and sickness rates, better productivity, technological innovation and improved amenities.

It is encouraging to note that governmental demonstration that "pollution-prevention pays" has impressed some sectors of private industry. Pollution is largely a function of waste, and private companies are finding that it makes no sense to allow the waste, quite literally, to go to waste. In Switzerland, the United Kingdom and the Federal Republic of Germany, a number of companies increased their profits up to 40 per cent through retrieving pollutants.

Despite these examples and many others, environmental cost-benefit analysis remains something of an infant science. Or at least there are many imponderables. We are trying to shed light. The secretariat of the OECD Environment Committee is engaged, at the moment, in the preparation of an environmental economics report, which it hopes could be presented to the Session of a Special Character. Taken together, these efforts will advance the state of knowledge on the subject.

I am aware, however, of a strong current of opinion in the environment movement which considers environmental protection an ethical issue and which baulks at expressing its benefits in dollars and cents. Cost-benefit analysis is not intended to replace the other weapons in the environmentalists' arsenal but to add one more.

One of the reasons for holding the Session of a Special Character is to take a closer look at the Stockholm Declaration and see how our understanding, our "perceptions" of the environment have altered and advanced. We have identified those principles and approaches which we think have emerged in the ten years. They embrace such areas as interdependence between states, interconnexions between various components of the environment, alternative lifestyles, environmental uncertainties and surprises, and the interrelationships of people, resources, environment and development. They are set out in a "Consolidated Document", which has been circulated to governments for review. UNEP would welcome any thoughts and views you may have.

I anticipate that the May 1982 Session will not feel any inclination to alter in any fundamental way the Stockholm Plan of Action. Even a cursory glance at the Stockholm Plan reveals that many of the problems and challenges it identifies are as relevant today as they were a decade ago. It can be added to, adapted, to meet changing circumstances — but its underlying principles are immutable.

The implementation of the Plan over the past nine years confirmed the basic message that we live in an interdependent world and showed why you, in Europe, with your particular problems, some of them the consequences of prosperity, should be vitally concerned with the gathering pace of environmental deterioration taking place in faraway lands.

At an obvious level, all nations, for example, should be concerned about man's impact on the atmosphere. The buildup of carbon dioxide, caused by the burning of more coal, shale oil and tar and by the destruction of the tropical forests could result in what we have termed the "greenhouse effect", which, if it occurs, could certainly alter the climate and affect food production in all areas of the world.

Food production is dependent, too, on the conservation of the range of genetic material present in wild plants and animals. In Europe, there is no such thing as a home-grown meal — your agriculture (and also your pharmaceutical and certain other industries) depends upon infusions of fresh germ plasm imported from the genetic powerhouses, which, except for a part of the Mediterranean, are all located in the developing countries.

Again, we need look no further than the Stockholm Plan to find the major cause of the environmental deterioration which destabilizes nations and creates both social and political problems for all of us. This is poverty. In the developing world, steadily increasing numbers of poor are locked into a vicious cycle: in their efforts merely to meet basic needs like food, shelter and heat, they are being forced to destroy the very resources upon which their future survival — let alone, their prosperity — depends. And as poverty bites deeper, the markets for Europe's manufactured goods become more restricted.

One of my principal disappointments over the past ten years has been the failure of the message of environmental interdependence to get through to the person in the street. Ask the average European what he or she considers the term "environment" to indicate, and, nine times out of ten, he or she will say pollution and, maybe, nature conservation in its narrow sense.

But there are always bright spots if we look hard enough: the coverage given to our annual State of the Environment reports has been encouraging, and the media support, last year, for the launch of the World Conservation Strategy with its completely new re-orientation of the meaning of the word, "conservation", far exceeded our expectations. As you recall, the Strategy demonstrates sentence by sentence, page by page, that sustainable development cannot take place without conservation and that conservation is pointless without development. And I am pleased to report that almost 40 Governments are now taking specific action to follow-up the Strategy's recommendations.

There is a growing recognition that sustainable development must be based on sound environmental management.

I believe that one of our signal achievements, as a catalytic agency, was to promote the 1980 "Declaration on Environmental Policies and Procedures Relating to Economic Development", signed by the EDF, the World Bank, UNDP and six more of the world's leading multilateral development financing agencies, which, between them, spend in excess of US$14,000 million on projects every year. The Declaration has since been followed by the establishment of a Committee of International Development Institutions on the Environment to review and monitor its implementation.

UNEP is now looking to the bilateral donors to make a similar move. One important priority for European nations is to make sure that environmental considerations are taken fully into account in their aid programmes. Projects and programmes approved within these aid programmes should contain provisions for preparing environmental impact assessments, and the cost of such assessments should be included in the aid package. UNEP is currently engaged in a project to turn environmental impact assessments into better management tools through defining a simplified, cost-effective format for environmental impact assessments, particularly keeping the technical expertize and financial abilities of developing countries in view.

There are hopeful pointers in this respect. Both Denmark and Holland have recently approached UNEP for assistance, and, even more encouraging, was the recent declaration on environment-based development made by the OECD Development Assistance Committee.

UNEP sets store by the public statement on the subject made by Herr Rainer Offergeld, the Federal Republic of Germany's Minister of Economic Cooperation. The Minister, who made the statement in Bonn during August, said that all decisions on aid to developing countries must give as much priority to environmental factors as to economic and industrial ones. He said that, henceforth, this would be a matter of fundamental policy for his ministry.

These actions and declarations are counted among the successes of the impact of the environment programme over the last ten years. But not all the signs have been positive. There have also been failures.

Governments, for example, have not been ready to provide the data needed to set up a register of radioactive releases called for by the Stockholm Plan of Action. Similarly, Governments have been reluctant to conform to an important Stockholm principle, which related to the use of shared natural resources.

The Stockholm Action Plan also contained within it some seeds of failure. It is clear, now, that, in the light of funds that were made available, it was overly ambitious. Implementation might have gone ahead more quickly, if the Plan had conveyed a clearer sense of priorities.

However, none of these failures offset the very definite progress made in the last decade. Probably our most important overall achievement has been to raise the general level of environmental awareness in decision-making circles. The priority given to the environment in the New International Development Strategy; the prominence given to eco-development in the Brandt Report; the growth in membership of the conservation conventions; the regional environment pacts — these can all be taken as evidence of a remarkable expansion in the priority decision-makers now give to the environment.

As a catalytic agency — the role bequeathed to us by the Stockholm Conference — we have been a prime mover behind many of the more positive developments. But this catalytic role has often appeared to us a thankless brief, because, unlike, for instance, WHO or FAO, we cannot say at the end of the day that we eradicated a disease here or planted so many thousands of hectares of rice fields there.

We are inviting Governments to assess the effectiveness of this catalytic role. Should it be modified or reinforced? This will be an issue for the Session of a Special Character to decide.

In this, as in all matters before the Session, it is conceivable that Europe could take a lead in support of the global environment programme. What I can reasonably expect, I think is that the EEC nations will make reasoned and detached judgements, that they will come forward with wise counsel in determining the future of the Programme, the future for UNEP if you will, but, much more, for the environment cause, which the United Nations System, as a whole, is preparing to take up with more resolution and purpose.

The point of decision will be reached at the Nairobi meeting. Is the environment programme to be advanced or retarded? Do we try to maintain the momentum we have put so much effort into building up over the last decade or do we begin to run it down?

If the assembly of statesmen here today — of people who make the decisions — can set in motion increased support for the environment, both in your own countries and abroad through aid programmes, then the environmental outlook for the next ten years could be much better than the one we foresee today.

There are a series of fundamental questions which the Session will need to address. Principal among them is a question that concerns the developing world. How do we respond to a clear awakening among the developing nations on the issues and concerns of the environment?

The search for solutions to environmental problems can transcend political divisions in the developing regions. Accords on the combat against desertification and on the protection of the Caribbean environment are two examples — and there are others in various stages of negotiation, e.g., on tropical forest destruction, on the wider application of environmental law and conventions.

There are also many initiatives which now require the means for development. In this instance, not necessarily any massive financial or technical assistance, merely the transfer of ideas, of guidance, of maturing experience.

The fact is that the developing countries want more, much more, from the Environment Programme. They want an expansion of activities beyond the level approved by Governments for the next two years, and far beyond the level of funding we can now expect from the voluntary contribution of states.

As of now we are cutting back. There is no alternative. There are no firm indications that the traditional, generous support of principal donors to the Environment Fund will be maintained. There is one hopeful sign, however, that some nations, for example, the Swedish Government, are coming forward with increased support. There is also a concerted effort to find a way of providing additional resources for funding environmental programmes in developing countries. However, on balance, the indications are for a substantial deficit on the desirable target for contributions set for the next two years, of US$120 million.

I am in Europe as an advocate of the cause of the environment. The decisions at Nairobi will not be taken by the Western European nations, alone, of course. But the power of their influence — their potential leadership in debate — is not underestimated.

A judgement by nations in favour of the renewed commitment we seek would also involve a considerable increase in the present level of financial contributions. It would also mean a re-allocation of priorities for expenditure.

I am putting forward a challenge to Europe. In a sense, throwing down the gauntlet. You either leave it where it is, or pick it up — and, in so doing, ensure that the intent of Stockholm will be preserved.

That intent was "to safeguard and enhance the human environment for present and future generations of man". I hope, fervently, that objective will be reaffirmed in Nairobi by the nations of the world following the example of Europe.

ABBREVIATIONS

ACC	Administrative Committee on Coordination
ALECSO	Arab League Education, Scientific and Cultural Organization
ASEAN	Association of South-East Asian Nations
CEC	Commission of the European Communities
ECA	Economic Commission for Africa
ECE	Economic Commission for Europe
ECLA	Economic Commission for Latin America
ECU	Environmental Coordination Unit
ECWA	Economic Commission for Western Asia
EDF	European Development Fund
EEC	European Economic Community
EMEP	European Monitoring and Evaluation Programme
EPA	Environmental Protection Agency of the United States of America
ESCAP	Economic and Social Commission for Asia and the Pacific
FAO	Food and Agriculture Organization of the United Nations
GEMS	Global Environmental Monitoring System
IAEA	International Atomic Energy Agency
IARC	International Agency for Research on Cancer
ICSU	International Council of Scientific Unions
IFAD	International Fund for Agricultural Development
IFIAS	International Federation of Institutes for Advanced Study
IIASA	International Institute for Applied Systems Analysis
ILO	International Labour Organization
IMCO	Inter-Governmental Maritime Consultative Organization
INFOTERRA	International Referral system for sources of environmental information
IRPTC	International Register of Potentially Toxic Chemicals
IUCN	International Union for the Conservation of Nature and Natural Resources
IWC	International Whaling Commission
MAB	Man and the Biosphere Programme
MARC	Monitoring and Assessment Research Centre
MARPOLMON	IOC/WMO Marine Pollution Monitoring Programme
NIDS	New International Development Strategy
NIEO	New International Economic Order
NGO	Non-Governmental Organization

OAS	Organization of American States
OAU	Organization of African Unity
OECD	Organization for Economic Cooperation and Development
PAHO	Pan-American Health Organization
SCOPE	Scientific Committee on Problems of the Environment
SPC	South Pacific Commission
SWMTEP	System-wide Medium-term Environment Programme
UNCHS	United Nations Centre for Human Settlements (Habitat)
UNCOD	United Nations Conference on Desertification
UNCTAD	United Nations Conference on Trade and Development
UNDP	United Nations Development Programme
UNDRO	Office of the United Nations Disaster Relief Co-ordinator
UNEP	United Nations Environment Programme
UNESCO	United Nations Educational, Scientific and Cultural Organization
UNFPA	United Nations Fund for Population Activities
UNICEF	United Nations Children's Fund
UNIDO	United Nations Industrial Development Organization
UNSO	United Nations Statistical Office
WCS	World Conservation Strategy
WFC	World Food Council
WFP	World Food Programme
WHO	World Health Organization
WMO	World Meteorological Organization
WWF	World Wildlife Fund

INDEX

Abidjan, 28
Acid Rain, 116, 137, 144, 150, 155, 170, 181
Aerosols, 151
Africa, 2, 4, 26, 51, 53, 57, 71, 73, 74, 77, 78, 98, 113, 115, 121, 122, 128, 129, 161, 166, 177
Agrarian Reform, 101-105
Agriculture, Slash-and-burn, 2, 104; Subsistence, 37; Yield, 2
Aircraft, Supersonic, 16, 24
Air Pollution, 10, 15, 23, 29, 46, 51, 64, 68, 85, 87, 135, 144, 147-152, 155, 163; Abatement; 150, 151; Transfrontier, 22, 150
Air Quality Management, 147-152, 168
Aleppo, 175
Alexandria, 175
Algiers, 175
Andes, 113, 121
Antarctica, 145
Aquaculture, 106, 160
Aquifers, 75
Arab Countries, 171-180
Arabian Peninsula, 75
Arctic Ice, 99
Argentina, 59, 74, 93, 147, 197
Aridity Index, 74
Armaments, 40, 42, 88-92, 117, 129
Arms: Control, 88, 89; Race, 88, 89, 90, 91, 109, 130; Tax, 91; Trade, 90
Asia, 75, 113, 115, 121, 122, 128, 129, 161, 163
Atmospheric Circulation, 99

Attica, 87, 181
Attitudes, 17, 120
Australia, 74
Austria, 106

Baghdad, 175
Bangkok, 163
Bangladesh, 2
Barcelona, 17, 26, 56
Basic Needs, 10, 11, 13, 14, 16, 17, 20, 25, 29, 30, 33, 36, 41-42, 44, 48, 49, 54, 57, 60, 62, 63-70, 82, 91, 94, 153, 173, 174, 184
Bauxite, 117, 125, 128
Beijing, 118
Beirut, 175
Belgium, 181
Bilharzia, *See* Schistosomiasis
Bioaccumulation, 159
Biogas, 43, 103, 114, 179
Bioproductivity, 66
Biosphere, 21, 22, 31, 32, 48, 50, 63, 172
Birth Control, 37
Biswas, A.K., 16, 74, 179
Biswas, M.R., 74
Bombay, 116, 163
Bonn, 185
Brandt Report, 185
Brussels, 181
Bucharest, 11, 29, 37, 59
Budapest, 35
Buenos Aires, 93, 147, 149, 179
Burundi, 116, 123

Cadmium, 116
Cairo, 175
Calcutta, 163
Canada, 6, 116, 150, 155
Cancer, 82, 130
Carbon Dioxide, 85, 98, 99, 107, 112, 116, 121, 122, 137, 143, 144, 150, 151, 160, 170, 184
Carbon Monoxide, 149
Carcinogen, 164
Caribbean Action Plan, 161, 186
Carrying Capacity, 42, 48, 49, 52, 88, 107, 145, 163
Chad, 55
Chemicals, Toxic, 53, 120, 137, 143, 144
Chile, 74, 127
China, 74, 114, 118, 123
Chlorofluoromethanes, 151
Cholera, 37
Chromium, 159
Clevelan, H., 64
Climate, 4, 10, 14, 23, 54, 72, 73, 74, 78, 85; Anomalies, 98; Change, 15, 24, 66, 73, 97, 98, 99, 107, 121, 128, 151, 170, 184; Forecast, 4; Fluctuations, 55, 98; Impacts, 15, 29, 98-99, 143; Models, 4; Temperate, 4; Tropical, 4
Club of Rome, 111, 125
Coal Liquefaction, 144
Cocoyoc, *See* Declaration, Cocoyoc
College, Chelsea, 10
Communications, 7, 25, 47, 55, 84, 142, 177
Compost, 179
Conferences: Gdansk, 26; Helsinki, 26; World Climate, 97-100, 112; World Employment, 28, 36
Contamination: Bacteriological, 159; Viral, 159
Convention, Barcelona, 17, 26, 56
Copper, 117, 125
Cost-benefit Analysis, 119, 143, 182, 183
Cycle: Carbon, 99, 112, 125, 160; Geochemical, 99, 112, 125, 151; Nitrogen, 112, 125; Phosphorus, 112; Sulphur, 112, 125

Damascus, 175
Dandora Project, 53
Decade: Development, 32; International Drinking Water, Supply and Sanitation, 164, 176
Declaration: Cocoyoc, 5, 33, 48, 49, 91; Helsinki, 22; Human Rights, 69; Philadelphia, 102; Lima, 122

Deforestation, 2, 29, 42, 53, 54, 64, 86, 87, 98, 103, 104, 107, 108, 113, 119, 120, 121, 128, 167, 168, 169, 173, 181, 184, 186
Denmark, 185
Desalination, 176
Deserts, 10, 75, 96, 146, 158; Technology, 72
Desertification, 20, 37, 42-43, 52, 55, 56, 71-81, 83, 89, 96, 98, 104, 113, 119, 120, 121, 122, 128, 137, 143, 144, 153, 167, 169, 173, 186
Development: Agricultural, 10, 29, 40, 52; Alternative Patterns, 9, 12, 30, 33, 44, 49, 60, 65, 67, 94, 107, 120, 127-135, 137, 143, 153, 173; Economic, 20, 29, 30, 35-36, 38, 39-41, 47, 57, 60, 85, 91, 111, 118, 120, 123, 127, 130, 135; Industrial, 10, 42, 43, 106, 108, 122, 123, 128, 177; Negative, 10, 29; New, 12-13, 21, 30; Rural, 101-106; Social, 20, 30, 47, 57, 60, 91, 118, 135; Strategies, 5, 38-39, 48, 49, 101; Sustainable, 3, 9, 12, 13, 14, 16, 21, 22, 25, 27, 30, 31, 32, 33, 35-44, 49, 57, 63, 65, 66, 67, 83, 90, 91, 94, 95, 102, 104, 105, 106, 114, 117, 118, 125, 130, 133, 134, 135, 138, 147, 164, 174, 184
Disarmament, 88-92, 109
Diseases, 11, 20, 29, 47, 55, 60, 64, 85, 86, 87, 103, 104, 114, 120, 143, 156, 164; Itai-Itai, 115; Minamata, 115; Parasitic, 107; Waterborne, 4, 60
Drought, 54, 55, 56, 71, 73, 75, 98, 113, 122

Earthwatch, 9, 14, 15, 16, 22, 23, 24, 49, 50, 66, 67, 84, 97
Ecodevelopment, 17, 25
Economic Commission for Europe, 145, 150
Ecosystem: Deterioration, 73, 86; Fragile, 11, 20, 29, 64, 73, 86, 107
Effluents: Industrial, 13, 21, 116, 120; Standards, 156
El-Hinnawi, E., 169
Employment, 7, 11, 20, 25, 29, 36, 38, 41, 42, 43, 53, 62, 63, 102, 115, 118, 119, 123, 128, 129, 130, 131, 132, 165, 182
Energy, 5, 10, 12, 13, 143, 166, 167, 168-170, 177, 178; and Food, 2, 14, 128; Conservation, 31, 42, 43, 116, 123, 130, 150, 168, 170, 178; Demands, 29, 103; Mixes, 123, 168, 169; New Sources, 53, 85, 95, 107, 168-170; Nuclear, 85, 107, 116, 122, 130, 155, 170; Offshore, 56, 116, 159; Options, 99, 169; Renewable,

INDEX

17, 21, 25, 27, 85, 107, 108, 116, 122, 123, 130, 164, 168-170; Solar, 21, 32, 103; Tidal, 32; Wind, 103
Environmental: Assessment, 9, 14-16, 17, 22, 26, 27, 40, 50, 60, 65, 66, 67, 83-84, 86, 97, 131, 154, 161; Awareness, 82, 83, 85, 154, 182, 185; Catastrophe, 17, 37, 44; Conservation, 59, 64, 184; Constraints, 9, 14, 25, 33, 65, 86, 107, 172; Data, 50; Degradation, 2, 36, 38, 40, 48, 64, 67, 83, 86, 93, 103, 104, 105, 107, 117, 119, 120, 122, 125, 132, 145, 165, 166, 169, 171, 177; Education, 11, 12, 20, 27, 29, 31, 36, 41, 42, 60, 62, 63, 82-87, 104, 114, 120, 143, 154, 178; Enhancement, 41, 160; Hazards, 4, 85, 89, 112, 117, 122, 145; Impacts, 14, 27, 46, 51, 60, 85, 89, 99, 116, 124, 143, 151, 155, 158, 161, 169, 170, 176, 185; Law, 26, 27, 51, 54, 62, 120, 143, 148, 149, 182, 186; Management, 16-17, 22, 24-25, 26, 27, 44, 45-58, 65, 66, 67, 83, 84, 86, 95, 97, 105, 131, 154, 160, 161, 165, 184, 185; Pollution, 1, 10, 11, 13, 30, 38, 46, 53, 56, 60, 64, 85-86, 94, 103, 108, 115, 116, 118, 123, 131, 148, 156, 158; Protection, 3, 28-34, 41, 42, 44, 54, 83, 97, 118, 119, 125, 130, 132, 143, 144, 148, 158, 168, 182, 183; Standards, 46, 61, 134; Trends, 15, 23, 49, 182; Quality, 16, 25, 51, 61, 82, 88-89, 136, 148
Environment and Development, 1, 7, 8-9, 11, 19, 20, 28-34, 44, 46-49, 83, 85, 93, 119, 120, 132-133, 134, 153, 165-167, 168
Estuaries, 158, 159
Europe, 22, 129, 133, 150, 181, 182, 184, 185, 187
European Economic Community, 147, 182, 183, 186
Evaporation, 99

FAO, 1, 26, 57, 74, 98, 106, 121, 136, 166, 186
Fertilizers, 3, 14, 114; Biological, 1; Efficient Use, 3, 103; Nitrogen, 3, 16, 24
Fisheries, 1, 56, 60, 61, 103, 113, 116, 128, 137, 144, 158, 159, 160
Floods, 2, 55, 61, 98, 121, 128, 178
Floret, C. 74
Fluorocarbons, 16, 24
Food: Aid, 1; Chains, 3, 15, 23; Conservation, 4, 178; Consumption, 1; Contamination, 4; Distribution, 1, 5, 178, 179; Handling, 4; Losses, 14, 103, 114; Marketing, 2; Processing, 4, 178-179; Production, 2, 3, 4, 14, 72, 98, 99, 102, 103, 106, 108, 112, 114, 121, 128, 166, 173, 177, 178, 179, 184; Security, 1; Storage, 2, 4, 103, 114, 178; Surplus, 5, 14; Transportation, 2, 103, 114; Webs, 3, 155
Forests, 1, 52, 69, 73, 83, 87, 98, 106, 113, 116, 135, 136, 137, 146, 166, 169, 173, 177; Tropical, 2, 21, 27, 32, 98, 103, 104, 120, 121, 122, 128, 132, 143, 144, 153, 184, 186
Fossil Fuels, 10, 29, 85, 98, 99, 107, 112, 117, 121, 122, 125, 128, 129, 130, 131, 134, 144, 145, 149, 150, 151, 155, 159, 170, 184
Founex, 47
France, 142, 182
Fuelwood, 37, 52, 103, 143, 169, 170; Plantation, 169

Gabon, 121
Gambia, 55
Gastroenteritis, 61, 164
GEMS, 15, 23, 50, 66, 95, 97
Geneva, 133, 142
Genetic: Diversity, 32, 114; Resources, 136, 184
Genetics, 99
Germany, F.R., 111, 142, 183, 185
Ghana, 53, 114
Gigiri, 52
Glaciers, 154
Global Commons, 22, 125, 132
Greece, 59
Greenbelts, 75, 77
Greenhouse Effect, 99, 184
Green Revolution, 166
Groundwater, 61, 154, 155-156, 164, 176, 177, 178
Gulf of Guinea, 161
Gulf of Mexico, 159

HABITAT, *See* UN Conference on Human Settlements
Health, 4, 11, 13, 15, 21, 23, 27, 29, 32, 36, 41, 42, 50, 59, 60, 62, 63, 68, 82, 89, 103, 106, 107, 115, 116, 119, 120, 130, 161, 164, 179
Hepatitis, 37
Heseltine, M., 182
Himalayas, 2, 113, 121
Houston, 63
Human Rights, 7, 34

Human Settlements, 6-9, 11, 19, 25, 27, 41, 42, 47, 53, 73, 80, 86, 107, 108, 120, 121, 129, 146, 163-164, 172, 174-177, 179; Marginal, 17, 25, 41, 105, 107, 173, 179
Hungary, 35
Hydropower, 103, 114

ICSU, 122
IIASA, 166
ILO, 41
Income Distribution, 35, 36, 38, 39, 41, 48, 65, 68, 86, 131, 135, 175
India, 2, 74, 130, 139, 144
Indonesia, 2, 17, 25
Inflation, 118
Information Exchange, 14, 15, 16, 22, 23, 24, 42, 50, 60, 66, 67, 84, 87, 94, 120, 154, 157, 178, 179
Information Gap, 95
INFOTERRA, 15, 23, 24, 66, 95, 108, 143
Inner Limits, 34, 91
Inter-American Development Bank, 147
Interdependence, 5, 44, 47, 93, 119, 169, 184
International Law Commission, 62
Interrelationship, 8, 27, 32, 35, 40, 66, 69, 85, 93, 97, 101, 111, 131, 132, 143, 145, 151, 165-167
Iran, 74
Iraq, 74, 174
IRPTC, 15, 23, 24, 66, 95
Irrigation, 4, 14, 53, 74, 98, 104, 113, 114, 121, 177
Islamic Tradition, 177, 179
Israel, 74
Italy, 1, 101
IUCN, 136, 157
Ivory Coast, 28

Jakarta, 163
Japan, 137

Katowice, 19
Kenya, 45, 52, 53, 54, 71, 116, 136, 142, 165, 168
Kenyatta, President, 54
Khartoum, 175
Krill, 145
Kuwait, 171, 174, 175, 176
Kuwait Action Plan, 161

Lake Chad, 55
Land: Arable, 2, 26, 61, 64, 86, 113, 122, 137, 144; Arid, 17, 25, 27, 73, 74, 82, 86, 104, 113, 122, 128, 176; Degradation, 72, 73, 76, 78, 81, 87, 104, 122, 134, 173 (*See also* Desertification *and* Soil Loss); Fragmentation, 105; Marginal, 37, 103; Reclamation, 26, 75, 78, 81; Semi-arid, 17, 25, 73, 83, 86, 104, 113, 122, 128, 176; Tenure, 104, 105; Use, 15, 23, 26, 73, 75, 76, 98, 103, 155, 166, 177, 178
Latin America, 74, 75, 113, 122, 128, 129, 135, 149
Lead, 117, 125, 128, 159
Libreville, 121
Lifestyles, 12, 13, 33, 48, 59, 65, 68, 86, 107, 119, 143, 169; New, 20, 39, 44, 49, 53, 173, 178
Lima, 43
Livestock 13, 52, 54, 58, 75, 104
London, 10, 129, 181
Los Angeles, 149

Mabutt, J., 74
Malacca Straits, 26
Malaria, 37, 60, 107
Malaysia, 113, 121, 128
Mali, 55
Malnutrition, 11, 20, 29, 55, 86, 104, 120
Malta, 17, 26
Manila, 163
Mar del Plata, 59
Marine: Ecosystems, 15, 23, 160, 161; Environment, 17, 56, 57, 158, 159, 160; Pollution, 15, 23, 26, 46, 53, 56, 57, 158, 159, 160, 161; Resources, 134, 135, 158, 160
Mauritania, 54, 55
Mboya, T., 45
Mediterranean Action Plan, 56-57, 161
Mendoza, 74
Mercury, 116, 158, 159
Mexico, 5, 33, 48, 91, 149
Micotoxin, 103
Microbiology, 103
Microorganisms, 21, 33
Middle East, 113, 121
Military Expenditure, 40, 90, 129, 130
Models, Mathematical, 4, 148, 150, 166
Monitoring, 14, 15, 16, 22, 23, 26, 27, 50, 56, 60, 66, 67, 131, 156
Monoculture, 105, 114, 134
Mount Kenya, 50

Nairobi, 13, 45, 52, 53, 71, 72, 86, 136, 138, 139, 165, 168, 181, 186, 187
Natural Disasters, 15, 23, 27, 47

INDEX

Nepal, 113, 121, 128
Netherlands, 185
New York, 88, 116, 142
NGO, 79
NIDS, 7, 91, 110, 125, 134, 143, 153, 165, 185
NIEO, 7, 9, 13, 33, 43, 49, 64, 80, 83, 91, 102, 134
Niger, 55, 74
Nitrates, 3
Nitrogen, 159; Fixation, 3, 21, 32, 103, 106, 112, 114; Oxides, 112, 149, 155
Noise, 129
Nomads, 54, 55
Non-Proliferation Treaty, 89
North America, 150
Norway, 155
Nutrients, 158
Nutrition, 41, 47, 60, 113, 121

OAS, 148
Obsolescence, 12, 31
Ocean: Atlantic, 57; Indian, 121; Southern, 145
Odum, E. P., 172
OECD, 62, 149, 150, 169, 183, 185
Offergeld, R., 185
Oil Pollution, 22, 159
Oil Spill, 17, 26, 116
Onchocerciasis, 60
Organochlorines, 159
Outer Limits, 10, 15, 21, 24, 29, 32, 34, 48, 49, 57, 66, 85, 97, 107, 112, 120, 125; Social, 66
Outer Space, 89
Overfishing, 145
Overgrazing, 2, 52, 98, 104
Overstocking, 104
Ozone Layer, 15, 16, 21, 24, 32, 66, 85, 97, 99, 112, 137, 143, 144, 151

Pakistan, 2, 74
Paris, 108, 129, 148
Parkman, F., 69
Particulates, 149, 173
Patents, 108, 123
Peace, 22, 35-44, 69, 90, 91
Peccei, A., 111, 112, 114
Perceptions, 22, 43, 48, 118, 133, 139, 171-173, 183
Pest Control, 3, 14, 21, 32, 103; Integrated, 114
Pesticides, 3, 82, 103, 115; Concentration, 3; Efficient Use, 3, 103; Resistance, 128, 143

Philippines, 2, 17, 25, 163, 170
Phosphorus, 158
Photochemical Oxidants, 149, 150
Photosynthesis, 99, 106
Plato, 87, 181
Poland, 19
Political Will, 16, 17, 25, 27, 43, 63, 66, 81
Population, 14, 29, 33, 36-37, 38, 43, 47, 52, 53, 65, 72, 80, 93, 98, 102, 103, 104, 112, 114, 115, 121, 129, 134, 136, 144, 149, 163, 164, 165-167, 169, 173, 174, 175;Migration, 103, 107, 163, 175
Poverty, 11, 20, 35, 36, 37, 38, 40, 47, 59, 63, 64, 83, 87, 101, 102, 115, 119, 120, 129, 130, 131, 135, 137, 165, 184
Protein, 113, 128, 159, 160, 179
Public Participation, 35, 43, 84, 105, 120, 133, 166, 177

Quality of Life, 8, 11, 30, 35, 38, 39-41, 43, 44, 56, 65, 69, 83, 90, 94, 102, 116, 117, 123, 125, 126, 129, 130, 132, 133, 134, 138, 153, 168, 170, 173

Radiation, Ultraviolet, 16, 24, 32
Radioactivity, 116, 185
Rangeland, 17, 25, 52, 104
Reactor Accidents, 116
Recreation, 73, 150, 163, 178
Recycling, 13, 43, 51, 68, 69, 108, 178
Reaforestation, 52, 104, 178
Regional Seas, 26-27, 142, 154, 160, 161
Resettlement, 61, 103
Resources: Conservation, 1, 12, 21, 31, 43, 53, 54, 59, 69, 130, 137, 160; Depletion, 20, 29, 36, 38, 40, 47, 50, 51, 54, 65, 67, 85, 88, 106, 117, 120, 125, 132, 172; Irrational Use, 9, 13-14, 40, 42, 48, 50, 51, 67, 86, 89, 104, 107, 119, 122, 166; Management, 1, 50; Non-renewable, 21, 50-51, 67, 68, 80, 90, 107, 129; Rational Use, 13, 31, 51, 57, 59, 65, 68, 117, 134, 152, 156, 169, 176; Renewable, 21, 51, 68, 69, 80; Reuse, 12, 13, 21, 31, 43, 51; Shared, 99, 125, 132, 157, 185
River: Euphrates, 174; Niger, 55; Rhine, 181; Senegal, 55; Tana, 53; Tigris, 174; Volta, 53
Riyadh, 175
Rodents, 4, 114
Rome, 1, 59, 107
Rosso, 54

Sahara, 2, 55, 75

Sahel, 2, 54, 55, 56, 98
Salinization, 61, 73, 74, 103, 113, 121, 128
Sanitation, 41, 42, 47, 60, 103, 114, 115, 119, 123, 129, 132, 157, 163, 169, 177
Santiago, 127
Saudi Arabia, 175
Scandinavia, 150, 155, 181
Schistosomiasis, 17, 25, 53-54, 60, 107
SCOPE, 99, 150
Sea: Baltic, 26, 158; Caribbean, 26; East Asian, 161; Law of the, 158; Mediterranean, 17, 26, 27, 158, 174, 181, 184; North, 158, 159; Red, 26; Regional, *See* Regional Seas
Self-reliance, 9, 39, 48, 126, 130, 131
Senegal, 55, 170
Seveso Accident, 115
Sewage, 158, 179
Shelter, 7, 11, 20, 25, 29, 36, 62, 63, 70, 115, 129, 164, 184
Singapore, 163
Slums, 37, 107, 164, 166, 173, 175
Smog, 181
Social Justice, 35-44, 69, 102
Soil: Compaction, 26; Conservation, 95, 103, 108, 166, 173; Erosion, 2, 26, 37, 42, 52, 73, 103, 113, 119, 121, 128, 169, 173, 178, 179; Fertility, 26, 43, 52, 73, 76, 113, 116, 153, 173; Loss, 11, 13, 20, 26, 29, 47, 64, 103, 105, 120, 135, 137, 144, 146, 166, 181; Nutrients, 43, 113, 122; Pollution, 10, 26, 29, 64, 144, 173
South Pacific, 113, 121, 128, 161
Species Extinction, 137, 144
Sri Lanka, 170
Starvation, 5
Stockholm, 7, 46, 61, 64, 86, 89, 101, 139, 148, 181, 183, 187 (*see also* UN Conference on the Human Environment)
Strip Mining, 26
Sulphur, 13, 21; Dioxide, 116, 148, 150; Oxides, 149, 155; Removal, 150
Sweden, 155, 187
Switzerland, 47, 183
Sydney, 149

Tbilisi, 82, 86, 143
Technical Assistance, 27, 60, 84, 154, 186
Technology: Application, 106; Appropriate, 43, 51, 52, 69, 96, 108-109, 123-124; Capital-intensive, 107; Choice, 68, 95, 123, 133; Cooperation, 38, 93-96; Developments, 50, 68; Environmentally Sound, 8, 9, 21, 42, 51, 68, 95, 108-109, 117, 122, 123-124, 126, 148; Failures, 95; Hazardous, 134; Imported, 12, 39, 46, 133; Innovations, 31, 183; Low Cost, 8; Low-waste, 69, 108, 116, 133; Modern, 30, 94, 106; Sugar, 51; Traditional, 108, 124; Transfer, 2, 80, 94
Terracing, 2, 43
Texas, 63
Thailand, 113, 121, 128
Tokyo, 148, 149
Torrey Canyon, 181
Tourism, 13, 56, 73
Training, 8, 27, 60, 84, 87, 120, 154, 157
Transportation, 42, 47, 56, 103, 115, 129, 159, 163
Tunis, 175
Tunisia, 73
Typhoid, 37

USSR, 74, 82, 121, 129
United Kingdom, 10, 182, 183
United Nations, 6, 17, 23, 25, 26, 45, 55, 57, 58, 61, 63, 64, 71, 79, 80, 83, 91, 127, 134, 142, 143, 144, 147, 149, 154, 175, 181, 186; Conference on Agrarian Reform and Rural Development, 101-105; Conference on Desertification, 17, 25, 55, 56, 71-81, 83, 96, 101, 104, 122; *Action Plan,* 55, 56, 75-81, 96, 157; Conference on Food, 1-5, 28, 36, 37, 59, 80, 83, 101, 112, 121, 127; Conference on the Human Environment, 7, 14, 15, 23, 46, 47, 48, 61, 64, 86, 89, 95, 101, 115, 131, 157, 186; *Declaration,* 61; *Action Plan,* 7, 48, 139, 157, 183, 184, 185; Conference on Human Settlements, HABITAT, 6-9, 11, 28, 36, 53, 59, 80, 83, 101, 115; Conference on Population, 11, 28, 29, 59, 80, 83; Conference on New and Renewable Sources of Energy, 168-170; Conference on Science and Technology for Development, 80, 101, 106-110; Conference on Technical Cooperation Among Developing Countries, 80, 93-96, 101; Conference on Water, 59-62, 80, 83, 96, 101, 157; Economic and Social Council, 95, 140, 166; Economic Commission for Europe, 22; General Assembly, 27, 28, 43, 48, 55, 71, 72, 74, 75, 76, 79, 81, 83, 86, 88, 89, 91, 95, 122, 125, 134, 140, 165, 181
UNCTAD, 5, 33, 48
UNDP, 74, 147, 185

INDEX

UNEP, 3, 4, 5, 6, 7, 8, 14, 15, 16, 17, 19, 20, 22, 23, 24, 25, 26, 27, 28, 32, 36, 45, 48, 49, 51, 52, 53, 54, 57, 58, 62, 64, 65, 66, 71, 72, 74, 82, 83, 86, 89, 90, 95, 96, 97, 99, 102, 108, 110, 118, 119, 121, 122, 131, 136, 138, 139-146, 147, 148, 150, 151, 154, 156-157, 162, 166, 169, 170, 173, 181, 182, 183, 185, 186; Governing Council, 6, 7, 22, 26, 72, 78, 95, 139, 140, 141, 154, 157, 160, 165, 170
UNESCO, 41, 74, 86, 97, 121, 136
UNFPA, 166, 175
UNICEF, 57
United States, 2, 4, 63, 69, 74, 88, 116, 117, 121, 123, 125, 128, 130, 137, 149, 153, 155, 156
Upper Volta, 55
Urbanization, 42, 56, 69, 98, 102, 103, 107, 115, 120, 123

Vancouver, 6, 11, 59
Vienna, 106

Warsaw, 19
Washington, D.C., 153
Waste: Disposal, 37, 53, 60, 61, 68, 103, 114, 115, 123, 149, 155, 158, 164, 178, 179; Hazardous, 137, 144, 145, 146, 159; Industrial, 26, 64, 158; Minimization, 43, 179, 183; Organic, 103, 114, 159; Treatment, 57, 158

Water: Conservation, 81, 157, 178; Drinking, 20, 36, 37, 41, 42, 103, 104, 114, 115, 123, 129, 156, 164, 176; Management, 43, 50, 53, 59-61, 82, 98, 153-162, 166, 167, 176; Pollution, 10, 29, 46, 51, 53, 68, 87, 128, 144, 149, 163, 173, 178; *Transfrontier,* 61-62; Quality, 47, 59, 60, 62, 155, 156, 157, 159, 160, 164, 176, 177, 178; Salt Intrusion, 176; Shared, 61-62, 157; Treatment, 51, 68; Use, 15, 23, 61, 68, 155, 156, 164, 176, 177, 178
Waterlogging, 61, 73, 74, 103, 121, 128
Weapons, *See* Armaments
Weather Modification, 66, 97
West Berlin, 111
Wetlands, 61
White, G.F., 150
Wildlife, 13, 47, 52, 53, 60, 61, 118, 131, 132, 136, 177
World Bank, 36, 41, 147, 185
World Climate Programme, 99
World Conservation Strategy, 136-138, 153, 157, 184
WHO, 36, 41, 57, 148, 156, 164, 186
WMO, 24, 74, 97, 122, 150
World Peace Council, 35
World Wildlife Fund, 136, 157

Yemen, 116, 123, 174
Yugoslavia, 57

Zinc, 125, 128